Web Engineering
Handbook

Web Engineering Handbook

Jeremiah Downey

WILLFORD PRESS

www.willfordpress.com

Published by Willford Press,
118-35 Queens Blvd., Suite 400,
Forest Hills, NY 11375, USA

ISBN: 978-1-64728-033-8

Cataloging-in-Publication Data

Web engineering handbook / Jeremiah Downey.
    p. cm.
Includes bibliographical references and index.
ISBN 978-1-64728-033-8
1. Web services. 2. Web site development. 3. Software engineering. 4. World Wide Web.
5. Web sites--Design. 6. Web servers. I. Downey, Jeremiah.
TK5105.88813 .W43 2022
006.78--dc23

For information on all Willford Press publications
visit our website at www.willfordpress.com

TABLE OF CONTENTS

PREFACE

The purpose of this book is to help students understand the fundamental concepts of this discipline. It is designed to motivate students to learn and prosper. I am grateful for the support of my colleagues. I would also like to acknowledge the encouragement of my family.

Web engineering focuses on the techniques, tools and methodologies related to web application development. It also deals with their development, design, evolution and evaluation. Web engineering is a multidisciplinary field that encompasses various areas including software engineering, hypertext engineering, human computer interaction, user interface, information engineering, modeling and simulation, and project management. It utilizes the principles of software engineering. It includes new tools, methodologies, approaches and guidelines in order to meet the unique requirements of web-based applications. Some of the different types of applications where it is used are semantic web applications, workflow-based web applications, collaborative web applications, transactional web applications, interactive web applications and portal-oriented web applications. This book presents the complex subject of web engineering in the most comprehensible and easy to understand language. There has been rapid progress in this field and its applications are finding their way across multiple industries. This book will provide comprehensive knowledge to the readers.

A foreword for all the chapters is provided below:

Chapter – Introduction to Web Engineering

World Wide Web is the platform that delivers complex applications in different domains. The branch of engineering that deals with the design, development and evolution of the world wide web is referred to as Web Engineering. This is an introductory chapter which will briefly introduce all the significant aspects of Web Engineering.

Chapter – Web Development and its Tools

Web Development is defined as the building, organizing and maintaining of websites. Some of the aspects that fall under its domain are web application development, UML, web design, case tools for the development of web applications, web modeling, web modeling language (WebML), etc. This chapter closely examines these aspects of web development and its tools to provide an extensive understanding of the subject.

Chapter – Web Development Languages

Programming languages are the sets of instructions which are used to command the computer to perform specific tasks. Languages used for performing actions such as content creation, web security, web design, etc. are defined as web development languages. The languages elaborated in this chapter will help in gaining a better perspective about web development.

Chapter – Web Protocols

World Wide Web depends upon numerous protocols for maintaining the efficiency in its functioning. A few of such protocols are hypertext transfer protocol, common gateway interface, web services for remote portlets, websocket, etc. This chapter has been carefully written to provide an easy understanding of these different web protocols.

Chapter – Web Application Programming Interface

API is a set of functions that allows user to access specific functions, OS and other services. Web API is a concept that allows it to be accessed over the internet via HTTP, HTML5 audio, Cross-Origin Resource Sharing, W3C Geolocation API, HTML5 Video, WebRTC, etc. are some of its components. The diverse applications of Web API have been thoroughly discussed in this chapter.

Chapter – Website Maintenance and Management

Website maintenance and management is referred as the act of checking website for issues and continuously keeping it updated and seamless. Various sub-fields included are web audits, website governance, website monitoring, website tracking, web content lifecycle, etc. The following chapter elucidates the varied aspects associated with website maintenance and management.

Jeremiah Downey

Introduction to Web Engineering

World Wide Web is the platform that delivers complex applications in different domains. The branch of engineering that deals with the design, development and evolution of the world wide web is referred to as Web Engineering. This is an introductory chapter which will briefly introduce all the significant aspects of Web Engineering.

Web engineering is neither a clone, nor a subset of software engineering, although both involve programming and software development. While web Engineering uses software engineering principles, it encompasses new approaches, methodologies, tools, techniques, and guidelines to meet the unique requirements of web-based applications.

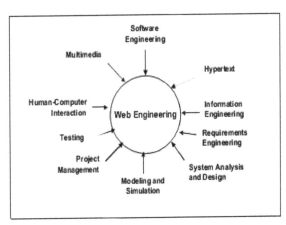

Web Engineering and Software Engineering

Though Web engineering involves some programming and software development, and adopts some of the principles of the software engineering, Web-based system development is different from software development, and also Web engineering is different from software engineering.

- Now-a-days almost all web-based systems are documentoriented containing static or dynamic Web pages.

- Web-based systems will continuously focus on look and feel, favouring visual creativity and incorporation of multimedia (in varying degrees) in presentation and interface. More emphasis will be placed on visual creativity and presentation as regards to the front-end interface with which a user interacts.

- Most Web-based systems will continue to be contentdriven–often Web-based systems development include development of the content presented.

- Multiplicity of user profiles – Most Web-based systems need to cater to users with diverse skills and capability, complicating human-computer interaction, user interface and information presentation.

- The nature and characteristics of the medium of Web is not well understood as the software medium.

- The Web exemplifies a greater bond between art and science than generally encountered in software development.

- Most Web-based systems need to be developed within a short time, making it difficult to apply the same level of formal planning and testing as used in software development.

- Also Web is different from software as related to the delivery medium.

- Further, the type of individuals who build/develop Webbased systems are vastly varied in their background, skills, knowledge and system understanding, and as well as their perception of Web and quality Web -based system.

Managing Software Projects versus Web Projects

Management Objectives

Software project management enables an engineering-style software development through extending the technical product development cycle (plan – produce – check) with the economical and social tasks of management, development, and monitoring. Thus, software development becomes an iterative, feedback-controlled process that includes a controlled, continuous adaptation of the orientation towards the objectives. Software project management therefore combines the technical development of software with its economical production.

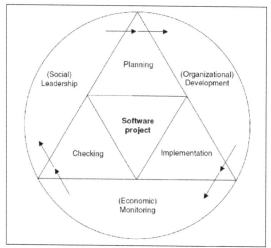

Project Management Objective: An
Engineering Approach to Software Development.

Distinguishing Web Projects from Software Projects

Generally one can observe that many monolithic software applications of former times are being replaced by a number of highly interacting, small web applications. This trend necessitates shorter development cycles, reducing the necessity to develop software from scratch according to specified requirements. Instead, components are combined following an agile process and a – hopefully – useable design is being created "on the job" by means of refactoring. This circumstance leads to a different characteristics for web project management from general software project management.

Many young developers are not familiar with traditional models and methods that ensure and increase development maturity. And time to learn and apply these models is frequently not available. Process development, discipline, or estimation skills are typically shed as unnecessary ballast. Web projects differ from traditional software projects in their results, too:

- Traditional software systems are comprised of parts grouped by functions, where the key metric of these parts is functionality. In contrast, software functionality and con-tent depend on each other in web applications, and the joint availability of both elements is essential from the very first delivery.

- The design and the creation of the content are at least as important as the application's functionality. For web applications, the structuring into design components is done in different ways by the different development communities, using different naming.

These areas have to be coordinated and – ideally – developed jointly. While information design aims at the content, interface design deals with user interaction and navigation in the web application. Program design comprises the functionality and communication with the application in the backend (databases, data warehousing systems, etc.). The main objective of web project management is to optimally match the presentation of information, access, and functionality of a web application, and coordinate all these areas with the content from the product perspective.

Disciplines Contributing Towards Web Engineering

As Web Engineering is not a single activity or task. It deals with all aspects of Web-based system development, starting from conception and development to implementation, performance evaluation, and continual maintenance. Various disciplines which affect Web-based development have been mentioned in the context of specific discussions. We will first enumerate all of them and then discuss them in brief with respect to their contribution in Web Engineering. It cannot be overemphasized that this list must be placed in the overall context of a good process model but every web-based application must be built in conjunction with it.

- Software Engineering,

- Hypertext, Multimedia and Information Structuring,

- (Information Engineering),

- Requirements Engineering,

- System Analysis and Design,

- Modeling and simulation,

- Project Management,

- Testing,

- Human-Computer Interaction.

Software Engineering

Software development can be a part of web development, but web development is not always so. When you need a website or a web segment to run on it, you are looking for website development services. But, if you want a program that runs only on your PC or all the interconnected computers in your organization, you might be on your way to a desktop application or software. So, while desktop software runs off the web, a webbased software application is intended to run in the web environment.

Software engineering is applicable and necessary at the application and project management levels. While there are many differences between Web development and Software development, there are also similarities between them. These include:

- Need for methodologies,

- Requirements elicitation,

- Programming,

- Testing, and

- Maintenance of those parts that deal with programming and functionalities.

Web Engineering has much to learn from software engineering in these areas but, in the light of the differences enumerated before, software engineering methods may have to be modified or new methods devised.

However, there is one major difference that Web developers/engineers have to bear in mind, as the discussion below clarifies. Web development, and in particular, Web site creation and maintenance, are not merely technical activities. Software development is generally regarded as the province of computing professionals. Web development affects the entire organization, including its interfaces with the world, and has to accommodate non-developers, especially management, when designing or recommending architecture and policies. This is particularly true of content management.

Hypertext, Multimedia and Information Engineering

With regard to information, information systems until now have dealt with largely transactional data in predominantly numerical form, with a bit of textual information, which can be more easily normalised, structured, sorted and searched. Webbased information systems contain text and multimedia, which are difficult to structure, cannot be normalised and are very hard to sort and search. Furthermore, they mix documentorientation with database access through the hypertext and hypermedia metaphor. As content, they are at this time 'integrated inextricably with procedural processing. Furthermore, they raise questions of information ownership, and are mired in matters of legal, ethical, social and legal issues. Software developers did not deal with these issues in the past. Web developers must take them into account in creating Web applications. The implication is that if proper policies and procedures are not created, the work of Web developers may not achieve what the client wants.

Databases and Storage Systems, storehouses for large quantities of information, are the foundation of many Web applications. In a typical e-commerce Web site, databases store such items as product information and current inventory status, as well as customer data ranging from name and address to prior shopping history. Deep understanding of the principles and application of database and storage systems allows Web engineers to design their data repositories to scale as the application grows. Database and Storage System principles include:

- Data design, including the entity relationship and semantic data models, and their translation into relational database schemas.

- Database query languages for retrieval of information, including commercial search query languages such as SQL and QBE.

- Theory of Internet search engines. Foundations of information retrieval, and recent work on search engine hit ranking.

Physics of storage devices, including disk, tape, and memorybased systems. Principles of filesystem design, including interactions with the physical storage device.

Information structuring isn't a new topic for application developers because database design strategies pay explicit attention to information structuring. However, the introduction of hyper-links, multimedia, and hypermedia now complicates the scene, going beyond the traditional numbers and text that developers have dealt with previously. Structuring this information for efficient and reliable management is an area where a lot of research occurs and new methods are being devised.

Hypermedia is concerned with linked information objects. Specifically, hypermedia is interested in the architectural properties of systems (such as the Web) that support hypermedia linking, and hypermedia link traversal, the design of large hypermedia linked corpuses of information (such as a Web site), as well as the rhetorical and narrative properties of specific hypermedia link structures. Hypermedia areas of particular interest for Web engineers include:

- Design. Techniques for structuring and decomposing an information space into individual hypermedia pages. Decomposition of hypermedia pages into more fine-grain objects that can be reused across multiple pages, and their reintegration.

- Visualization. Graphical techniques for conveying an overview image of a Web site.

- Usability. Design and analysis techniques for ensuring a Web site can be efficiently used to accomplish a specific task.

- Collaboration tools. Software tools that allow a hypermedia network to be developed, simultaneously, by multiple people, including those from multiple organizations.

Requirements Engineering

Insufficient requirements specifications and constant evolution are two major differences between Web applications and other software. User-centric approaches and methods to build applications have an unrealised potential in arriving at better specifications. The openness of the Web makes it feasible to get user feedback (and requirements) on-line as opposed to more laborious and expensive traditional methods, such as meetings, interviews, paper-based surveys and focus groups. The on-line methods have not been tried out yet in any great measure and could prove to be very interesting. It is also likely that users now will have a greater say in application development. Again, Agile methods and extreme programming may offer compatible solutions.

System Analysis and Design

Analysis

The first essential step in developing a Web-based system is "context analysis," where we elicit and understand the system's major objectives and requirements, as well as the needs of the system's typical users and the organisation that needs the system. It is important to realise at this stage that requirements will change and evolve — even during system development and after its deployment. It is also important to study briefly the operation for which a Web application is to be developed, and the potential implications of introduction of the new system on the organisation. This study should normally include: how information (to be made available on the Web) is created and managed; organisational policy on ownership and control (centralised or decentralised) of information; its current and future plans and business objectives; possible impact of the introduction of Web-based applications on the organisation; the resulting changes in its business and business processes; and emerging trends in the industry sector. Before starting Web development, therefore, developers need to elicit and understand the system's major objectives and requirements, gather information about the operational and application environment, and identify the profile of typical system users. In addition to the functional requirements, potential demands on the scalability, maintainability, availability, and performance of the system need to be specifically elicited and understood by the developers at the beginning of the development process. Based on this information, developers then arrive at the system's functional, technical, and non-technical requirements, which, in turn, influence the system's architectural design.

Context analysis can minimize or eliminate the major problems plaguing large Web-based system development. But, many developers and project managers overlook this essential first step in Web system development and face the problems later when it is hard to correct them.

Design

System Design

In system architecture design, we decide on various components of the system and how they are linked. At this stage, we design:

- An overall system architecture describing how the network and the various servers (Web servers, application servers and database servers) interact;

- An application architecture depicting various information modules and the functions they support; and

- A software architecture identifying various software and database modules required to implement the application architecture.

Web Page Design

Web page design is an important activity; it determines what information is presented and how it is presented to the users. A prototype usually contains a set of sample pages to evaluate the page layout, presentation, and navigation (within and among different pages). Based on the feedback from the stakeholders, the page design is suitably modified. This process may go through a few iterations until the stakeholders and designers are satisfied with the page layout, presentation and the navigation structure.

Web page content development needs to take into consideration the stakeholders requirements, users' cognitive abilities, technical issues and considerations, nontechnical issues, experiences of developers and users, and lessons learned from similar Web applications.

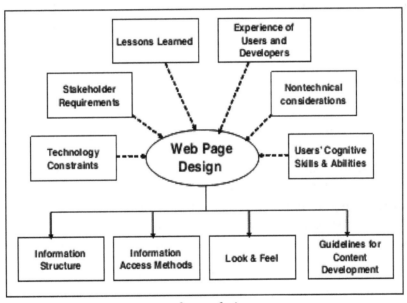

Web page design.

Modelling and Simulation

To help to reduce the difficulty in building Web-based systems we need a process model that describe the phases of Web-based system development - some of the aspects that make Web-system difficult include complexity, changeability, invisibility and unrealistic schedule. A process model should help developers "to address the complexities of Web-based systems, minimize risks of development, deal with likelihood of change, and deliver the site quickly, while providing feedback for management as the project goes along." Further, the progress of Web-based development should be monitor able and tractable. The process besides being easy to apply should facilitate continual update/refinement and evolution, based on feedback from users/clients.

Simulation consists on the observation of a systems response over time when a known set of stimuli is present at its input. Simulation is regarded as the evaluation of the extent to which the web application design supports interaction with the user, and aim to monitor and draw inferences of what occurs internally.

Web applications projects have reached a level of complexity that demand modelling techniques to tackle their design intricacies. Several modelling languages such as OOHDM, UML and WebML have been proposed as aids to Web application design, development and implementation.

Project Management

The purpose of project management is to ensure that all the key processes and activities work in harmony. Building successful Web-based applications requires close coordination among various efforts involved in the Web development cycle. Many studies, however, reveal that poor project management is the major cause of Web failures both during development and subsequently in the operational phase. Poor project management will defeat good engineering; good project management is a recipe for success. Successfully managing a large, complex Web development is a challenging task requiring multidisciplinary skills and is, in some ways, different from managing traditional IT projects. Quality control, assurance and documentation are other important activities, but they are often neglected. Like project management, these activities need to spread throughout the Web development life cycle.

Testing, Metrics and Quality

Web testing has many dimensions in addition to conventional software testing. Each unit of a Web application such as page, code, site, navigation, standards, legal requirements must be tested. Usability testing has also become a big and somewhat controversial issue. Services like W3C's HTML, CSS and XHTML certification, and Bobby for accessibility are freely available to Web developers. Consultants in Web site auditing also provide a testing service. However, Web engineers need to create explicit testing strategies that include the relevant tests. Web metrics and quality are interlinked, and like software metrics, under-utilised. However, more tools are becoming available and Web engineers need to evolve conscious policies to test their sites and applications.

The test planning needs to be carried out early in the project lifecycle. A test plan provides a roadmap so that the Web site can be evaluated through requirements or design stage. It also helps to estimate the time and effort needed for testing — establishing a test environment, finding test personnel, writing test procedures before any testing can actually start, and testing and evaluating the system.

- Browser compatibility,

- Page display,

- Session management,

- Usability,

- Content analysis,

- Availability,

- Backup and recovery,

- Transactions,

- Shopping, order processing,

- Internalization,

- Operational business procedures,

- System integration,

- Performance,

- Login and security.

Human-Computer Interaction

The era of end user computing started with the mass arrival of PCs in the mid 1980s. Information technology professionals have justifiably criticized it for its deficiencies—its lack of formal methods, insufficient understanding of theory, and poor maintenance, for example. The Web greatly amplifies the end users' reach— beyond the desktop PC to the Internet—both in accessing and publishing information. The end users will harness this power to solve their problems, regardless of whether information technology professionals help. It's imperative that we devise methods and processes to assist end users, develop their applications, and take the message of systematic development, testing, and maintenance to them along with the responsibilities of deploying the applications on the Web. Software engineering is meant to address problems of large, team-based projects. End user projects are unlikely to fall into this category but must be addressed now, to increase the reliability of applications and at the same time release the creative power of people in general.

Web Development and its Tools

Web Development is defined as the building, organizing and maintaining of websites. Some of the aspects that fall under its domain are web application development, UML, web design, case tools for the development of web applications, web modeling, web modeling language (WebML), etc. This chapter closely examines these aspects of web development and its tools to provide an extensive understanding of the subject.

WEB DEVELOPMENT

Web development refers to building, creating, and an maintaining websites. It includes aspects such as web design, web publishing, web programming, and database management.

While the terms "web developer" and "web designer" are often used synonymously, they do not mean the same thing. Technically, a web designer only designs website interfaces using HTML and CSS. A web developer may be involved in designing a website, but may also write web scripts in languages such as PHP and ASP. Additionally, a web developer may help maintain and update a database used by a dynamic website.

Web development includes many types of web content creation. Some examples include hand coding web pages in a text editor, building a website in a program like Dreamweaver, and updating a blog via a blogging website. In recent years, content management systems like WordPress, Drupal, and Joomla have also become popular means of web development. These tools make it easy for anyone to create and edit their own website using a web-based interface.

While there are several methods of creating websites, there is often a trade-off between simplicity and customization. Therefore, most large businesses do not use content management systems, but instead have a dedicated Web development team that designs and maintains the company's website(s). Small organizations and individuals are more likely to choose a solution like WordPress that provides a basic website template and simplified editing tools.

WEB APPLICATION DEVELOPMENT

Web application development is the creation of application programs that reside on remote servers and are delivered to the user's device over the Internet. A web application (web app) does not need to be downloaded and is instead accessed through a network. An end user can access a web application through a web browser such as Google Chrome, Safari, or Mozilla Firefox. A majority of web applications can be written in JavaScript, Cascading Style Sheets (CSS), and HTML5.

Web application development will typically have a short development life-cycle lead by a small development team. Front-end development for web applications is accomplished through client-side programming. Client refers to a computer application such as a web browser. Client-side programming will typically utilize HTML, CSS and JavaScript. HTML programming will instruct a browser how to display the on-screen content of web pages, while CSS keeps displayed information in the correct format. JavaScript will run JavaScript code on a web page, making some of the content interactive.

Server-side programming powers the client-side programming and is used to create the scripts that web applications use. Scripts can be written in multiple scripting languages such as Ruby, Java and Python. Server-side scripting will create a custom interface for the end-user and will hide the source code that makes up the interface.

A database such as MySQL or MongoDB can be used to store data in web application development.

Best Practices

Web applications will have a large amount of information that may contain mistakes, so the testing process for web applications tend to be more in-depth than other forms of software. Web application development tests may include security, performance, load, stress, accessibility, usability and quality assurance tests. Other tests that can be performed for web applications include HTML/CSS validation or cross-browser tests. Many of these tests can and should be automated whenever possible.

Tools

Helpful web application development tools include:

- Bootstrap an automation framework which manages HTML and CSS.
- jQuery and Ruby on Rails: for JavaScript libraries and frameworks respectively.
- js: is a JavaScript runtime used as a back-end programming tool.

VS Native and Hybrid Apps

Web applications are sometimes contrasted with native apps and hybrid apps. Native apps are applications that are developed specifically for a particular platform or device and installed on that device. Native apps can use device-specific hardware, such as GPS or cameras. Native apps typically have an advantage in functionality over web or hybrid apps.

Hybrid apps are a combination of native and web apps. The inner workings of a hybrid application are similar to a web application but are installed similar to how a native app would be. Hybrid applications have access to internal APIs which can access device-specific resources similar to (but not as efficiently as) a native application. For example, native apps are faster and perform more efficiently because native apps are designed to be platform specific. Hybrid apps have the same navigational elements as web apps since hybrid apps are based on web applications. Additionally, there is no off-line mode for hybrid applications.

Life Cycle Models

Extreme Programming

Extreme programming (XP) is a software development methodology which is intended to improve software quality and responsiveness to changing customer requirements. As a type of agile software development, it advocates frequent "releases" in short development cycles, which is intended to improve productivity and introduce checkpoints at which new customer requirements can be adopted.

Other elements of extreme programming include: programming in pairs or doing extensive code review, unit testing of all code, avoiding programming of features until they are actually needed, a flat management structure, code simplicity and clarity, expecting changes in the customer's requirements as time passes and the problem is better understood, and frequent communication with the customer and among programmers. The methodology takes its name from the idea that the beneficial elements of traditional software engineering practices are taken to "extreme" levels. As an example, code reviews are considered a beneficial practice; taken to the extreme, code can be reviewed continuously, i.e. the practice of pair programming.

Concept

Goals

Extreme Programming Explained describes extreme programming as a software-development discipline that organizes people to produce higher-quality software more productively.

XP attempts to reduce the cost of changes in requirements by having multiple short development cycles, rather than a long one. In this doctrine, changes are a natural, inescapable and desirable aspect of software-development projects, and should be planned for, instead of attempting to define a stable set of requirements.

Extreme programming also introduces a number of basic values, principles and practices on top of the agile programming framework.

Activities

XP describes four basic activities that are performed within the software development process: coding, testing, listening, and designing. Each of those activities is described below.

Coding

The advocates of XP argue that the only truly important product of the system development process is code – software instructions that a computer can interpret. Without code, there is no working product.

Coding can be used to figure out the most suitable solution. Coding can also help to communicate thoughts about programming problems. A programmer dealing with a complex programming problem, or finding it hard to explain the solution to fellow programmers, might code it in a simplified manner and use the code to demonstrate what he or she means. Code, say the proponents of this position, is always clear and concise and cannot be interpreted in more than one way. Other programmers can give feedback on this code by also coding their thoughts.

Testing

Testing is central to extreme programming. Extreme programming's approach is that if a little testing can eliminate a few flaws, a lot of testing can eliminate many more flaws.

- Unit tests determine whether a given feature works as intended. Programmers write as many automated tests as they can think of that might "break" the code; if all tests run successfully, then the coding is complete. Every piece of code that is written is tested before moving on to the next feature.

- Acceptance tests verify that the requirements as understood by the programmers satisfy the customer's actual requirements.

System-wide integration testing was encouraged, initially, as a daily end-of-day activity, for early detection of incompatible interfaces, to reconnect before the separate sections diverged widely from coherent functionality. However, system-wide integration testing has been reduced, to weekly, or less often, depending on the stability of the overall interfaces in the system.

Listening

Programmers must listen to what the customers need the system to do, what "business logic" is needed. They must understand these needs well enough to give the customer feedback about the technical aspects of how the problem might be solved, or cannot be solved. Communication between the customer and programmer is further addressed in the planning game.

Designing

From the point of view of simplicity, of course one could say that system development doesn't need more than coding, testing and listening. If those activities are performed well, the result should always be a system that works. In practice, this will not work. One can come a long way without designing but at a given time one will get stuck. The system becomes too complex and the dependencies within the system cease to be clear. One can avoid this by creating a design structure that organizes the logic in the system. Good design will avoid lots of dependencies within a system; this means that changing one part of the system will not affect other parts of the system.

Values

Extreme programming initially recognized four values in 1999: communication, simplicity, feedback, and courage. A new value, respect, was added in the second edition of Extreme Programming Explained.

Communication

Building software systems requires communicating system requirements to the developers of the system. In formal software development methodologies, this task is accomplished through documentation. Extreme programming techniques can be viewed as methods for rapidly building and disseminating institutional knowledge among members of a development team. The goal is to give all developers a shared view of the system which matches the view held by the users of the system. To this end, extreme programming favors simple designs, common metaphors, collaboration of users and programmers, frequent verbal communication, and feedback.

Simplicity

Extreme programming encourages starting with the simplest solution. Extra functionality can then be added later. The difference between this approach and more conventional system development methods is the focus on designing and coding for the needs of today instead of those of tomorrow, next week, or next month. This is sometimes summed up as the "You aren't gonna need it" (YAGNI) approach. Proponents of XP acknowledge the disadvantage that this can sometimes entail more effort tomorrow to change the system; their claim is that this is more than compensated for by the advantage of not investing in possible future requirements that might change before they become relevant. Coding and designing for uncertain future requirements implies the risk of spending resources on something that might not be needed, while perhaps delaying crucial features. Related to the "communication" value, simplicity in design and coding should improve the quality of communication. A simple design with very simple code could be easily understood by most programmers in the team.

Feedback

Within extreme programming, feedback relates to different dimensions of the system development:

- Feedback from the system: By writing unit tests, or running periodic integration tests, the programmers have direct feedback from the state of the system after implementing changes.

- Feedback from the customer: The functional tests (aka acceptance tests) are written by the customer and the testers. They will get concrete feedback about the current state of their system. This review is planned once in every two or three weeks so the customer can easily steer the development.

- Feedback from the team: When customers come up with new requirements in the planning game the team directly gives an estimation of the time that it will take to implement.

Feedback is closely related to communication and simplicity. Flaws in the system are easily communicated by writing a unit test that proves a certain piece of code will break. The direct feedback from the system tells programmers to recode this part. A customer is able to test the system periodically according to the functional requirements, known as *user stories*. To quote Kent Beck, "Optimism is an occupational hazard of programming. Feedback is the treatment."

Courage

Several practices embody courage. One is the commandment to always design and code for today and not for tomorrow. This is an effort to avoid getting bogged down in design and requiring a lot of effort to implement anything else. Courage enables developers to feel comfortable with refactoring their code when necessary. This means reviewing the existing system and modifying it so that future changes can be implemented more easily. Another example of courage is knowing when to throw code away: courage to remove source code that is obsolete, no matter how much effort was used to create that source code. Also, courage means persistence: a programmer might be stuck on a complex problem for an entire day, then solve the problem quickly the next day, but only if they are persistent.

Respect

The respect value includes respect for others as well as self-respect. Programmers should never commit changes that break compilation, that make existing unit-tests fail, or that otherwise delay the work of their peers. Members respect their own work by always striving for high quality and seeking for the best design for the solution at hand through refactoring.

Adopting the four earlier values leads to respect gained from others in the team. Nobody on the team should feel unappreciated or ignored. This ensures a high level of motivation and encourages loyalty toward the team and toward the goal of the project. This value is dependent upon the other values, and is oriented toward teamwork.

Rules

The first version of rules for XP was published in 1999 by Don Wells at the XP website. 29 rules are given in the categories of planning, managing, designing, coding, and testing. Planning, managing and designing are called out explicitly to counter claims that XP doesn't support those activities.

Another version of XP rules was proposed by Ken Auer in XP/Agile Universe 2003. He felt XP was defined by its rules, not its practices (which are subject to more variation and ambiguity). He defined two categories: "Rules of Engagement" which dictate the environment in which software development can take place effectively, and "Rules of Play" which define the minute-by-minute activities and rules within the framework of the Rules of Engagement.

Here are some of the rules (incomplete):

Coding

- The customer is always available.
- Code the unit test first.
- Only one pair integrates code at a time.
- Leave optimization until last.
- No overtime.

Testing

- All code must have unit tests.
- All code must pass all unit tests before it can be released.

- When a bug is found, tests are created before the bug is addressed (a bug is not an error in logic; it is a test that was not written).

- Acceptance tests are run often and the results are published.

Principles

The principles that form the basis of XP are based on the values just described and are intended to foster decisions in a system development project. The principles are intended to be more concrete than the values and more easily translated to guidance in a practical situation.

Feedback

Extreme programming sees feedback as most useful if it is done frequently and promptly. It stresses that minimal delay between an action and its feedback is critical to learning and making changes. Unlike traditional system development methods, contact with the customer occurs in more frequent iterations. The customer has clear insight into the system that is being developed, and can give feedback and steer the development as needed. With frequent feedback from the customer, a mistaken design decision made by the developer will be noticed and corrected quickly, before the developer spends much time implementing it.

Unit tests contribute to the rapid feedback principle. When writing code, running the unit test provides direct feedback as to how the system reacts to the changes made. This includes running not only the unit tests that test the developer's code, but running in addition all unit tests against all the software, using an automated process that can be initiated by a single command. That way, if the developer's changes cause a failure in some other portion of the system that the developer knows little or nothing about, the automated all-unit-test suite will reveal the failure immediately, alerting the developer of the incompatibility of their change with other parts of the system, and the necessity of removing or modifying their change. Under traditional development practices, the absence of an automated, comprehensive unit-test suite meant that such a code change, assumed harmless by the developer, would have been left in place, appearing only during integration testing – or worse, only in production; and determining which code change caused the problem, among all the changes made by all the developers during the weeks or even months previous to integration testing, was a formidable task.

Assuming Simplicity

This is about treating every problem as if its solution were "extremely simple". Traditional system development methods say to plan for the future and to code for reusability. Extreme programming rejects these ideas.

The advocates of extreme programming say that making big changes all at once does not work. Extreme programming applies incremental changes: for example, a system might have small releases every three weeks. When many little steps are made, the customer has more control over the development process and the system that is being developed.

Embracing Change

The principle of embracing change is about not working against changes but embracing them.

For instance, if at one of the iterative meetings it appears that the customer's requirements have changed dramatically, programmers are to embrace this and plan the new requirements for the next iteration.

Practices

Extreme programming has been described as having 12 practices, grouped into four areas:

Fine-scale Feedback

- Pair programming,
- Planning game,
- Test-driven development,
- Whole team.

Continuous Process

- Continuous integration,
- Refactoring or design improvement,
- Small releases.

Shared Understanding

- Coding standards,
- Collective code ownership,
- Simple design,
- System metaphor.

Programmer Welfare

- Sustainable pace.

Controversial Aspects

The practices in XP have been heavily debated. Proponents of extreme programming claim that by having the on-site customer request changes informally, the process becomes flexible, and saves the cost of formal overhead. Critics of XP claim this can lead to costly rework and project scope creep beyond what was previously agreed or funded.

Change-control boards are a sign that there are potential conflicts in project objectives and constraints between multiple users. XP's expedited methods are somewhat dependent on programmers being able to assume a unified client viewpoint so the programmer can concentrate on coding, rather than documentation of compromise objectives and constraints. This also applies when multiple programming organizations are involved, particularly organizations which compete for shares of projects.

Other potentially controversial aspects of extreme programming include:

- Requirements are expressed as automated acceptance tests rather than specification documents.

- Requirements are defined incrementally, rather than trying to get them all in advance.

- Software developers are usually required to work in pairs.

- There is no Big Design Up Front. Most of the design activity takes place on the fly and incrementally, starting with "the simplest thing that could possibly work" and adding complexity only when it's required by failing tests. Critics compare this to "debugging a system into appearance" and fear this will result in more re-design effort than only re-designing when requirements change.

- A customer representative is attached to the project. This role can become a single-point-of-failure for the project, and some people have found it to be a source of stress. Also, there is the danger of micro-management by a non-technical representative trying to dictate the use of technical software features and architecture.

Critics have noted several potential drawbacks, including problems with unstable requirements, no documented compromises of user conflicts, and a lack of an overall design specification or document.

Scalability

ThoughtWorks has claimed reasonable success on distributed XP projects with up to sixty people.

In 2004, industrial extreme programming (IXP) was introduced as an evolution of XP. It is intended to bring the ability to work in large and distributed teams. It now has 23 practices and flexible values.

Scrum

Scrum is an agile process framework for managing complex knowledge work, with an initial emphasis on software development, although it has been used in other fields and is slowly starting to be explored for other complex work, research and advanced technologies. It is designed for teams of ten or fewer members, who break their work into goals that can be completed within timeboxed iterations, called sprints, no longer than one month and most commonly two weeks, then track progress and re-plan in 15-minute time-boxed stand-up meetings, called daily scrums.

Name

Scrum is occasionally seen written in all-capitals, as SCRUM. The word is not an acronym, so this stylization is not correct; it likely arose due to an early paper by Ken Schwaber which capitalized SCRUM in its title.

While the trademark on the term *Scrum* itself has been allowed to lapse, it is deemed as owned by the wider community rather than an individual, so the leading capital for *Scrum*

Many of the terms used in Scrum are typically written with leading capitals (e.g., Scrum Master, Daily Scrum). However, to maintain an encyclopedic tone, use normal sentence case for these terms (e.g., scrum master, daily scrum) — unless they are recognized marks (such as Certified Scrum Master).

Key Ideas

Scrum is a lightweight, iterative and incremental framework for managing complex work. The framework challenges assumptions of the traditional, sequential approach to product development, and enables teams to self-organize by encouraging physical co-location or close online collaboration of all team members, as well as daily face-to-face communication among all team members and disciplines involved.

A key principle of Scrum is the dual recognition that customers will change their minds about what they want or need (often called requirements volatility) and that there will be unpredictable challenges—for which a predictive or planned approach is not suited.

As such, Scrum adopts an evidence-based empirical approach — accepting that the problem cannot be fully understood or defined up front, and instead focusing on how to maximize the team's ability to deliver quickly, to respond to emerging requirements, and to adapt to evolving technologies and changes in market conditions.

Roles

There are three roles in the Scrum framework. These are ideally co-located to ensure optimal communication among team members. Together these three roles form the scrum team. While many organizations have other roles involved with defining and delivering the product, Scrum defines only these three.

Product Owner

The product owner, representing the product's stakeholders and the voice of the customer (or may represent the desires of a committee), is responsible for delivering good business results. Hence, the product owner is accountable for the product backlog and for maximizing the value that the team delivers. The product owner defines the product in customer-centric terms (typically user stories), adds them to the product backlog, and prioritizes them based on importance and dependencies. A scrum team should have only one product owner (although a product owner could support more than one team). This role should not be combined with that of the scrum master. The product owner should focus on the business side of product development and spend the majority of their time liaising with stakeholders and the team. The product owner should not dictate how the team reaches a technical solution, but rather will seek consensus among the team members. This role is crucial and requires a deep understanding of both sides: the business and the engineers (developers) in the scrum team. Therefore a good product owner should be able to communicate what the business needs, ask why they need it (because there may be better ways to achieve that), and convey the message to all stakeholders including the delivery Team using a technical language, as required. The Product Owner uses Scrum's empirical tools to manage highly complex work, while controlling risk and achieving value.

Communication is a core responsibility of the product owner. The ability to convey priorities and empathize with team members and stakeholders is vital to steer product development in the right direction. The product owner role bridges the communication gap between the team and its stakeholders, serving as a proxy for stakeholders to the team and as a team representative to the overall stakeholder community.

As the face of the team to the stakeholders, the following are some of the communication tasks of the product owner to the stakeholders:

- Define and announce releases.

- Communicate delivery and team status.

- Share progress during governance meetings.

- Share significant RIDAs (risks, impediments, dependencies, and assumptions) with stakeholders.

- Negotiate priorities, scope, funding, and schedule.

- Ensure that the product backlog is visible, transparent and clear.

Empathy is a key attribute for a product owner to have—the ability to put one's self in another's shoes. A product owner converses with different stakeholders, who have a variety of backgrounds, job roles, and objectives. A product owner must be able to see from these different points of view. To be effective, it is wise for a product owner to know the level of detail the audience needs. The development team needs thorough feedback and specifications so they can build a product up to expectation, while an executive sponsor may just need summaries of progress. Providing more information than necessary may lose stakeholder interest and waste time. A direct means of communication is the most preferred by seasoned agile product owners.

A product owner's ability to communicate effectively is also enhanced by being skilled in techniques that identify stakeholder needs, negotiate priorities between stakeholder interests, and collaborate with developers to ensure effective implementation of requirements.

Development Team

The development team has from three to nine members who carry out all tasks required to build increments of valuable output every sprint.

While team members are referred to as developers in some literature, the term refers to anyone who plays a role in the development and support of the system or product, and can include researchers, architects, designers, data specialists, statisticians, analysts, engineers, programmers, and testers, among others. However, due to the confusion that can arise when some people do not feel the term 'developer' applies to them, they are often referred to just as team members.

The team is self-organizing. While no work should come to the team except through the product owner, and the scrum master is expected to protect the team from too much distraction, the team should still be encouraged to interact directly with customers and/or stakeholders to gain maximum understanding and immediacy of feedback.

Scrum Master

Scrum is facilitated by a scrum master, who is accountable for removing impediments to the ability of the team to deliver the product goals and deliverables. The scrum master is not a traditional team lead or project manager but acts as a buffer between the team and any distracting influences. The scrum master ensures that the scrum framework is followed. The scrum master helps to ensure the team follows the agreed processes in the Scrum framework, often facilitates key sessions, and encourages the team to improve. The role has also been referred to as a team facilitator or servant-leader to reinforce these dual perspectives.

The core responsibilities of a scrum master include (but are not limited to):

- Helping the product owner maintain the product backlog in a way that ensures the needed work is well understood so the team can continually make forward progress.

- Helping the team to determine the definition of done for the product, with input from key stakeholders.

- Coaching the team, within the Scrum principles, in order to deliver high-quality features for its product.

- Promoting self-organization within the team.

- Helping the scrum team to avoid or remove impediments to its progress, whether internal or external to the team.

- Facilitating team events to ensure regular progress.

- Educating key stakeholders on Agile and Scrum principles.

- Coaching the development team in self-organization and cross-functionality.

The scrum master helps people and organizations adopt empirical and lean thinking, leaving behind hopes for certainty and predictability.

One of the ways the scrum master role differs from a project manager is that the latter may have people management responsibilities and the scrum master does not. A scrum master provides a limited amount of direction since the team is expected to be empowered and self-organizing. Scrum does not formally recognise the role of project manager, as traditional command and control tendencies would cause difficulties.

Workflow

Sprint

A sprint (also known as iteration or timebox) is the basic unit of development in Scrum. The sprint is a timeboxed effort; that is, the length is agreed and fixed in advance for each sprint and is normally between one week and one month, with two weeks being the most common.

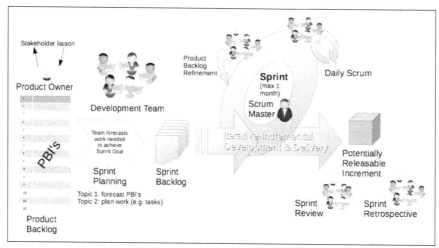

Scrum framework.

Each sprint starts with a sprint planning event that establishes a sprint goal and the required product backlog items. The team accepts what they agree is ready and translate this into a sprint backlog, with a breakdown of the work required and an estimated forecast for the sprint goal. Each sprint ends with a sprint review and sprint retrospective, that reviews progress to show to stakeholders and identify lessons and improvements for the next sprints.

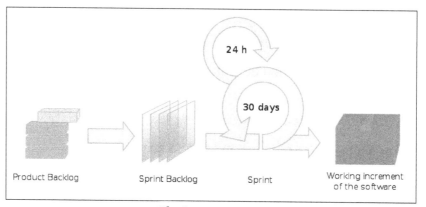

The Scrum process.

Scrum emphasizes valuable, useful output at the end of the sprint that is really done. In the case of software, this likely includes that the software has been fully integrated, tested and documented, and is potentially releasable.

Sprint Planning

At the beginning of a sprint, the scrum team holds a sprint planning event to:

- Mutually discuss and agree on the scope of work that is intended to be done during that sprint.

- Select product backlog items that can be completed in one sprint.

- Prepare a sprint backlog that includes the work needed to complete the selected product backlog items.

- Agree the sprint goal, a short description of what they are forecasting to deliver at the end of the sprint.

- The recommended duration is four hours for a two-week sprint (pro-rata for other sprint durations).

  ◦ During the first half, the whole scrum team (development team, scrum master, and product owner) selects the product backlog items they believe could be completed in that sprint.

  ◦ During the second half, the development team identifies the detailed work (tasks) required to complete those product backlog items; resulting in a confirmed sprint backlog.

    ▪ As the detailed work is elaborated, some product backlog items may be split or put back into the product backlog if the team no longer believes they can complete the required work in a single sprint.

- Once the development team has prepared their sprint backlog, they forecast (usually by voting) which tasks will be delivered within the sprint.

Daily Scrum

A daily scrum in the computing room. This
centralized location helps the team start on time.

Each day during a sprint, the team holds a daily scrum (or stand-up) with specific guidelines:

- All members of the development team come prepared. The daily scrum:

  ◦ Starts precisely on time even if some development team members are missing.

  ◦ Should happen at the same time and place every day.

  ◦ Is limited (timeboxed) to fifteen minutes.

- Anyone is welcome, though only development team members should contribute.

- During the daily scrum, each team member typically answers three questions:

  ○ What did I complete yesterday that contributed to the team meeting our sprint goal?

  ○ What do I plan to complete today to contribute to the team meeting our sprint goal?

  ○ Do I see any impediment that could prevent me or the team from meeting our sprint goal?

Any impediment (e.g., stumbling block, risk, issue, delayed dependency, assumption proved unfounded) identified in the daily scrum should be captured by the scrum master and displayed on the team's scrum board or on a shared risk board, with an agreed person designated to working toward a resolution (outside of the daily scrum). While the currency of work status is the whole team's responsibility, the scrum master often updates the sprint burndown chart. Where the team does not see the value in these events, it is the responsibility of the scrum master to find out why. This is part of the responsibility of educating the team and stakeholders about the Scrum principles.

No detailed discussions should happen during the daily scrum. Once the meeting ends, individual members can get together to discuss issues in detail; such a meeting is sometimes known as a 'breakout session' or an 'after party'.

Sprint Review

At the end of a sprint, the team holds two events: the sprint review and the sprint retrospective.

At the sprint review, the team:

- Reviews the work that was completed and the planned work that was not completed.

- Presents the completed work to the stakeholders (a.k.a. the demo).

- Collaborates with the stakeholders on what to work on next.

Guidelines for sprint reviews:

- Incomplete work cannot be demonstrated.

- The recommended duration is two hours for a two-week sprint (proportional for other sprint-durations).

Sprint Retrospective

At the sprint retrospective, the team:

- Reflects on the past sprint.

- Identifies and agrees on continuous process improvement actions.

Guidelines for sprint retrospectives:

- Three main questions are asked in the sprint retrospective: What went well during the sprint? What did not go well? What could be improved for better productivity in the next sprint?

- The recommended duration is one-and-a-half hours for a two-week sprint (proportional for other sprint duration(s)).

- This event is facilitated by the scrum master.

Backlog Refinement

Backlog refinement (formerly called grooming) is the ongoing process of reviewing product backlog items and checking that they are appropriately prepared and ordered in a way that makes them clear and executable for teams once they enter sprints via the sprint planning activity. Product backlog items may be broken into multiple smaller ones. Acceptance criteria may be clarified. Dependencies may be identified and investigated.

Although not originally a core Scrum practice, backlog refinement has been added to the Scrum Guide and adopted as a way of managing the quality of product backlog items entering a sprint, with a recommended investment of up to 10% of a team's sprint capacity.

The backlog can also include technical debt (also known as design debt or code debt). This is a concept in software development that reflects the implied cost of additional rework caused by choosing an easy solution now instead of using a better approach that would take longer.

Cancelling a Sprint

The product owner can cancel a sprint if necessary. The product owner may do so with input from the team, scrum master or management. For instance, management may wish the product owner to cancel a sprint if external circumstances negate the value of the sprint goal. If a sprint is abnormally terminated, the next step is to conduct a new sprint planning, where the reason for the termination is reviewed.

Artifacts

Product Backlog

The product backlog is a breakdown of work to be done and contains an ordered list of product requirements that a scrum team maintains for a product. Common formats include user stories and use cases. The requirements define features, bug fixes, non-functional requirements, etc.—whatever must be done to deliver a viable product. The product owner prioritizes product backlog items (PBIs) based on considerations such as risk, business value, dependencies, size, and date needed.

The product backlog is what will be delivered, ordered into the sequence in which it should be delivered. It is visible to everyone but may only be changed with the consent of the product owner, who is ultimately responsible for ordering product backlog items for the development team to choose.

The product backlog contains the product owner's assessment of business value and the development team's assessment of development effort, which are often, but not always, stated in story points using the rounded Fibonacci scale. These estimates help the product owner to gauge the timeline and may influence the ordering of product backlog items; for example, if two features have the same business value, the product owner may schedule earlier delivery of the one with the lower development effort (because the return on investment is higher) or the one with higher development effort (because it is more complex or riskier, and they want to retire that risk earlier).

The product backlog and the business value of each product backlog item is the responsibility of the product owner. The effort to deliver each item is estimated by the development team in story points, or time. By estimating in story points, the team reduces the dependency in individual developers; this is useful especially in dynamic teams where developers are often assigned to other projects after sprint delivery. For instance, if a user story is estimated as a 5 in effort (using Fibonacci sequence), it remains 5 regardless of how many developers are working on it.

Story points define the effort in a time-box, so they do not change with time. For instance, in one hour an individual can walk, run, or climb, but the effort expended is clearly different. The gap progression between the terms in the Fibonacci sequence encourages the team to deliver carefully considered estimates. Estimates of 1, 2 or 3 imply similar efforts (1 being trivial), but if the team estimates an 8 or 13 (or higher), the impact on both delivery and budget can be significant. The value of using story points is that the team can reuse them by comparing similar work from previous sprints, but it should be recognized that estimates are relative to the team. For example, an estimate of 5 for one team could be a 2 for another having senior developers and higher skills.

Every team should have a product owner, although in many instances a product owner could work with more than one team. The product owner is responsible for maximizing the value of the product. The product owner gathers input and takes feedback from, and is lobbied by, many people, but ultimately makes the call on what gets built.

The product backlog:

- Captures requests to modify a product—including new features, replacing old features, removing features, and fixing issues.

- Ensures the development team has work that maximizes business benefit to the product owner.

Typically, the product owner and the scrum team work together to develop the breakdown of work; this becomes the product backlog, which evolves as new information surfaces about the product and about its customers, and so later sprints may address new work.

Management

A product backlog, in its simplest form, is merely a list of items to work on. Having well-established rules about how work is added, removed and ordered helps the whole team make better decisions about how to change the product.

The product owner prioritizes product backlog items based on which are needed soonest. The team then chooses which items they can complete in the coming sprint. On the scrum board, the team moves items from the product backlog to the sprint backlog, which is the list of items they will build. Conceptually, it is ideal for the team to only select what they think they can accomplish from the top of the list, but it is not unusual to see in practice that teams are able to take lower-priority items from the list along with the top ones selected. This normally happens because there is time left within the sprint to accommodate more work. Items at the top of the backlog, the items to work on first, should be broken down into stories that are suitable for the development team to work on. The further down the backlog goes, the less refined the items should be. As Schwaber and Beedle put it "The lower the priority, the less detail until you can barely make out the backlog item."

As the team works through the backlog, it must be assumed that change happens outside their environment—the team can learn about new market opportunities to take advantage of, competitor threats that arise, and feedback from customers that can change the way the product was meant to work. All of these new ideas tend to trigger the team to adapt the backlog to incorporate new knowledge. This is part of the fundamental mindset of an agile team. The world changes, the backlog is never finished.

Sprint Backlog

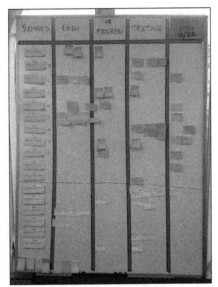

A scrum task board.

The sprint backlog is the list of work the development team must address during the next sprint. The list is derived by the scrum team progressively selecting product backlog items in priority order from the top of the product backlog until they feel they have enough work to fill the sprint. The development team should keep in mind its past performance assessing its capacity for the new sprint, and use this as a guideline of how much 'effort' they can complete.

The product backlog items may be broken down into tasks by the development team. Tasks on the sprint backlog are never assigned (or pushed) to team members by someone else; rather team members sign up for (or pull) tasks as needed according to the backlog priority and their own skills and capacity. This promotes self-organization of the development team and developer buy-in.

The sprint backlog is the property of the development team, and all included estimates are provided by the development team. Often an accompanying task board is used to see and change the state of the tasks of the current sprint, like to do, in progress and done.

Once a sprint backlog is committed, no additional work can be added to the sprint backlog except by the team. Once a sprint has been delivered, the product backlog is analyzed and reprioritized if necessary, and the next set of functionality is selected for the next sprint.

Increment

The *increment* is the potentially releasable output of the sprint that meets the sprint goal. It is formed from all the completed sprint backlog items, integrated with the work of all previous sprints. The increment must be complete, according to the scrum team's *definition of done* (DoD), fully functioning, and in a usable condition regardless of whether the product owner decides to actually deploy and use it.

Extensions

The following artifacts and techniques can be used to help people use Scrum:

Sprint Burndown Chart

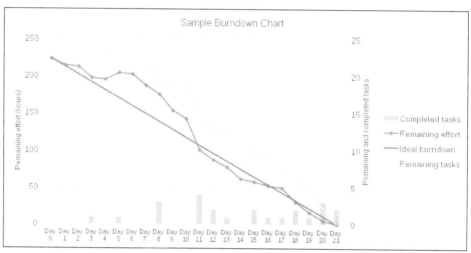

A sample burndown chart for a completed sprint,
showing remaining effort at the end of each day.

The sprint burndown chart is a publicly displayed chart showing remaining work in the sprint backlog. Updated every day, it gives a simple view of the sprint progress. It also provides quick visualizations for reference. The horizontal axis of the sprint burndown chart shows the days in a sprint, while the vertical axis shows the amount of work remaining each day (typically representing the estimate of hours of work remaining).

During sprint planning, the ideal burndown chart is plotted. Then, during the sprint, each member picks up tasks from the sprint backlog and works on them. At the end of the day, they update the remaining hours for tasks to be completed. In such a way, the actual burndown chart is updated day by day.

Release Burn-up Chart

The release burn-up chart is a way for the team to provide visibility and track progress toward a release. Updated at the end of each sprint, it shows progress toward delivering a forecast scope. The horizontal axis of the release burn-up chart shows the sprints in a release, while the vertical axis shows the amount of work completed at the end of each sprint (typically representing cumulative story points of work completed). Progress is plotted as a line that grows up to meet a horizontal line that represents the forecast scope; often shown with a forecast, based on progress to date, that indicates how much scope might be completed by a given release date or how many sprints it will take to complete the given scope.

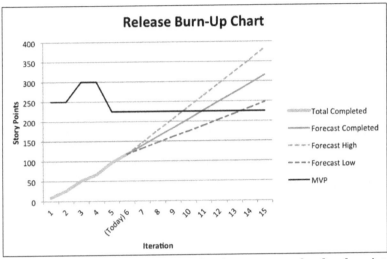

A sample burn-up chart for a release, showing scope completed each sprint.

The release burn-up chart makes it easy to see how much work has been completed, how much work has been added or removed (if the horizontal scope line moves), and how much work is left to be done.

Definition of Ready (DoR)

The start criteria to determine whether the specifications and inputs are set enough to start the work item, i.e. a user story.

Definition of Done (DoD)

The exit-criteria to determine whether a product backlog item is complete. In many cases, the DoD requires that all regression tests be successful. The definition of done may vary from one scrum team to another but must be consistent within one team.

Velocity

The total effort a team is capable of in a sprint. The number is derived by evaluating the work (typically in user story points) completed in the last sprint. The collection of historical velocity data is a guideline for assisting the team in understanding how much work they can likely achieve in a future sprint.

Spike

A time-boxed period used to research a concept or create a simple prototype. Spikes can either be planned to take place in between sprints or, for larger teams, a spike might be accepted as one of many sprint delivery objectives. Spikes are often introduced before the delivery of large or complex product backlog items in order to secure budget, expand knowledge, or produce a proof of concept.

The duration and objective(s) of a spike is agreed between product owner and development team before the start. Unlike sprint commitments, spikes may or may not deliver tangible, shippable, valuable functionality. For example, the objective of a spike might be to successfully reach a decision on a course of action. The spike is over when the time is up, not necessarily when the objective has been delivered.

Tracer Bullet

Also called a drone spike, a tracer bullet is a spike with the current architecture, current technology set, current set of best practices that result in production quality code. It might just be a very narrow implementation of the functionality but is not throwaway code. It is of production quality, and the rest of the iterations can build on this code. The name has military origins as ammunition that makes the path of the bullet visible, allowing for corrections. Often these implementations are a 'quick shot' through all layers of an application, such as connecting a single form's input field to the back-end, to prove the layers connect as expected.

Limitations

The benefits of Scrum may be more difficult to achieve when:

- Teams whose members are geographically dispersed or part-time: In Scrum, developers should have close and ongoing interaction, ideally working together in the same space most of the time. While recent improvements in technology have reduced the impact of these barriers (e.g., being able to collaborate on a digital whiteboard), the Agile manifesto asserts that the best communication is face to face.

- Teams whose members have very specialized skills: In Scrum, developers should have T-shaped skills, allowing them to work on tasks outside of their specialization. This can be encouraged by good Scrum leadership. While team members with very specific skills can and do contribute well, they should be encouraged to learn more about and collaborate with other disciplines.

- Products with many external dependencies: In Scrum, dividing product development into short sprints requires careful planning; external dependencies, such as user acceptance testing or coordination with other teams, can lead to delays and the failure of individual sprints.

- Products that are mature or legacy or with regulated quality control: In Scrum, product increments should be fully developed and tested in a single sprint; products that need large amounts of regression testing or safety testing (e.g., medical devices or vehicle control) for each release are less suited to short sprints than to longer waterfall releases.

From a business perspective, Scrum has many virtues, one of which is that it is designed to yield the best business solutions. However, the efficiency by which it does so in any given organization can vary widely and is largely dependent on the ability of the organization to adhere to the implementation guidelines. Every company has its own distinct organizational structure, culture, and set of business practices, and some are more naturally amenable to this methodology than others.

Tools for Implementation

Like other agile methods, effective adoption of Scrum can be supported through a wide range of tools.

Many companies use universal tools, such as spreadsheets to build and maintain artifacts such as the sprint backlog. There are also open-source and proprietary software packages for Scrum—which are either dedicated to product development using the Scrum framework or support multiple product development approaches including Scrum.

Other organizations implement Scrum without software tools and maintain their artifacts in hard-copy forms such as paper, whiteboards, and sticky notes.

Scrum Values

Scrum is a feedback-driven empirical approach which is, like all empirical process control, underpinned by the three pillars of transparency, inspection, and adaptation. All work within the Scrum framework should be visible to those responsible for the outcome: the process, the workflow, progress, etc. In order to make these things visible, scrum teams need to frequently inspect the product being developed and how well the team is working. With frequent inspection, the team can spot when their work deviates outside of acceptable limits and adapt their process or the product under development.

These three pillars require trust and openness in the team, which the following five values of Scrum enable:

- Commitment: Team members individually commit to achieving their team goals, each and every sprint.

- Courage: Team members know they have the courage to work through conflict and challenges together so that they can do the right thing.

- Focus: Team members focus exclusively on their team goals and the sprint backlog; there should be no work done other than through their backlog.

- Openness: Team members and their stakeholders agree to be transparent about their work and any challenges they face.

- Respect: Team members respect each other to be technically capable and to work with good intent.

Adaptations

The hybridization of Scrum with other software development methodologies is common as Scrum does not cover the whole product development lifecycle; therefore, organizations find the need to add in additional processes to create a more comprehensive implementation. For example, at the start of product development, organizations commonly add process guidance on the business case, requirements gathering and prioritization, initial high-level design, and budget and schedule forecasting.

Various authors and communities of people who use Scrum have also suggested more detailed techniques for how to apply or adapt Scrum to particular problems or organizations. Many refer to these methodological techniques as 'patterns' - by analogy with design patterns in architecture and software. Such patterns have extended Scrum outside of the software development domain into Manufacturing, Finance and Human Resources.

Scrumban

Scrumban is a software production model based on Scrum and Kanban. Scrumban is especially suited for product maintenance with frequent and unexpected work items, such as production defects or programming errors. In such cases the time-limited sprints of the Scrum framework may be perceived to be of less benefit, although Scrum's daily events and other practices can still be applied, depending on the team and the situation at hand. Visualization of the work stages and limitations for simultaneous unfinished work and defects are familiar from the Kanban model. Using these methods, the team's workflow is directed in a way that allows for minimum completion time for each work item or programming error, and on the other hand ensures each team member is constantly employed.

To illustrate each stage of work, teams working in the same space often use post-it notes or a large whiteboard. In the case of decentralized teams, stage-illustration software such as Assembla, JIRA or Agilo.

The major differences between Scrum and Kanban is that in Scrum work is divided into sprints that last a fixed amount of time, whereas in Kanban the flow of work is continuous. This is visible in work stage tables, which in Scrum are emptied after each sprint, whereas in Kanban all tasks are marked on the same table. Scrum focuses on teams with multifaceted know-how, whereas Kanban makes specialized, functional teams possible.

Scrum of Scrums

The scrum of scrums is a technique to operate Scrum at scale, for multiple teams working on the same product, allowing them to discuss progress on their interdependencies, focusing on how to coordinate delivering software, especially on areas of overlap and integration. Depending on the cadence (timing) of the scrum of scrums, the relevant daily scrum for each scrum team ends by designating one member as an ambassador to participate in the scrum of scrums with ambassadors from other teams. Depending on the context, the ambassadors may be technical contributors or each team's scrum master.

Rather than simply a progress update, the scrum of scrums should focus on how teams are collectively working to resolve, mitigate, or accept any risks, impediments, dependencies, and assumptions (RIDAs) that have been identified. The scrum of scrums tracks these RIDAs via a backlog of its own, such as a risk board (sometimes known as a ROAM board after the initials of resolved, owned, accepted, and mitigated), which typically leads to greater coordination and collaboration between teams.

This should run similar to a daily scrum, with each ambassador answering the following four questions:

- What risks, impediments, dependencies, or assumptions has your team resolved since we last met?

- What risks, impediments, dependencies, or assumptions will your team resolve before we meet again?

- Are there any new risks, impediments, dependencies, or assumptions slowing your team down or getting in their way?

- Are you about to introduce a new risk, impediment, dependency, or assumption that will get in another team's way?

As Jeff Sutherland commented,

> Since I originally defined the Scrum of Scrums (Ken Schwaber was at IDX working with me), I can definitively say the Scrum of Scrums is not a 'meta Scrum'. The Scrum of Scrums as I have used it is responsible for delivering the working software of all teams to the Definition of Done at the end of the sprint, or for releases during the sprint. PatientKeeper delivered to production four times per Sprint. Ancestry.com delivers to production 220 times per two-week Sprint. Hubspot delivers live software 100-300 times a day. The Scrum of Scrums Master is held accountable for making this work. So the Scrum of Scrums is an operational delivery mechanism.

Large-scale Scrum

Large-scale Scrum (LeSS) is a product development framework that extends Scrum with scaling rules and guidelines without losing the original purposes of Scrum.

There are two levels to the framework: the first LeSS level is designed for up to eight teams; the second level, known as 'LeSS Huge', introduces additional scaling elements for development with up to hundreds of developers. "Scaling Scrum starts with understanding and being able to adopt standard real one-team Scrum. Large-scale Scrum requires examining the purpose of single-team Scrum elements and figuring out how to reach the same purpose while staying within the constraints of the standard Scrum rules."

Bas Vodde and Craig Larman evolved the LeSS framework from their experiences working with large-scale product development, especially in the telecoms and finance industries. It evolved by taking Scrum and trying many different experiments to discover what works. In 2013, the experiments were solidified into the LeSS framework rules. The intention of LeSS is to 'descale' organization complexity, dissolving unnecessary complex organizational solutions, and solving them in simpler ways. Less roles, less management, less organizational structures.

Timeboxing

In time management, timeboxing allocates a fixed time period, called a timebox, within which planned activity takes place. It is employed by several project management approaches and for personal time management.

Many successful software development projects use timeboxing, especially smaller ones. Adopting timeboxing more than tripled developer productivity at DuPont in the '80s. In some cases, applications were completely delivered within the time estimated to complete just a specification. However, Steve McConnell argues that not every product is suitable and that timeboxing should only be used after the customer agrees to cut features, not quality. There is little evidence for strong adoption amongst the largest class of projects.

Timeboxing has been adopted by some notable software development methodologies:

- Dynamic systems development method (DSDM).

- In lean software development, pull scheduling with Kanban provides short term time management. When developing a large and complex system, when long term planning is required timeboxing is layered above.

- Rapid application development (RAD) software development process features iterative development and software prototyping. According to Steve McConnell, timeboxing is a "Best Practice" for RAD and a typical timebox length should be 60–120 days.

- Scrum was influenced by ideas of timeboxing and iterative development. Regular timeboxed units known as sprints form the basic unit of development. A typical length for a sprint is less than 30 days. Sprint planning, sprint retrospective and sprint review meetings are timeboxed.

- In Extreme programming methodologies, development planning is timeboxed into iterations typically 1, 2 or 3 weeks in length. The business revalues pending user stories before each iteration.

Agile software development advocates moving from plan driven to value driven development. Quality and time are fixed but flexibility allowed in scope. Delivering the most important features first leads to an earlier return on investment than the waterfall model.

A lack of detailed specifications typically is the result of a lack of time, or the lack of knowledge of the desired end result (solution). In many types of projects, and especially in software engineering, analyzing and defining all requirements and specifications before the start of the realization phase is impossible. Timeboxing can be a favorable type of contracting for projects in which the deadline is the most critical aspect and when not all requirements are completely specified up front. This also allows for new feedback or insights discovered during the project to be reflected in the end result.

Feature Drivem Development

Feature-driven development (FDD) is an iterative and incremental software development process. It is a lightweight or Agile method for developing software. FDD blends a number of industry-recognized best practices into a cohesive whole. These practices are driven from a client-valued functionality (feature) perspective. Its main purpose is to deliver tangible, working software repeatedly in a timely manner in accordance with the Principles behind the Agile Manifesto.

FDD was initially devised by Jeff De Luca to meet the specific needs of a 15-month, 50-person software development project at a large Singapore bank in 1997. This resulted in a set of five processes that covered the development of an overall model and the listing, planning, design, and building of features. The first process is heavily influenced by Peter Coad's approach to object modelling. The second process incorporates Coad's ideas of using a feature list to manage functional requirements and development tasks. The other processes are a result of Jeff De Luca's experience. There have been several implementations of FDD since its successful use on the Singapore project.

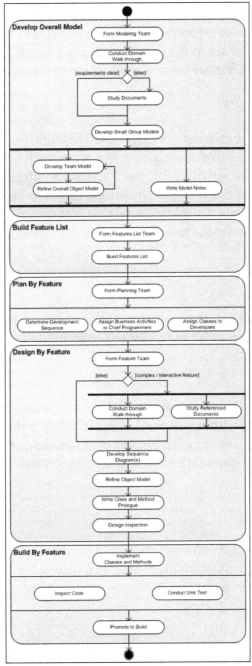

Process model for FDD.

FDD is a model-driven short-iteration process that consists of five basic activities. For accurate state reporting and keeping track of the software development project, milestones that mark the progress made on each feature are defined. This topic gives a high level overview of the activities. In the figure on the right, the meta-process model for these activities is displayed. During the first two sequential activities, an overall model shape is established. The final three activities are iterated for each feature.

Develop Overall Model

The FDD project starts with a high-level walkthrough of the scope of the system and its context. Next, detailed domain models are created for each modelling area by small groups and presented for peer review. One or more of the proposed models are selected to become the model for each domain area. Domain area models are progressively merged into an overall model.

Build Feature List

Knowledge gathered during the initial modeling is used to identify a list of features by functionally decomposing the domain into subject areas. Subject areas each contain business activities, and the steps within each business activity form the basis for a categorized feature list. Features in this respect are small pieces of client-valued functions expressed in the form "<action> <result> <object>", for example: 'Calculate the total of a sale' or 'Validate the password of a user'. Features should not take more than two weeks to complete, else they should be broken down into smaller pieces.

Plan by Feature

After the feature list is completed, the next step is to produce the development plan and assign ownership of features (or feature sets) as classes to programmers.

Design by Feature

A design package is produced for each feature. A chief programmer selects a small group of features that are to be developed within two weeks. Together with the corresponding class owners, the chief programmer works out detailed sequence diagrams for each feature and refines the overall model. Next, the class and method prologues are written and finally a design inspection is held.

Build by Feature

After a successful design inspection for each activity to produce a feature is planned, the class owners develop code for their classes. After unit testing and successful code inspection, the completed feature is promoted to the main build.

Milestones

Since features are small, completing a feature is a relatively small task. For accurate state reporting and keeping track of the software development project, it is important to mark the progress made on each feature. FDD therefore defines six milestones per feature that are to be completed sequentially. The first three milestones are completed during the Design By Feature activity, and the last three are completed during the Build By Feature activity. To track progress, a percentage complete is assigned to each milestone. In the table below the milestones and their completion percentage are shown. At the point that coding begins, a feature is already 44% complete (Domain Walkthrough 1%, Design 40% and Design Inspection 3% = 44%).

Table: Milestones					
Domain Walkthrough	Design	Design Inspection	Code	Code Inspection	Promote To Build
1%	40%	3%	45%	10%	1%

Best Practices

Feature-driven development is built on a core set of software engineering best practices aimed at a client-valued feature perspective.

- Domain Object modelling: Domain Object modelling consists of exploring and explaining the domain of the problem to be solved. The resulting domain object model provides an overall framework in which to add features.

- Developing by Feature: Any function that is too complex to be implemented within two weeks is further decomposed into smaller functions until each sub-problem is small enough to be called a feature. This makes it easier to deliver correct functions and to extend or modify the system.

- Individual Class (Code) Ownership: Individual class ownership means that distinct pieces or grouping of code are assigned to a single owner. The owner is responsible for the consistency, performance, and conceptual integrity of the class.

- Feature Teams: A feature team is a small, dynamically formed team that develops a small activity. Multiple minds are always applied to each design decision, and multiple design options are evaluated before one is chosen.

- Inspections: Inspections are carried out to ensure good quality design and code primarily by detection of defects.

- Configuration Management: Configuration management helps with identifying the source code for all features that have been completed to date and maintaining a history of changes to classes as feature teams enhance them.

- Regular Builds: Regular builds ensure there is always an up-to-date system that can be demonstrated to the client and helps highlight integration errors of source code for the features early.

- Visibility of progress and results: Managers steer a project using frequent, appropriate, and accurate progress reporting from all levels inside and outside the project based on completed work.

Metamodel (Metamodelling)

Metamodelling helps visualize both the processes and the data of a method. This allows methods to be compared, and method fragments in the method engineering process can easily be reused. Usage of this technique is consistent with UML standards.

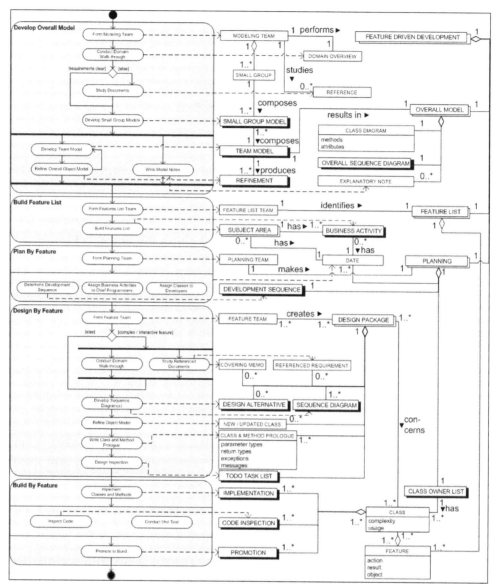

Process-Data Model for FDD.

The left side of the metadata model shows the five basic activities involved in a software development project using FDD. The activities all contain sub-activities that corresponding to sub-activities in the FDD process description. The right side of the model shows the concepts involved. These concepts originate from the activities depicted in the left side of the diagram.

Web Application Framework

A web framework (WF) or web application framework (WAF) is a software framework that is designed to support the development of web applications including web services, web resources, and web APIs. Web frameworks provide a standard way to build and deploy web applications on the World Wide Web. Web frameworks aim to automate the overhead associated with common activities performed in web development. For example, many web frameworks provide libraries for database access, templating frameworks, and session management, and they often promote code reuse. Although they often target development of dynamic web sites, they are also applicable to static websites.

Types of Framework Architectures

Most web frameworks are based on the model–view–controller (MVC) pattern.

Model–View–Controller (MVC)

Many frameworks follow the MVC architectural pattern to separate the data model with business rules from the user interface. This is generally considered a good practice as it modularizes code, promotes code reuse, and allows multiple interfaces to be applied. In web applications, this permits different views to be presented, such as web pages for humans, and web service interfaces for remote applications.

Push-based vs. Pull-based

Most MVC frameworks follow a push-based architecture also called "action-based". These frameworks use actions that do the required processing, and then "push" the data to the view layer to render the results. Django, Ruby on Rails, Symfony, Spring MVC, Stripes, Sails.js, Diamond, CodeIgniter are good examples of this architecture. An alternative to this is pull-based architecture, sometimes also called "component-based". These frameworks start with the view layer, which can then "pull" results from multiple controllers as needed. In this architecture, multiple controllers can be involved with a single view. Lift, Tapestry, JBoss Seam, JavaServer Faces, (μ)Micro, and Wicket are examples of pull-based architectures. Play, Struts, RIFE, and ZK have support for both push- and pull-based application controller calls.

Three-tier Organization

In three-tier organization, applications are structured around three physical tiers: client, application, and database. The database is normally an RDBMS. The application contains the business logic, running on a server and communicates with the client using HTTP. The client on web applications is a web browser that runs HTML generated by the application layer. The term should not be confused with MVC, where, unlike in three-tier architecture, it is considered a good practice to keep business logic away from the controller, the "middle layer".

Framework Applications

Frameworks are built to support the construction of internet applications based on a single programming language, ranging in focus from general purpose tools such as Zend Framework and Ruby on Rails, which augment the capabilities of a specific language, to native-language programmable packages built around a specific user application, such as content management systems, some mobile development tools and some portal tools.

General-purpose Website Frameworks

Web frameworks must function according to the architectural rules of browsers and web protocols such as HTTP, which is stateless. Webpages are served up by a server and can then be modified by the browser using JavaScript. Either approach has its advantages and disadvantages.

Server-side page changes typically require that the page be refreshed, but allow any language to be used and more computing power to be utilized. Client-side changes allow the page to be updated in small chunks which feels like a desktop application, but are limited to JavaScript and run in the user's browser, which may have limited computing power. Some mix of the two is typically used. Applications which make heavy use of JavaScript are called single-page applications and typically make use of a client-side JavaScript web framework to organize the code.

Server-side

- ASP.NET Core,
- CakePHP,
- Catalyst,
- CppCMS,
- Django,
- Express.js,
- Gridfyx PHP,
- Laravel,
- Mojolicious,
- Ruby on Rails,
- Sails.js,
- Spring MVC,
- Wt (web toolkit),
- Zend Framework.

Client-side

Examples include Backbone.js, AngularJS, Angular, EmberJS, ReactJS and Vue.js.

Features

Frameworks typically set the control flow of a program and allow the user of the framework to "hook into" that flow by exposing various events. This "inversion of control" design pattern is considered to be a defining principle of a framework, and benefits the code by enforcing a common flow for a team which everyone can customize in similar ways. For example, some popular "microframeworks" such as Ruby's Sinatra (which inspired Express.js) allow for "middleware" hooks prior to and after HTTP requests. These middleware functions can be anything, and allow the user to define logging, authentication and session management, and redirecting.

Caching

Web caching is the caching of web documents in order to reduce bandwidth usage, server load, and perceived "lag". A web cache stores copies of documents passing through it; subsequent requests may be satisfied from the cache if certain conditions are met. Some application frameworks provide mechanisms for caching documents and bypassing various stages of the page's preparation, such as database access or template interpretation.

Security

Some web frameworks come with authentication and authorization frameworks, that enable the web server to identify the users of the application, and restrict access to functions based on some defined criteria. Drupal is one example that provides role-based access to pages, and provides a web-based interface for creating users and assigning them roles.

Database Access, Mapping and Configuration

Many web frameworks create a unified API to a database backend, enabling web applications to work with a variety of databases with no code changes, and allowing programmers to work with higher-level concepts. Additionally, some object-oriented frameworks contain mapping tools to provide object-relational mapping, which maps objects to tuples.

Some frameworks minimize web application configuration through the use of introspection and/ or following well-known conventions. For example, many Java frameworks use Hibernate as a persistence layer, which can generate a database schema at runtime capable of persisting the necessary information. This allows the application designer to design business objects without needing to explicitly define a database schema. Frameworks such as Ruby on Rails can also work in reverse, that is, define properties of model objects at runtime based on a database schema.

Other features web frameworks may provide include transactional support and database migration tools.

URL Mapping

A framework's URL mapping or routing facility is the mechanism by which the framework interprets URLs. Some frameworks, such as Drupal and Django, match the provided URL against pre-determined patterns using regular expressions, while some others use rewriting techniques to translate the provided URL into one that the underlying engine will recognize. Another technique is that of graph traversal such as used by Zope, where a URL is decomposed in steps that traverse an object graph (of models and views).

A URL mapping system that uses pattern matching or rewriting to route and handle requests allows for shorter more "friendly URLs" to be used, increasing the simplicity of the site and allowing for better indexing by search engines. For example, a URL that ends with "/page.cgi?cat=-science&topic=physics" could be changed to simply "/page/science/physics". This makes the URL easier for people to remember, read and write, and provides search engines with better information about the structural layout of the site. A graph traversal approach also tends to result in the creation of friendly URLs. A shorter URL such as "/page/science" tends to exist by default as that is simply a shorter form of the longer traversal to "/page/science/physics".

AJAX

Ajax, shorthand for "Asynchronous JavaScript and XML", is a web development technique for creating web applications. The intent is to make web pages feel more responsive by exchanging small amounts of data with the server behind the scenes, so that the entire web page does not have to be reloaded each time the user requests a change. This is intended to increase a web page's interactivity, speed, and usability.

Due to the complexity of Ajax programming in JavaScript, there are numerous Ajax frameworks that exclusively deal with Ajax support. Some Ajax frameworks are even embedded as a part of larger frameworks. For example, the jQuery JavaScript library is included in Ruby on Rails.

With the increased interest in developing "Web 2.0" rich media applications, the complexity of programming directly in Ajax and JavaScript has become so apparent that compiler technology has stepped in, to allow developers to code in high-level languages such as Java, Python and Ruby. The first of these compilers was Morfik followed by Google Web Toolkit, with ports to Python and Ruby in the form of Pyjs and RubyJS following some time after. These compilers and their associated widget set libraries make the development of rich media Ajax applications much more akin to that of developing desktop applications.

Web Services

Some frameworks provide tools for creating and providing web services. These utilities may offer similar tools as the rest of the web application.

Web Resources

A number of newer Web 2.0 RESTful frameworks are now providing resource-oriented architecture (ROA) infrastructure for building collections of resources in a sort of Semantic Web ontology, based on concepts from Resource Description Framework (RDF).

UML

The Unified Modeling Language (UML) is a general-purpose, developmental, modeling language in the field of software engineering that is intended to provide a standard way to visualize the design of a system.

The creation of UML was originally motivated by the desire to standardize the disparate notational systems and approaches to software design. It was developed by Grady Booch, Ivar Jacobson and James Rumbaugh at Rational Software in 1994–1995, with further development led by them through 1996.

In 1997, UML was adopted as a standard by the Object Management Group (OMG), and has been managed by this organization ever since. In 2005, UML was also published by the International Organization for Standardization (ISO) as an approved ISO standard. Since then the standard has been periodically revised to cover the latest revision of UML.

Generations of UML

Before UML 1.0

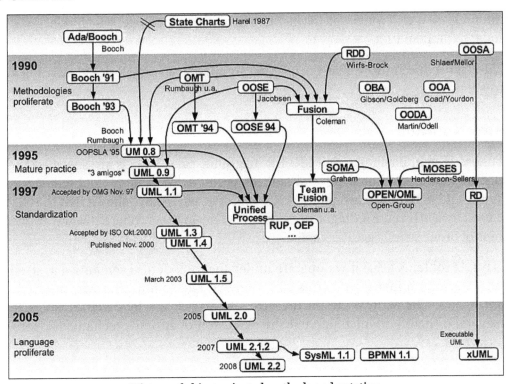

History of object-oriented methods and notation.

UML has been evolving since the second half of the 1990s and has its roots in the object-oriented programming methods developed in the late 1980s and early 1990s. The timeline shows the highlights of the history of object-oriented modeling methods and notation.

It is originally based on the notations of the Booch method, the object-modeling technique (OMT) and object-oriented software engineering (OOSE), which it has integrated into a single language.

Rational Software Corporation hired James Rumbaugh from General Electric in 1994 and after that the company became the source for two of the most popular object-oriented modeling approaches of the day: Rumbaugh's object-modeling technique (OMT) and Grady Booch's method. They were soon assisted in their efforts by Ivar Jacobson, the creator of the object-oriented software engineering (OOSE) method, who joined them at Rational in 1995.

UML 1.x

Under the technical leadership of those three (Rumbaugh, Jacobson and Booch), a consortium called the UML Partners was organized in 1996 to complete the Unified Modeling Language (UML) specification, and propose it to the Object Management Group (OMG) for standardisation. The partnership also contained additional interested parties (for example HP, DEC, IBM and Microsoft). The UML Partners' UML 1.0 draft was proposed to the OMG in January 1997 by the consortium. During the same month the UML Partners formed a group, designed to define the exact meaning of language constructs, chaired by Cris Kobryn and administered by Ed Eykholt, to finalize the specification and integrate it with other standardization efforts. The result of this work, UML 1.1, was submitted to the OMG in August 1997 and adopted by the OMG in November 1997.

After the first release a task force was formed to improve the language, which released several minor revisions, 1.3, 1.4, and 1.5.

The standards it produced (as well as the original standard) have been noted as being ambiguous and inconsistent.

Cardinality Notation

As with database Chen, Bachman, and ISO ER diagrams, class models are specified to use "look-across" cardinalities, even though several authors prefer same-side or "look-here" for roles and both minimum and maximum cardinalities. Recent researchers have shown that the "look-across" technique used by UML and ER diagrams is less effective and less coherent when applied to n-ary relationships of order strictly greater than 2.

Feinerer says: "Problems arise if we operate under the look-across semantics as used for UML associations. Hartmann investigates this situation and shows how and why different transformations fail.", and: "As we will see on the next few pages, the look-across interpretation introduces several difficulties which prevent the extension of simple mechanisms from binary to n-ary associations."

UML 2

UML 2.0 major revision replaced version 1.5 in 2005, which was developed with an enlarged consortium to improve the language further to reflect new experience on usage of its features.

Although UML 2.1 was never released as a formal specification, versions 2.1.1 and 2.1.2 appeared in 2007, followed by UML 2.2 in February 2009. UML 2.3 was formally released in May 2010. UML 2.4.1 was formally released in August 2011. UML 2.5 was released in October 2012 as an "In progress" version and was officially released in June 2015. Formal version 2.5.1 was adopted in December 2017.

There are four parts to the UML 2.x specification:

- The Superstructure that defines the notation and semantics for diagrams and their model elements.

- The Infrastructure that defines the core metamodel on which the Superstructure is based.

- The Object Constraint Language (OCL) for defining rules for model elements.

- The UML Diagram Interchange that defines how UML 2 diagram layouts are exchanged.

The current versions of these standards are:

- UML Superstructure version 2.4.1.

- UML Infrastructure version 2.4.1.

- OCL version 2.3.1.

- UML Diagram Interchange version 1.0.

It continues to be updated and improved by the revision task force, who resolve any issues with the language.

Design

UML offers a way to visualize a system's architectural blueprints in a diagram, including elements such as:

- Any activities (jobs);

- Individual components of the system; and how they can interact with other software components;

- How the system will run;

- How entities interact with others (components and interfaces);

- External user interface.

Although originally intended for object-oriented design documentation, UML has been extended to a larger set of design documentation and been found useful in many contexts.

Software Development Methods

UML is not a development method by itself; however, it was designed to be compatible with the leading object-oriented software development methods of its time, for example OMT, Booch method, Objectory and especially RUP that it was originally intended to be used with when work began at Rational Software.

Modeling

It is important to distinguish between the UML model and the set of diagrams of a system. A diagram is a partial graphic representation of a system's model. The set of diagrams need not completely cover the model and deleting a diagram does not change the model. The model may also contain documentation that drives the model elements and diagrams (such as written use cases).

UML diagrams represent two different views of a system model:

- Static (or structural) view: emphasizes the static structure of the system using objects, attributes, operations and relationships. It includes class diagrams and composite structure diagrams.

- Dynamic (or behavioral) view: emphasizes the dynamic behavior of the system by showing collaborations among objects and changes to the internal states of objects. This view includes sequence diagrams, activity diagrams and state machine diagrams.

UML models can be exchanged among UML tools by using the XML Metadata Interchange (XMI) format.

In UML, one of the key tools for behavior modelling is the use-case model, caused by OOSE. Use cases are a way of specifying required usages of a system. Typically, they are used to capture the requirements of a system, that is, what a system is supposed to do.

Diagrams

UML 2 has many types of diagrams, which are divided into two categories. Some types represent structural information, and the rest represent general types of behavior, including a few that represent different aspects of interactions. These diagrams can be categorized hierarchically as shown in the following class diagram:

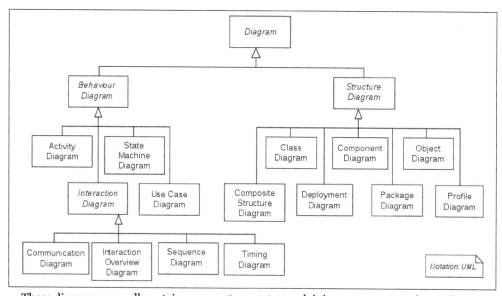

These diagrams may all contain comments or notes explaining usage, constraint, or intent.

Structure Diagrams

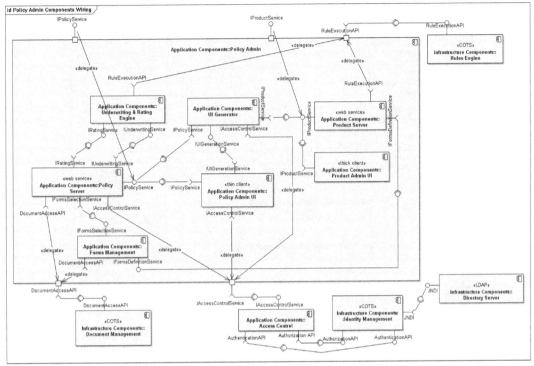

Component diagram.

Structure diagrams emphasize the things that must be present in the system being modeled. Since structure diagrams represent the structure, they are used extensively in documenting the software architecture of software systems. For example, the component diagram describes how a software system is split up into components and shows the dependencies among these components.

BankAccount
owner : String balance : Dollars = 0
deposit (amount : Dollars) withdrawal (amount : Dollars)

Class diagram.

Behavior Diagrams

Behavior diagrams emphasize what must happen in the system being modeled. Since behavior diagrams illustrate the behavior of a system, they are used extensively to describe the functionality of software systems. As an example, the activity diagram describes the business and operational step-by-step activities of the components in a system.

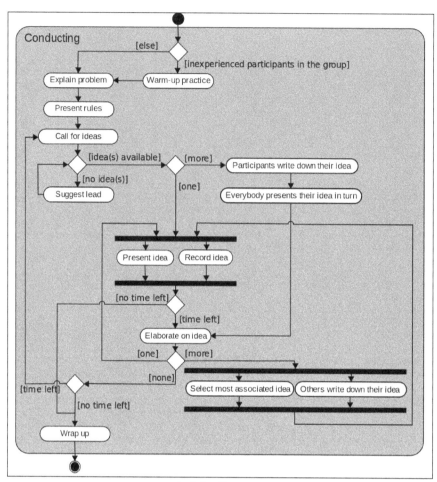

Activity diagram.

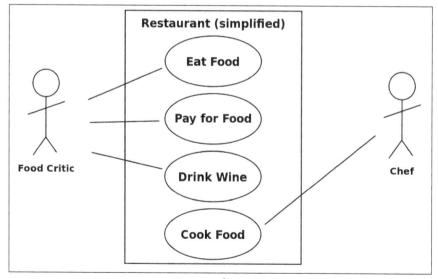

Use case diagram.

Interaction Diagrams

Interaction diagrams, a subset of behavior diagrams, emphasize the flow of control and data among the things in the system being modeled. For example, the sequence diagram shows how objects communicate with each other regarding a sequence of messages.

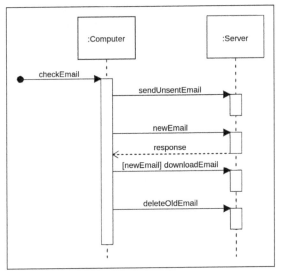

Sequence diagram.

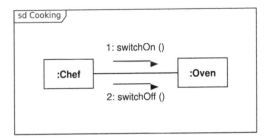

Communication diagram.

Metamodeling

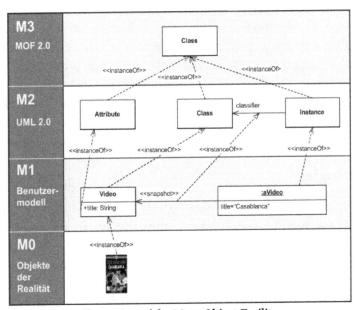

Illustration of the Meta-Object Facility.

The Object Management Group (OMG) has developed a metamodeling architecture to define the UML, called the Meta-Object Facility. MOF is designed as a four-layered architecture, as shown in the image at right. It provides a meta-meta model at the top, called the M3 layer. This M3-model is the language used by Meta-Object Facility to build metamodels, called M2-models.

The most prominent example of a Layer 2 Meta-Object Facility model is the UML metamodel, which describes the UML itself. These M2-models describe elements of the M1-layer, and thus M1-models. These would be, for example, models written in UML. The last layer is the M0-layer or data layer. It is used to describe runtime instances of the system.

The meta-model can be extended using a mechanism called stereotyping. This has been criticised as being insufficient/untenable by Brian Henderson-Sellers and Cesar Gonzalez-Perez in "Uses and Abuses of the Stereotype Mechanism in UML 1.x and 2.0".

Adoption

UML has been marketed for many contexts.

It has been treated, at times, as a design silver bullet, which leads to problems. UML misuse includes overuse (designing every part of the system with it, which is unnecessary) and assuming that novices can design with it.

It is considered a large language, with many constructs. Some people (including Jacobson) feel that UML's size hinders learning (and therefore, using) it.

WEB DESIGN

Web design encompasses many different skills and disciplines in the production and maintenance of websites. The different areas of web design include web graphic design; interface design; authoring, including standardised code and proprietary software; user experience design; and search engine optimization. Often many individuals will work in teams covering different aspects of the design process, although some designers will cover them all. The term web design is normally used to describe the design process relating to the front-end (client side) design of a website including writing markup. Web design partially overlaps web engineering in the broader scope of web development. Web designers are expected to have an awareness of usability and if their role involves creating markup then they are also expected to be up to date with web accessibility guidelines.

Tools and Technologies

Web designers use a variety of different tools depending on what part of the production process they are involved in. These tools are updated over time by newer standards and software but the principles behind them remain the same. Web designers use both vector and raster graphics editors to create web-formatted imagery or design prototypes. Technologies used to create websites include W3C standards like HTML and CSS, which can be hand-coded or generated by WYSIWYG editing software. Other tools web designers might use include mark up validators and other testing tools for usability and accessibility to ensure their websites meet web accessibility guidelines.

Skills and Techniques

Marketing and Communication Design

Marketing and communication design on a website may identify what works for its target market. This can be an age group or particular strand of culture; thus the designer may understand the trends of its audience. Designers may also understand the type of website they are designing, meaning, for example, that (B2B) business-to-business website design considerations might differ greatly from a consumer targeted website such as a retail or entertainment website. Careful consideration might be made to ensure that the aesthetics or overall design of a site do not clash with the clarity and accuracy of the content or the ease of web navigation, especially on a B2B website. Designers may also consider the reputation of the owner or business the site is representing to make sure they are portrayed favourably.

User Experience Design and Interactive Design

User understanding of the content of a website often depends on user understanding of how the website works. This is part of the user experience design. User experience is related to layout, clear instructions and labeling on a website. How well a user understands how they can interact on a site may also depend on the interactive design of the site. If a user perceives the usefulness of the website, they are more likely to continue using it. Users who are skilled and well versed with website use may find a more distinctive, yet less intuitive or less user-friendly website interface useful nonetheless. However, users with less experience are less likely to see the advantages or usefulness of a less intuitive website interface. This drives the trend for a more universal user experience and ease of access to accommodate as many users as possible regardless of user skill. Much of the user experience design and interactive design are considered in the user interface design.

Advanced interactive functions may require plug-ins if not advanced coding language skills. Choosing whether or not to use interactivity that requires plug-ins is a critical decision in user experience design. If the plug-in doesn't come pre-installed with most browsers, there's a risk that the user will have neither the know how or the patience to install a plug-in just to access the content. If the function requires advanced coding language skills, it may be too costly in either time or money to code compared to the amount of enhancement the function will add to the user experience. There's also a risk that advanced interactivity may be incompatible with older browsers or hardware configurations. Publishing a function that doesn't work reliably is potentially worse for the user experience than making no attempt. It depends on the target audience if it's likely to be needed or worth any risks.

Page Layout

Part of the user interface design is affected by the quality of the page layout. For example, a designer may consider whether the site's page layout should remain consistent on different pages when designing the layout. Page pixel width may also be considered vital for aligning objects in the layout design. The most popular fixed-width websites generally have the same set width to match the current most popular browser window, at the current most popular screen resolution, on the current most popular monitor size. Most pages are also center-aligned for concerns of aesthetics on larger screens.

Fluid layouts increased in popularity around 2000 as an alternative to HTML-table-based layouts and grid-based design in both page layout design principle and in coding technique, but were very slow to be adopted. This was due to considerations of screen reading devices and varying windows sizes which designers have no control over. Accordingly, a design may be broken down into units (sidebars, content blocks, embedded advertising areas, navigation areas) that are sent to the browser and which will be fitted into the display window by the browser, as best it can. As the browser does recognize the details of the reader's screen (window size, font size relative to window etc.) the browser can make user-specific layout adjustments to fluid layouts, but not fixed-width layouts. Although such a display may often change the relative position of major content units, sidebars may be displaced below body text rather than to the side of it. This is a more flexible display than a hard-coded grid-based layout that doesn't fit the device window. In particular, the relative position of content blocks may change while leaving the content within the block unaffected. This also minimizes the user's need to horizontally scroll the page.

Responsive Web Design is a newer approach, based on CSS3, and a deeper level of per-device specification within the page's style sheet through an enhanced use of the CSS. In March 2018 Google announced they would be rolling out mobile-first indexing.Sites using responsive design are well placed to ensure they meet this new approach.

Typography

Web designers may choose to limit the variety of website typefaces to only a few which are of a similar style, instead of using a wide range of typefaces or type styles. Most browsers recognize a specific number of safe fonts, which designers mainly use in order to avoid complications.

Font downloading was later included in the CSS3 fonts module and has since been implemented in Safari 3.1, Opera 10 and Mozilla Firefox 3.5. This has subsequently increased interest in web typography, as well as the usage of font downloading.

Most site layouts incorporate negative space to break the text up into paragraphs and also avoid center-aligned text.

Motion Graphics

The page layout and user interface may also be affected by the use of motion graphics. The choice of whether or not to use motion graphics may depend on the target market for the website. Motion graphics may be expected or at least better received with an entertainment-oriented website. However, a website target audience with a more serious or formal interest (such as business, community, or government) might find animations unnecessary and distracting if only for entertainment or decoration purposes. This doesn't mean that more serious content couldn't be enhanced with animated or video presentations that is relevant to the content. In either case, motion graphic design may make the difference between more effective visuals or distracting visuals.

Motion graphics that are not initiated by the site visitor can produce accessibility issues. The World Wide Web consortium accessibility standards require that site visitors be able to disable the animations.

Quality of Code

Website designers may consider it to be good practice to conform to standards. This is usually done via a description specifying what the element is doing. Failure to conform to standards may not make a website unusable or error prone, but standards can relate to the correct layout of pages for readability as well making sure coded elements are closed appropriately. This includes errors in code, more organized layout for code, and making sure IDs and classes are identified properly. Poorly-coded pages are sometimes colloquially called tag soup. Validating via W3C can only be done when a correct DOCTYPE declaration is made, which is used to highlight errors in code. The system identifies the errors and areas that do not conform to web design standards. This information can then be corrected by the user.

Generated Content

There are two ways websites are generated: statically or dynamically.

Static Websites

A static website stores a unique file for every page of a static website. Each time that page is requested, the same content is returned. This content is created once, during the design of the website. It is usually manually authored, although some sites use an automated creation process, similar to a dynamic website, whose results are stored long-term as completed pages. These automatically-created static sites became more popular around 2015, with generators such as Jekyll and Adobe Muse.

The benefits of a static website are that they were simpler to host, as their server only needed to serve static content, not execute server-side scripts. This required less server administration and had less chance of exposing security holes. They could also serve pages more quickly, on low-cost server hardware. These advantage became less important as cheap web hosting expanded to also offer dynamic features, and virtual servers offered high performance for short intervals at low cost.

Almost all websites have some static content, as supporting assets such as images and style sheets are usually static, even on a website with highly dynamic pages.

Dynamic Websites

Dynamic websites are generated on the fly and use server-side technology to generate webpages. They typically extract their content from one or more back-end databases: some are database queries across a relational database to query a catalogue or to summarise numeric information, others may use a document database such as MongoDB or NoSQL to store larger units of content.

In the design process, dynamic pages are often mocked-up or wireframed using static pages. The skillset needed to develop dynamic web pages is much broader than for a static pages, involving server-side and database coding as well as client-side interface design. Even medium-sized dynamic projects are thus almost always a team effort.

When dynamic web pages first developed, they were typically coded directly in languages such as Perl, PHP or ASP. Some of these, notably PHP and ASP, used a 'template' approach where a server-side page resembled the structure of the completed client-side page and data was inserted into places defined by 'tags'. This was a quicker means of development than coding in a purely procedural coding language such as Perl.

Both of these approaches have now been supplanted for many websites by higher-level application-focused tools such as content management systems. These build on top of general purpose coding platforms and assume that a website exists to offer content according to one of several well recognised models, such as a time-sequenced blog, a thematic magazine or news site, a wiki or a user forum. These tools make the implementation of such a site very easy, and a purely organisational and design-based task, without requiring any coding.

Editing the content itself (as well as the template page) can be done both by means of the site itself, and with the use of third-party software. The ability to edit all pages is provided only to a specific category of users (for example, administrators, or registered users). In some cases, anonymous users are allowed to edit certain web content, which is less frequent (for example, on forums - adding messages).

Homepage Design

Usability experts, including Jakob Nielsen and Kyle Soucy, have often emphasised homepage design for website success and asserted that the homepage is the most important page on a website. However practitioners into the 2000s were starting to find that a growing number of website traffic was bypassing the homepage, going directly to internal content pages through search engines, e-newsletters and RSS feeds. Leading many practitioners to argue that homepages are less important than most people think. Jared Spool argued in 2007 that a site's homepage was actually the least important page on a website.

In 2012 and 2013, carousels (also called 'sliders' and 'rotating banners') have become an extremely popular design element on homepages, often used to showcase featured or recent content in a confined space. Many practitioners argue that carousels are an ineffective design element and hurt a website's search engine optimisation and usability

CASE TOOLS FOR THE DEVELOPMENT OF WEB APPLICATIONS

One of the basic ideas behind the creation of CASE tools is the possibillity to shorten the implentation phase of the software engineering process that ususally consumes up to 60% of the project time. Considerable time would be saved by automatic code generation based on the process and data diagrams crated and inserted through the CASE tool editors and into the data dictionary. The generated code would be consistent with the created models, syntax error free, and test data could also be autometically generated to help the developers test the software. The overall quality of the software is always based on the quality and accuracy of the requirements, models and constraints put in the CASE tools by all the members of the software development team. Full code generation of general software is one of the botllenecks of CASE tool technology but it has been made functional in focused areas by providing a set of process patterns that can be customized and connected to the data model.

As web applications have become ubiquitous and web interfaces to the classic infomation systems a default feature, we feel that an online CASE tool for the development of web applications as well as web application interfaces to large information systems would improve and facilitate the development and quality of such applications. The time for development would be shortened by using the CASE tool generators and the quality would be enhanced by the metodical process used to describe the application being generated which is an important fact, given the research results of the web software development.

CASE tools embedd methods and techniques for software development, software engineering knowledge and methodologies as well as the apropriate user interfaces.

Today, most of the CASE tools are focused on some parts of the SE process like source control management, configuration management, prototyping, data dictionarys, user interface generators.

Sommerville proposes a classification of CASE tools on tools (focused), workbenches (multiple tools supporting a particular SE phase) and environments (support the software life cycle, consist of more workbenches). This classification can be seen in figure. The figure does not display the herarhical nature of the classification.

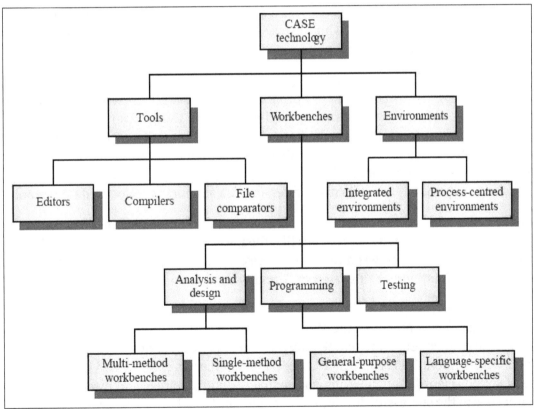

CASE tool classification.

CASE tools are usually categorized by the phases of the SE process they support. Usually they are divided in only two groups: UpperCASE (analysis and design) and LowerCASE (development, debugging, testing, QA. Brumec proposes a more detailed categorization ranging from application generators to Integrated CASE environments. The categorization is displayed in figure.

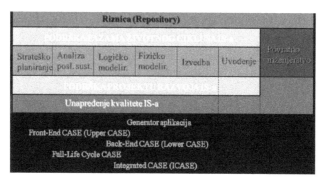

CASE tool categories.

Software Methodologies and Case Tools

Full Life Cycle tools often support some defined set of activities, rules and tasks e.g. software engineering methodologies.

In 1990s Oracle developed the CASE Method based on the structural approach. It is a highly structured top-down process consisting of strategy, analysis, design, build and documentation, transition and production phases. Each phase has a defined set of activities and artifacts it generates that are used in the next phases. The whole process is supported by a set of CASE tools (Dictionary, Designer, Generator, Project, Bridge).

In the following years object oriented analysis and design and object oriented development has been developed (powered by UML and OO programming languages) as well as iterative and component approaches to SE. New methodologies that integrate these advancements have been developed. One of such methodologies is the Rational Unified Process (RUP) developed in IBM. The basic characteristics of this process are iterative development, requirements management, component architecture, visual modeling in UML, risk management, quality assurance, configuration and change management. Most of its disciplines are also supported by focused CASE tools.

All of these methodologies use various modeling techniques to describe the processes and data of the clients business. Today, new approaches like Business Process Modeling (BPM) are being used to eliminate the differences between the real business process and the model of the process crated by analysts. BPM Notation is being used to formally describe and model the current and future processes.

Following the fast development of the World Wide Web and its economy, complex web applications have been created. Experts became interested in applying existing or creating new approaches to their development. These efforts created "web engineering" described in as "establishment and use of sound scientific, engineering and management principles and disciplined and systematic approaches to the successful development, deployment and maintenance of high quality Web-based systems and applications".

Further development of the WWW yielded even more interest which resulted in the creation of "The framework for Web Science" by a group of scientists at MIT.

Web engineering created many methodologies for web application development of which we would like to mention two: WAE2 and WebML.

WAE2 (Web application engineering) is a method created in IBM, strongly influenced by RUP. It uses UML for the analysis and UML extension called "Web Application Extension" for the design phase. Web Application Extension is a set of stereotypes representing all the standard parts of web sites and applications like pages, server pages, hyperlinks, forms, fields, frames, etc. It introduces the User Experience (UX) model that contains modeled screens, storyboards and realizations, navigational paths and map, user input, screen compartments, etc., used to model the hypertext part of the web application.

WebML – Web Modeling Language is a part of the methodology supported by the WebRatio CASE tool. This tool is a Java based software application.

Using CASE tools for supporting the methodological approach should have the synergic effect on the final software product. The formal and disciplined approach should ensure quality (software meets specifications and purpose), and code generation by CASE tools should shorten the implementation phase, reduce number of errors, and testing.

WADOC(T) – Online Case Tool for Development of Web

WADOCT is an acronym for Web Application Development Online Case Tool which clearly describes some of its most important characteristics. To further explain the ideas behind this project we can analyze parts of the name:

"WEB APPLICATION DEVELOPMENt" – States that the purpose of this tool is to support the development of web applications. Here we must clearly define and differ the terms web page, web site and web application. A "web page" is a:

- Text document containing some information structured using HTML (HyperText Markup Language) – this web page is called static.

- Text document containing code written in some server-side scripting language that is interpreted aftera client request and generates some information structured using HTML. The code is executed on the server and can access multiple data sources and prepare the data (information) for presentation – this web page is called a dynamic.

A static or a dynamic page can be part of a web site which is a set of web pages interconnected using hyperlinks into a clear and informative structure, stored at a web server at a unique named location (URL) which makes it available to users worldwide.

A web application is defined in as: "software system based on technologies and standards provided by World Wide Web Consortium (W3C) that provides Web specific resources such as content and services through a user interface, the Web browser". This definition should be extended because it mentions only the static technologies governed by W3C like HTML, and does not consider the programming languages, DMBS's, "third party" applications (that ensure required and needed additional functionality of the web browser) and other services and data sources every web application is based on. Therefore we could make a wider definition and define a web application as a software system based on a hyperlinked structure of dynamic pages containing code written in server-side programming languages, backed up by a database management system and other data sources and services, delivering the required content to the client in the form of information structured by technologies and standards of the W3C through a user interface, the Web browser application.

"ONLINE" – One of the special characteristics of this tool is the fact that it would be available on the World Wide Web making it unique to the best of our knowledge. Its online availability gives it the same advantages (and some disadvantages) all web applications have to classic desktop applications. "CASE"– This is a CASE tool that supports the process of engineering a complete web application. The basic plan of WADOC creation is to deploy a functional application generator in the first phase then add more functionality to support the full life cycle of the web application of web information system.

WADOC Specifics

While having mentioned its most specific characteristics – the fact that this tool would be available online and the fact that it is CASE tool for web application development there are six aspects of this tool to be pointed out:

* The (web) software that a user is developing is created and located on a test web server after the first iteration which makes it readily available for access and testing. After the first iteration that creates a minimal functional system we can define more functionality, define other modules and data structures and create another version. There is no additional software or installation procedure required. In this way the development team and clients can be physically distant but still work together online. The clients can see the software, comment it, and answer questions e.g. be involved with the project.

* WADOC has no need for custom interpreters and a compiler considering it is already located on a web server that has all the needed software for executing server side code and a DBMS installed. The proposed CASE tool would be created and would generate web applications based on free open source technologies known as the LAMP platform (LAMP = Linux OS, Apache web server, MySQL DBMS and PHP programming language). In this way the construction of the tool is simplified.

* By applying Web 2.0 approach and technologies the usage paradigm of a classic web application will be changed to fit the classic application usage – users will be able to insert and upload data or documents, create and edit models and code seamlessly. The user interface would be created according to W3C standards and user experience best practices and follow the usual programming metaphors software professionals are used to.

* WADOC enables an unlimited number of users per project. An initial user could register and add numerous other users (in various roles) to the new project. They will be able to work at different parts of the project at the same time, while the integrity of the work would be secured by the locking mechanisms and source control.

* Another Web 2.0 characteristic is the active participation of users. As WADOC would create a full data dictionary for each project, new users could browse through the database of finished projects or use some parts of their functionality which would further facilitate the development of new projects.

* One of the most complex part of the system would be full integration of all artifacts thru ought the project, from the list of requirements down to the functions and modules. This system would enable users get additional information about any part of the project (e.g. from what requirement was some module created or for a finished process we could open a code view for some part of the process model).

WADOC Structure

Brumec defines the following characteristics needed to consider an application generator a CASE tool:

- Keeps a system description for reuse WADOC has and internal database that keeps all data about projects like: relation schema, function lists, code generated, user interface parts, generated web pages with full HTML, CSS, JavaScript and other code. After the project has been finished a full application can be stored on the web server or prepared to be transferred to the client web server.

- Create a ERA model or a relation model of data Considering that WADOC is a Web 2.0 mashup application the relational database editor can be imported from existing web applications like PhpMyAdmin (a specialized web application offering a visual interface to the MySQL DBMS for editing an executing relational schemas). When the basic WADOC architecture is extended to Full Life Cycle ERA method visual editor will be integrated. In this case WADOC would use custom built or COTS JavaScript components like MxGraph. Such components would have to be edited to add special notation symbols as well as the formal rules behind the ERA method. From the visual model a relational schema can be exported and executed on the test web server.

- Use a data dictionary WADOC would create a data dictionary to keep all the necessary data about an application.

- Use a knowledge base (or patterns) for creating procedures As most web applications today are a part of larger information systems (for example e-banking web application is a part of the larger bank information system) we can state that the most of their functionality consist of reports (selects), forms (inserts), record changes (edit, delete). Because of this WADOC would in its application generator form offer a number of application procedure models which the user can then customize and connect to the data defined in the relational database or ERA model editor. The customizing process can be done using wizards or high level code editing or both. I the Full Life Cycle form WADOC would enable users to create a full process model using a visual editor (again based on custom build or COTS JavaScript components like MxGraph customized to enforce the formal rules of process modeling), from which a list of modules and functions can later be created and then customized by writing pseudo code. On such a detailed structure definition code would be generated by the WADOC code generator module that would combine the model created by the user and its own database of procedure models and the list of PHP functions.

- Connect program procedures based on the process model A web application is a set of connected dynamic pages. After a process model has been completed, a hierarchical list of modules would be derived. Based on that list the code generator would create a new virtual page per module and create functions bodies on the page. Each function would then be created based on the descriptions in the model, the data model and the pseudo code (if a custom procedure).

WADOC user interface editor would enable the users to create a model of the interface based on that (virtual) page list of procedures and a set of HTML symbols. For example many web applications that display a list of records have a form (mask) below the list to add new records. In this way the user can drag/ drop some procedure like "Display All Records" to the virtual page, define the area that procedure will take on the page, and then create a form and its field, and then connect the form with the necessary data. In this way a full set of user interface models for the application can be made.

The user interface editor will also be used to define the global navigation structure of the application. All the mentioned visual editors (process modeling editor, data modeling editor and user interface editor keep their data in two XML files. One file is used to preserve the layout of the model, and the other one to keep record of the model elements and their connections. The second XML file can easily be transferred into a database and later used for code generation. The WADOC structure is displayed in figure.

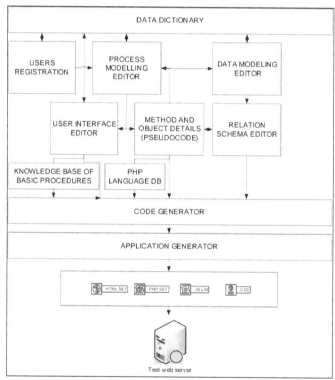

WADOC structure.

The code generator would use the data dictionary, the W3C standards for page structure, own procedure models and PHP function database to generate the code. The code would be connected to virtual dynamic pages. Each generated part of the code would be available for editing and review. As mentioned before full code generation is a bottleneck for many CASE systems but in this focused tool with a rather small list of used functions the code can be generated. The application generator is the final step of the process that consists of the following algorithm:

```
create application directory @web server

create application database

create users

execute the relational schema @database
```

```
create CSS

create CONFIG

copy JS LIB'S

WHILE have_virtual_pages

 create new file

 open file

 create method tree with QS vars

 WHILE have_methods

 create method

 add code

 close method

 LOOP

add user interface elements to page

set default method

add connection to CSS

add connection to CONFIG

add connection to JS lib's

LOOP
```

After the generation process the user will be able to use and test the web application. Ali files generated by user (or based on user input) can be edited while in production (test) phase. Also the models can be changed and the whole application generated again.

WEB 2.0 Technologies used in WADOC

XHTML and CSS 2.0

XHTML (HyperText Markup Language) is the only language used to structure information on the web pages. It is defined by the XHTML specification document issued by the World Wide Web Consortium. The basic structure of every web page is the same (every page consists of a heading (invisible – holds meta data and links the files that need to be included or referenced) and the body (visible to user, contains all the information structured by HTML)) which allows us to define the page creation process in the application generator. XHTML is a set of strict rules imposed on the general specification of the HTML. HTML is based on the box model meaning that elements that are opened/started first must be closed last. In this way we can create various structures to define the position and order of elements on a page.

CSS (Cascading Style Sheets) is a style sheet language used exclusively to format the information and structure of HTML elements. A style sheet consists of a list of rules. Each rule or rule-set consists of one or more selectors and a declaration block. A declaration-block consists of a list of semicolonseparated declarations in braces. Each declaration itself consists of a property, a colon

(:), a value, then a semi-colon (;). In CSS, selectors are used to declare which elements a style applies to, a kind of match expression. Selectors may apply to all elements of a specific type, or only those elements which match a certain attribute; elements may be matched depending on how they are placed relative to each other in the markup code, or on how they are nested within the document object model. CSS is heavily used in Web 2.0 applications to completely separate the content from the presentation as well as to create a classic application like interface. Also, separate CSS files are created for each application so that it can be modified to share the look and feel of the client's web site.

JavaScript Platforms

JavaScript is a scripting language most often used for client-side web development. It was the originating dialect of the ECMAScript standard. It is a dynamic, weakly typed, prototype-based language with firstclass functions. The primary use of JavaScript is to write functions that are embedded in or included from HTML pages and interact with the Document Object Model (DOM) of the page. JavaScript is heavily used in WADOC user interface in two ways: using JavaScript platforms (or libraries) to power online editors and using XmlHttpRequest object which is the main object behind AJAX that enables "behind the scenes" client->server communication.

JavaScript libraries are a set of objects, methods and special handlers built to add more functionality to a web application then initially made available by the browser's integrated JavaScript interpreter. On of the libraries used in this project is JQuery which will enable "classic application" like manipulation of records and tables in the WADOC user interface (for example sorting tables, sliding elements to and of the workspace, etc.).

Another JavaScript library that can be used to power the visual editors of WADOC id MxGraph which is a set of finished web based editors. This library would have to be modified with custom symbols and formal constraints that will support creating valid data models and process models.

AJAX (Asynchronous JavaScript and XML) is the common name for a set of existing and evolving technologies: standards-based presentation using XHTML and CSS; dynamic display and interaction using the Document Object Model; data interchange and manipulation using XML and XSLT; asynchronous data retrieval using XmlHttpRequest; and JavaScript as the language that binds the static and the dynamic part of the page. In WADOC most data manipulation will be made using XmlHttpRequest enabling the user to use this web tool like a classic desktop application.

WEB MODELING

Web modeling (aka model-driven Web development) is a branch of Web engineering which addresses the specific issues related to design and development of large-scale Web applications. In particular, it focuses on the design notations and visual languages that can be used for the realization of robust, well-structured, usable and maintainable Web applications. Designing a data-intensive Web site amounts to specifying its characteristics in terms of various orthogonal abstractions.

The main orthogonal models that are involved in complex Web application design are: data structure, content composition, navigation paths, and presentation model.

In the beginning of web development, it was normal to access Web applications by creating something with no attention to the developmental stage. In the past years, web design firms had many issues with managing their Web sites as the developmental process grew and complicated other applications. Web development tools have helped with simplifying data-intensive Web applications by using page generators. Microsoft's Active Server Pages and JavaSoft's Java Server Pages have helped by bringing out content and using user-programmed templates.

Several languages and notations have been devised for Web application modeling. Among them, we can cite:

- HDM - W2000,

- RMM,

- OOHDM,

- The Interaction Flow Modeling Language (IFML), adopted by the Object Management Group (OMG) in March 2013,

- ARANEUS,

- STRUDEL,

- TIRAMISU,

- WebML,

- Hera,

- UML Web Application Extension,

- UML-based Web Engineering (UWE),

- ACE,

- WebArchitect,

- OO-H.

WEB MODELING LANGUAGE

Web ML in a Nutshell

Web ML enables designers to express the core features of a site at a high level, without committing to detailed architectural details. Web ML concepts are associated with an intuitive graphic representation, which can be easily supported by CASE tools and effectively communicated to the non-technical members of the site development team (e.g., with the graphic designers and the content producers). Web ML also supports an XML syntax, which instead can be fed to software generators for automatically producing the implementation of a Web site. The specification of a site in Web ML consists of four orthogonal perspectives:

- Structural Model: It expresses the data content of the site, in terms of the relevant entities and relationships. Web ML does not propose yet another language for data modeling, but is compatible with classical notations like the E/R model, the ODMG object-oriented model, and UML class diagrams. To cope with the requirement of expressing redundant and calculated information, the structural model also offers a simplified, OQL-like query language, by which it is possible to specify derived information.

- Hypertext Model: It describes one or more hypertexts that can be published in the site. Each different hypertext defines a so-called site view . Site view descriptions in turn consist of two sub-models.

  ○ Composition Model: It specifies which *pages* compose the hypertext, and which content units make up a *page*. Six types of content units can be used to compose *pages*: data, multi-dat index, filter, scroller and direct units. Data units are used to publish the *information* of a single object (e.g., a music album), whereas the remaining types of units represent alternative ways to browse a set of objects (e.g., the set of tracks of an album). Composition units are defined on top of the structure schema of the site; the designer dictates the underlying entity or relationship on which the content of each unit is based. For example, the AlbumInfo data unit showing the *information* on an album in figure refers to the Album entity specified in the structure schema of figure.

  ○ Navigation Model: It expresses how pages and content units are linked to form the hypertext. Links are either non-contextual, when they connect semantically independent pages (e.g., the page of an artist to the home page of the site), or contextual, when the content of the destination unit of the link depends on the content of the source unit. For example, the page showing an artist's data is linked by a contextual link to the page showing the index of reviews of that specific artist. Contextual links are based on the structure schema, because they connect content units whose underlying entities are associated by relationships in the structure schema.

- Presentation Model: It expresses the layout and graphic appearance of pages, independently of the output device and of the rendition language, by means of an abstract XML syntax. Presentation specifications are either page-specific or generic. In the former case they dictate the presentation of a specific page and include explicit references to page content (e.g., they dictate the layout and the graphic appearance of the title and cover data of albums); in the latter, they are based on predefined models independent of the specific content of the page and include references to generic content elements (for instance, they dictate the layout and graphic appearance of all attributes of a generic object included in the page).

- Personalization Model: Users and user groups are explicitly modeled in the structure schema in the form of predefined entities called User and Group. The features of these entities can be used for storing group-specific or individual content, like shopping suggestions, list of favorites, and resources for graphic customization. Then, OQL-like declarative expressions can be added to the structure schema, which define derived content based on the profile data stored in the User and Group entities. This personalized content can be used both in the composition of units or in the definition of presentation specifications. Moreover, high-level business rules, written using a simple XML syntax, can be defined for reacting to site-related events, like user clicks and content updates. Business rules typically produce new user- related *information* (e.g., shopping histories) or update the site content (e.g., inserting new offers matching users' preferences). Queries and business rules provide two alternative paradigms (a declarative and a procedural one) for effectively expressing and managing personalization requirements.

In the Torii Soft tool suite, Web ML specifications are given as input to a code generator, which translates them into some concrete markup language (e.g. HTML or WML) for rendering the composition, navigation and presentation, and maps the abstract references to content elements inside *pages* into concrete data retrieval instructions in some server-side scripting language (e.g., JSP or ASP).

Web ML by Example

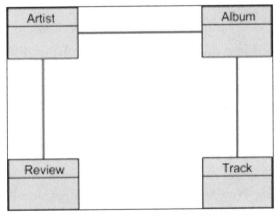

Example of structure schema.

Figure shows a simple structure schema for the publication of albums and artists information. Artists publish albums composed of tracks, and have biographic information and reviews of their work. To publish this information as a hypertext on the Web, it is necessary to specify criteria for composition and navigation, i.e., to define a site view.

Figure shows an excerpt from a site view specification, using Web ML graphical language. The hypertext consists of three pages, shown as dashed rectangles. Each page encloses a set of units (shown as solid rectangles with different icons) to be displayed together in the site. For example, page Album Page collects information on an album and its artist. It contains a data unit (Album Info) showing the information on the album, an index unit (Track Index) showing the list of the album's tracks, and another data unit (Artist Info) containing the essential information on the album's artist. The Album Info unit is connected to the Artist Info unit by an intermediate direct unit (To Artist), meaning that the Album Info refers to the (single) artist who composed the album shown in the page. The Artist Info unit has one outgoing link leading to a separate page containing the list of review, and one link to a direct unit pointing to the artist's biographic data, shown on a separate page. Note that changing the hypertext topology is extremely simple: for example, if the Review Index data unit is specified inside the Album Page instead of on a separate page, then the index of reviews is kept together with the album and artist info. Alternatively, if the Review Index unit is defined as a multi-data unit, instead of an index unit, all reviews (and not only their titles) are shown in the Reviews Page.

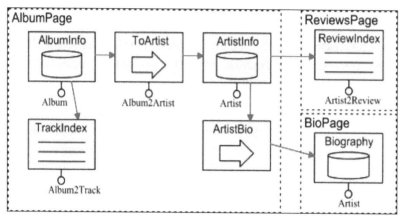

Example of Web ML composition and navigation specification.

Design Process in Web ML

Web application development is a multi-facet activity involving different players with different skills and goals. Therefore, separation of concerns is a key requirement for any Web modeling language. Web ML addresses this issue and assumes a development process where different kinds of specialists play distinct roles: 1) the data expert designs the structural model; 2) the application architect designs pages and the navigation between them; 3) the style architect designs the presentation styles of pages; 4) the site administrator designs users and personalization options, including business rules.

A typical design process using Web ML proceeds by iterating the following steps for each design cycle:

- Requirements Collection: Application requirements are gathered, which include the *main* objectives of the site, its target audience, examples of content, style guidelines, required personalization and constraints due to legacy data.

- Data Design: The data expert designs the structural model, possibly by reverse-engineering the exisiting logical schemas of legacy data sources.

- Hypertext Design "in the large": The Web application architect defines the structure "in the large" of the hypertext, by identifying pages and units, linking them, and mapping units to the main entities and relationships of the structure schema. In this way, he develops a "skeleton" site view, and then iteratively improves it. To support this phase, WebML-based tools must enable the production of fast prototypes to get immediate feedback on all design decisions.

- Hypertext Design "in the small": The Web application architect concentrates next in the design "in the small" of the hypertext, by considering each page and unit individually. At this stage, he may add non-contextual links between pages, consolidate the attributes that should be included within a unit, and introduce novel pages or units for special requirements (e.g., alternative index pages to locate objects, filters to search the desired information, and so on). During page design in the small, the Web application architect may discover that a page requires additional information, present in another concept semantically related to the one of the page currently being designed. Then, he may use the derivation language, to add ad hoc redundant data to the structure schema and include it in the proper units.

- Presentation Design: Once all *pages* are sufficiently stable, the Web style architect adds to each *page* a presentation style.

- User and Group Design: The Web administrator defines the features of user profiles, based on personalization requirements. Potential users and user groups are mapped to WebML users and groups, and possibly a different site view is created for each group. The design cycle is next iterated for each of the identified site views. "Copy-and-paste" of already designed site view *pages* and links may greatly speed up the generation of other site views.

- Customization Design: The Web administrator identifies profile-driven data derivations and business rules, which may guarantee an effective personalization of the site.

Some of the above stages can be skipped in the *case* of development of a simple WEB application. In particular, defaults help at all stages the production of simplified solutions. At one extreme, it is possible to develop a default initial site view directly from the structural schema, skipping all of the above stages except the first one.

The Structural Model

The fundamental elements of Web ML structure model are entities, which are containers of data elements, and relationships, which enable the semantic connection of entities. Entities have named attributes, with an associated type; properties with multiple occurrences can be organized by means of multi-valued components, which corresponds to the classical part-of relationship. Entities can be organized in generalization hierarchies. Relationships may be given cardinality constraints and role names.

```
<DOMAIN id="Support Type" values="CD Tape Vinyl">;

<ENTITY id="Album">

  <ATTRIBUTE id="title" type="String"/>

  <ATTRIBUTE id="cover" type="Image"/>

  <ATTRIBUTE id="year" type="Integer"/>

  <COMPONENT id="Support" minCard="1" maxCard="N">

    <ATTRIBUTE id="type" user Type="Support Type"/>

    <ATTRIBUTE id="list Price" type="Float"/>

    <ATTRIBUTE id="discount Percentage" type="Integer"/>

    <ATTRIBUTE id="current Price" type="Float"
```

```
                      value="Self list Price *

                        (1 - (Self discount Percentage / 100))"/>

  </COMPONENT>

  <RELATIONSHIP id="Album2Artist" to="Artist" inverse="ArtistT o Album"
               minCard="1" maxCard="1"/>

  <RELATIONSHIP id="Album2Track to="Track" inverse="Track2Album"
               minCard="1" maxCard="N"/>

</ENTITY>

  <ENTITY id="Artist">

  <ATTRIBUTE id="first Name" type="String"/>

  <ATTRIBUTE id="last Name" type="String"/>

  <ATTRIBUTE id="birth Date" type="Date"/>

  <ATTRIBUTE id="birth Place" type="String"/>

  <ATTRIBUTE id="photo" type="Image"/>

  <ATTRIBUTE id="biographic Info" type="Text"/>

  <RELATIONSHIP id="Artist2Album" to="Album" inverse="Album2Artist"
               minCard="1" maxCard="N"/>

  <RELATIONSHIP id="Artist2Review" to="Review" inverse="Review2Artist"
               minCard="0" maxCard="N"/>

  </ENTITY>

      <ENTITY id="Track">

      <ATTRIBUTE id="number" type="Integer"/>

      <ATTRIBUTE id="title" type="String"/>

      <ATTRIBUTE id="mpeg" type="URL"/>

      <ATTRIBUTE id="hqMpeg" type="URL"/>

      <RELATIONSHIP id="Track2Album" to="Album" inverse="Album2Track"
                   minCard="1" maxCard="1"/>

</ENTITY>

<ENTITY id="Review">

  <ATTRIBUTE id="text" type="Text"/>

  <ATTRIBUTE id="autho" type="String/>

  <RELATIONSHIP id="Review2Artist" to="Artist" inverse="Artist2Review"
               min Card="1" max Card="1"/>

</ENTITY>
```

The structural schema consists of four entities (Artist, Album, Review and Track) and three relationships (Artist2 Album, Artist2 Review, Album2 track). Entity Album has a multi-valued property represented by the Support component, which specifies the various issues of the album on vinyl, CD, and tape. *Note* that each issue has a discounted price, whose value is computed by applying a discount percentage to the list price, by means of a derivation query.

The Composition Model

The purpose of composition modeling is to define which nodes make up the hypertext contained in the Web site. More precisely, composition modeling specifies content units (units for short), i.e., the atomic information elements that may appear in the Web site, and pages, i.e., containers by means of which information is actually clustered for delivery to the user. In a concrete setting, e.g., an HTML or WML implementation of a Web ML site, pages and units are mapped to suitable constructs in the delivery language, e.g., units may map to HTML files and pages to HTML frames organizing such files on the screen.

Web ML supports six types of unit to compose an hypertext:

- Data units: They show information about a single object, e.g., an instance of an entity or of a component.

- Multi data units: They show information about a set of objects, e.g., all the instances of an entity or all the sub-components of a composite object.

- Index units: They show a list of objects (entity or component instances), without presenting the detailed information of each object.

- Scroller units: They show commands for accessing the elements of an ordered set of objects (the first, last, *previous*, next, i-th).

- Filter units: They show edit fields for inputting values used for searching within a set of object(s) those ones that meet a condition.

- Direct units: They do not display information, but are used to denote the connection to a single object that is semantically related to another object.

Data and multi data units present the actual content of the objects they refer to, whereas the remaining types of units permit one to locate objects. Data units refer to a single object. Multi data, index, filter, and scroller refer to a set of objects. Therefore, they are collectively called container units.

Data Units

Data units are defined to select a mix of information, which provides a meaningful view of a given concept of the structure schema. More than one unit can be defined for the same entity or component, to offer alternative points of view (e.g., a short or long, textual or multimedia version of the object).

The definition of a data unit requires 1) the indication of the concept (entity or component) to which the unit refers. 2) The selection of the attributes to include in the unit. Syntactically, data units are defined using the DATAUNIT element, which provides tags and attributes for the various aspects of unit definition. The selective inclusion of content in a unit is specified using the element

INCLUDE. Included attributes must be chosen among those declared in the structure schema for the entity or component. The INCLUDEALL element can be used to specify that all attributes are included. For example, the following definitions introduce two units for presenting the Artist entity. The goal of these definitions is to provide a short view of artists (limited to the first name, last name, and photo) and a complete view, including all data.

```
<DATAUNIT id="Short Artist" entity="Artist">

  <INCLUDE attribute="first Name"/>

  <INCLUDE attribute="last Name"/>

  <INCLUDE attribute="photo"/>

</DATAUNIT>

 <DATAUNIT id="Biography Unit" entity="Artist">

   <INCLUDEALL/>

 </DATAUNIT>
```

Figure shows the Web ML graphic notation for representing a data unit and its underlying entity, and a possible rendition of the Short Artist data unit in an HTML-based implementation.

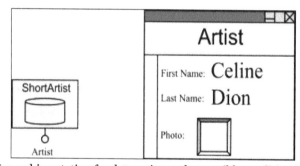

Web ML graphic notation for data units, and a possible rendition in HTML.

Multi-Data Units

Multi-data units present multiple instances of an entity or component together, by repeating the presentation of several, identical data units. Therefore, a multi-data unit specification has two parts: 1) the container which includes the instances to be displayed, which may refer to an entity, relationship, or component. 2) The data unit used for the presentation of each instance. Syntactically, a multi-data unit is represented by a MULTIDATAUNIT element, which includes a nested DATAUNIT element. The container is an *argument* of the external MULTIDATAUNIT element. The following example shows how all albums can be shown in the same multi data unit, by displaying all attributes of each individual album.

```
 <MULTIDATAUNIT id="Multi Album Unit" entity="Album">

   <DATAUNIT id="Album Unit" entity="Album">

     <INCLUDEALL/>

   </DATAUNIT>

 </MULTIDATAUNIT>
```

Figure shows the Web ML graphic notation for representing a multi data unit and a possible rendition of the multi data unit in an HTML-based implementation.

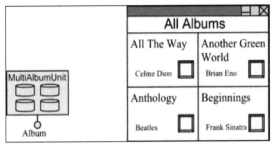

WebML graphic notation for multi data
units, and a possible rendition in HTML.

Index Units

Index units present multiple instances of an entity or component as a list, by denoting each object as an entry in the list. An index unit specification has two main parts: 1) the container which includes the instances to be displayed, which may be an entity, relationship, or component. 2) The attributes used as index key. Syntactically, an INDEXUNIT element is used, which includes a nested DESCRIPTION element. The following example shows how all albums can be shown in a list, by displaying only the title of each individual album. Figure shows the Web ML graphic notation for representing an index unit and a possible rendition of the index unit in an HTML-based implementation.

```
<INDEXUNIT id="Album Index" entity="Album">

  <DESCRIPTION Key="title"/>

</INDEXUNIT>
```

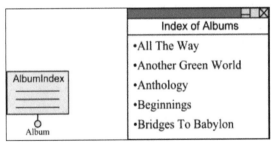

Web ML graphic notation for index
units, and a possible rendition in HTML.

Scroller Units

Scroller units provide commands to scroll through the objects in a container, e.g., all the instances of an entity or all the objects associated to another object via a relationship. A scroller unit is normally used in conjunction with a data unit, which represents the currently visualized element of the container. Syntactically, the SCROLLERUNIT element is used, which specifies the container (entity, relationship, or component) providing the set of objects to scroll, and suitable attributes to express which scrolling commands to use. For example, the following declaration introduces a unit for moving along the set of reviews of an artist, whereby it is possible to move to the first, *previous*, next and last review.

```
<SCROLLERUNIT id="Album
            Scroll"
            entity="Album"
            first="yes"
            last="yes"
            previous="yes"
            next="yes"/>
```

Figure shows the Web ML graphic notation for representing a scroller unit and a possible rendition in an HTML-based implementation.

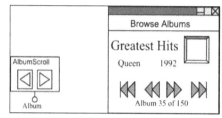

Web ML graphic notation for scroller
units, and a possible rendition in HTML.

Filter Units

Filter units provide input fields to search the objects in a container, e.g., all the instances of an entity whose attributes contain a given string. A filter unit is normally used in conjunction with an index or multi data unit, which present object matching the search condition. Syntactically, the FILTERUNIT element is used, which specifies the container (entity, relationship, or component) providing the set of objects to search. Inside the FILTERUNIT element, the SEARCHATTRIBUTE element is used to specify a search predicate on the value of a specific attribute. This element tells the attribute on which the search has to be performed and the comparison operator to use. In the following example, the Album Filter unit specifies a search form over the set of all albums. The form includes two input fields: the former for inputting a string to be located in the album's title, the latter for inputting the publication time interval of the album.

```
<FILTERUNIT id="Album Filter" entity="Album"/>
  </SEARCHATTRIBUTE name="title" predicate="like">
  </SEARCHATTRIBUTE name="year"  predicate="between">
</FILTERUNIT>
```

Figure shows the Web ML graphic notation for representing a filter unit and a possible rendition in an HTML-based implementation.

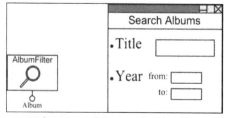

Web ML graphic notation for filter
units, and a possible rendition in HTML.

Direct Units

Direct units are a syntactic convenience to express a particular kind of index, which always contains a single object associated to another object by a one-to-one relationship. Differently from index units, direct units are not displayed, but merely support the specification of the relationship that associates the two related objects. Syntactically, direct units are expressed with the DIRECTUNIT element, as shown in the following example, which expresses the connection between an album and its unique artist:

```
<DIRECTUNIT id="To Artist" relation="Album2Artist"/>
```

Figure includes two direct units. The former (To Artist) connects each album to its (single) artist; the latter (Artist Bio) connects two data units over the same artist, one showing only a short presentation, the other including all biographic *information*.

Pages

The granularity of units may be too fine for the composition requirements of an application, which normally demand that the information contained in several units be delivered together (e.g., the data of an artist and the index of the albums he has published). To cope with this requirement, We bML provides a notion of page. A page is the abstraction of a self-contained region of the screen, which is treated as an independent interface block (e.g., it is delivered to the user independently and in one shot). Examples of concrete implementations of the abstract concept of page in specific languages may be a frame in HTML or a card in WML.

Pages may be internally organized into units and/or recursively other pages. In the latter case, sub-pages of a container page are treated as independent presentation blocks (similarly to the notion of frames within frame sets in HTML). Nested sibling sub-pages may be in conjunctive form (i.e., displayed together) or in disjunctive form (i.e., the display of one subpage is alternative to the display of another sibling sub-page).

AND/OR sub-pages permit one to represent many complex page structures occurring in practice. The simplest case occurs when a portion of a page is kept fixed (e.g., the left frame in an HTML page), and another portion may display variable information based on user commands (e.g., the information in the right frame may be replaced by different data after a user's click in the left frame).

Syntactically, the organization of units into *pages* is specified using the *PAGE* element, as shown in the XML fragment of figure, where a *page* portion (the sub-*page* named "leftmost") contains the indexes of past and recent issues, and the remaining portion (the sub-*page* named "rightmost") displays album *information*.

The graphic notation and possible HTML rendition of this XML specification is also illustrated in figure that *pages* are shown as dashed boxes around their enclosed units and/or sub-*pages*.

```
<PAGE id="outermost">

<PAGE id="leftmost"><UNIT id="past Index"/><UNIT id="this Year
Index"/></PAGE >
```

```
<PAGE id="rightmost"><UNIT id="Album Info"/></PAGE >

</PAGE>
```

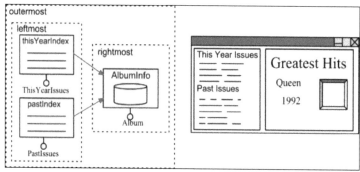

Web ML textual and graphic notation for nested AND pages.

Suppose now that we want a page to include the index of albums and artists, together with the information of either the album or the artist. This requires the introduction of alternative sub-pages, which is done in Web ML using the ALTERNATIVE element. The XML specification in Figure describes the needed page structure. Note that since the page composition (and not only the object to display) changes, if we select an artist or an album from the indexes, the ALTERNATIVE element is required to specify which alternative sub-pages should be used to display artist and album information. The graphic notation and possible HTML rendition of the XML specification are also shown in figure.

```
<PAGE id="outermost">

  <PAGE id="leftmost"> <UNIT id="artist Index"/> <UNIT id="album
  Index"/> </PAGE >

  <PAGE id="rightmost">

    <ALTERNATIVE>

      <PAGE id="rightmost1"> <UNIT id="artist Info"/> </PAGE >

      <PAGE id="rightmost2"> <UNIT id="album Info"/> </PAGE >

    </ALTERNATIVE>

  </PAGE >

</PAGE>
```

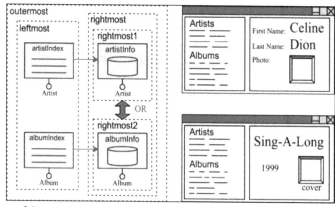

Web ML graphic notation nested AND/OR pages, and a possible rendition in HTML.

The Navigation Model

Units and *pages* do not exist in isolation, but must be connected to form a hypertext structure. The purpose of navigation modeling is to specify the way in which the units and *pages* are linked to form a hypertext. To this purpose, Web ML provides the notion of link. There are two variants of links:

- Contextual links: They connect units in a way coherent to the semantics expressed by the structure schema of the application. A contextual link carries some *information* (called context) from the source unit to the destination unit. Context is used to determine the actual object or set of objects to be shown in the destination unit.

- Non-contextual links: They connect *pages* in a totally free way, i.e., independently of the units they contain and of the semantic relations between the structural concepts included in those units. Syntactically, contextual and non-contextual links are denoted by element INFOLINK and HYPERLINK, respectively nested within units and *pages*.

The following example demonstrates the use of contextual links, by showing a piece of hypertext composed of three linked units: a data unit showing an artist's data, an index unit showing albums, and a data unit showing album's data.

```
<DATAUNIT id="Artist Unit" entity="Artist">

  <INCLUDEALL/>

  <INFOLINK id="link1" to="Album Index"/>

</DATAUNIT>

<INDEXUNIT id="Album Index" relation="Artist2Album>

  <DESCRIPTION key="title"/>

  <INFOLINK id="link2" to="Album Unit"/>

</INDEXUNIT>

<DATAUNIT id="Album Unit" entity="Album">

  <INCLUDEALL/>

</DATAUNIT>
```

The Artist Unit data unit, based on entity Artist, is linked via an INFOLINK to the index unit, which is based on the relationship Artist To Album. Such index unit in turn is linked by a second INFOLINK to the Album Unit data unit, based on entity Album. The semantics of the above contextual links is that:

- Due to the first link (link1) a navigation anchor is added inside the artist's data unit by means of which the user can navigate to the index unit listing all the albums of a specific artist.

- Due to the second link (link2), a set of navigation anchors (one per each entry in the index) is added to the index unit by means of which the user can navigate to one of the listed albums.

Context *information* flows along both links. The identifier of the artist whose albums are to be listed in the index unit flows from the source to the destination of the former link (link1). The identifier of the selected album flows from the source to the destination of the second link (link2), to determine the object shown in the data unit.

Figure shows the Web ML graphic notation for representing the above contextual links and a possible rendition of such piece of hypertext in an HTML-based implementation. In this example, each unit is placed in a separate page, therefore three distinct HTML pages are generated. Grouping units within pages and establishing contextual links are two orthogonal design primitives, as demonstrated by figure, where units Artist Unit and Album Index are kept on the same page. By linking data units and container units it is possible to obtain a variety of navigation modes, as shown in figure and where the index and album data unit are replaced by a multi data unit showing all albums of an artist together, both on the same page of the artist and in a separate page.

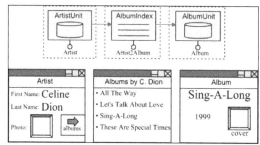

Index-based navigation (index in a separate page),
and a possible rendition in HTML.

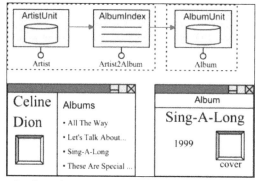

Index-based navigation (index in the source page),
and a possible rendition in HTML.

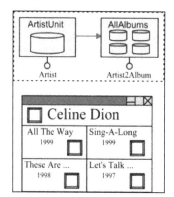

Composite page including one data and one related multi data unit.

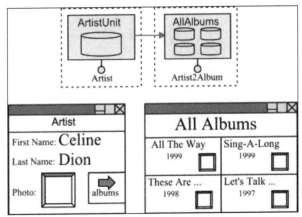

Separating the page including the artist data unit and the
page including the multi data unit showing all the artist's albums.

The following rules summarize the context information that flows out of a unit through a contextual link:

- Data Units: The identifier of the object currently shown in the unit.

- Index Units: The key value selected from the index list.

- Scroller Units: The identifier of the object selected by using the scrolling commands.

- Filter Unit: The attribute values given in input by the user in the data entry form.

- Direct units: The Key value of a single object.

- Multi data unit: The context *information* associated with the data units nested within the multi data unit.

Non-contextual links are demonstrated by the example of figure where the page of an artist is linked to a separate, unrelated page, which contains the index of all albums. In this case, no context information flows along the link, because the content of the unit in the destination page (All Albums) is totally independent of the source page of the navigation. Note that, to underline the absence of context flow between units, non-contextual links are drawn between pages.

```
<DATAUNIT id="Artist Unit" entity="Artist">

  <INCLUDEALL/>

</DATAUNIT>

<INDEXUNIT id="All Albums" entity="Album>

  <DESCRIPTION  key="title"/>

</INDEXUNIT>

<PAGE id="Artist Page">

  <UNIT id="Artist Unit"/>

  <HYPERLINK id="link1" to="All Albums Page"/>
```

```
</PAGE>

<PAGE id="All Albums Page">

  <UNIT id="All Albums"/>

</PAGE>
```

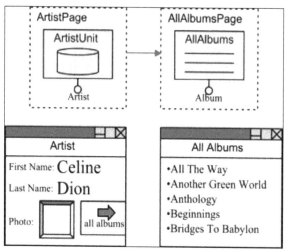

Web ML notation for non-contextual links.

Hidden Navigation

In many sites, the interaction between the user and the application is proactive in two senses: not only the user chooses what content to *see* by clicking on hyperlinks, but sometimes also the system autonomously determines which *page* to show, by "anticipating" the effect of some user clicks. This feature can be modeled in Web ML, by expressing the "filling semantics" of *pages* containing multiple units. For example, the user may access a *page*, which contains two units: an index unit over an entity pointing to a data unit on that entity. In this *case*, the content of the pointed data unit is "pending", i.e., it depends on the user's choice of one element in the preceding index unit. Web ML offers three alternatives to cope with pending units: 1) Leaving the pending unit empty, so that the user must explicitly perform a selection in one or *more* preceding units to display the content of the pending unit. 2) Filling the pending unit with a predefined default value (e.g., the first element chosen from a preceding index unit). 3) Filling the pending unit using with a default value expressed by means of a declarative query (e.g., the object of a preceding index unit that satisfies a given predicate).

Syntactically, the treatment of a pending unit is specified by choosing one of the above three options as the value of an ad hoc filling attribute, located in the "pointing" unit. If no value is specified, the pending unit is left empty.

Navigation Chains and "Web Patterns"

The typical configuration of a structured hypertext alternates data units, showing information on objects, with units that support the navigation from one object to another related object. Figure 9 shows two elementary forms of such a configuration, where an index unit and a multi data unit are used to move from an Artist to his/her Albums. Web ML units and links can be composed to express more complex navigation structures, where multiple intermediate pages support the navigation towards a data unit; we call these configurations "navigation chains". Frequently used navigation chains are sometimes referred to as "Web patterns". In this topic, briefly present a selection of representative examples of navigation chains, to show how WebML concepts can be composed to formally describe a wide variety of situations occurring in practice.

Figure shows an example of a navigation chain called multi-step index. A sequence of index units is defined over a given entity, such that each index unit specifies as its *description* key one of the attributes forming the key of the destination object. As shown in the figure, the semantics of this pattern is a hierarchical index, where the final object is located by means of a multi-step selection of its key value.

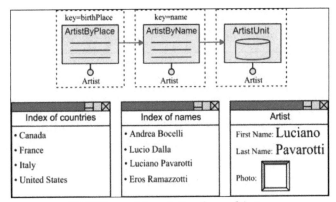

WebML graphic notation for multi-step
index, and a possible rendition in HTML.

Figure shows an example of a navigation chain configuration called filtered index. A sequence formed by a filter unit followed by an index unit is defined over a given entity. As shown in the figure, the semantics of this pattern is a three-step selection. First, the user provides input values to use as a search condition, then the objects matching such condition are presented in an index, finally the user may choose his object of interest from the (smaller) set shown in the index.

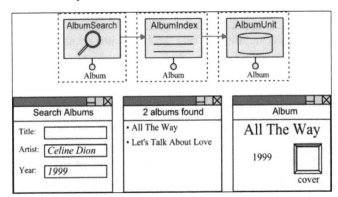

WebML graphic notation for filtered
index, and a possible rendition in HTML.

Figure shows an example of a navigation chain configuration called indexed guided tour. The configuration includes an index unit and a scroller unit which both are linked to the same data unit; in this *case*, the index and scroller units are synchronized: when the user performs a selection on either of them, the context of the other unit is changed so as to reflect the user's selection.

Usually, the user chooses his object of interest from the index, then he is presented the selected object together with commands to access the first, last, *previous*, next in the sequence, and thus he can explore the adjacent objects of the given one.

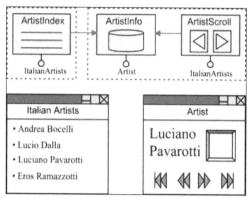

Web ML graphic notation for indexed
guided tour, and a possible rendition in HTML.

As a conclusive example, Figure shows a ring. In this configuration, two data units are linked via a direct unit defined over the identity relationship (i.e., the predefined relationship linking each object to itself). The two data units show different attributes of the same object (e.g., a long and a short presentation) thus enabling multiple views of the same item with variable details.

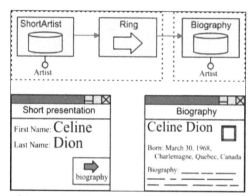

Web ML graphic notation for ring, and a possible rendition in HTML.

Site Views

The separation between the structure model and the hypertext model advocated by Web ML enables the definition of multiple views of the same data, which can be tuned to meet complex access requirements. For instance, different site views can be designed for alternative access devices or for distinct user groups. A Web ML site view comprises a set of *pages* and links, with associated presentation styles, all reachable from a designated home *page*. All the site views of a given Web application share the same structural schema, which represents at high level the data sources underlying the site. The structural schema, in turn, is mapped to one or *more* data sources, possibly embodied within legacy systems.

Default Hypertext

To enable fast prototyping, Web ML includes several shortcuts to obtain a running application from incomplete specifications. In particular, given the structural model, Web ML supports the notion of default hypertext, automatically generated *according* to the following rules:

- For each entity, a data unit is generated which includes all attributes.

- For each one-to-many or many-to-many relationship R between an entity A and an entity B, an index unit P is provided over the relationship R, based on the primary key of the entity B; two contextual links are established from the data unit of A to P and from P to the data unit of B.

- For each one-to-one or many-to-one relationship R between an entity A and an entity B, a direct unit P is provided over relationship R; two contextual links are established from the data unit of A to P and from P to the data unit of B.

- For each component C of an entity A, a multi-data unit P is provided over component C, and a contextual *link* is established from the data unit of A to P. For each entity, an index unit is created on the entity's primary key, which includes the list of all instances of the entity.

The default hypertext maps every concept of the structural model into exactly one unit and provides default indexes over all the defined entities. Given the default hypertext, a default site view is defined by associating units to *pages* as follows:

- Data unit over entities and index pages over relationships are put in distinct pages.

- Component multi-data units are kept in the same *page* as the data unit of the entity or component that encloses them.

- Index units over entities are put in distinct pages. An empty page is created as the home page, and connected by means of non-contextual links to the all these pages.

Figure illustrates the default site view for the structure schema of figure.

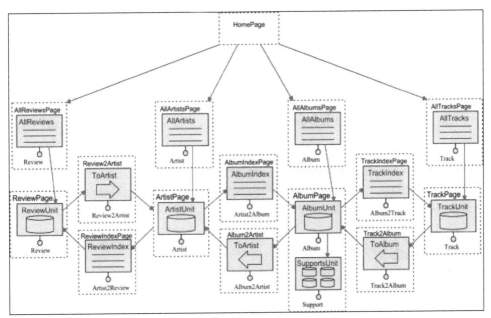

A default site view.

Validity of Web ML Hypertexts

Not all the Web ML specifications obtained by linking units and by clustering them into *pages* correspond to conceptually correct and practically implementable Web sites. First, we give a collection of rules for the progressive construction of correct logical hypertexts (units connected by contextual links) and then rules for verifying physical hypertexts (how units are clustered into *pages*).

A valid logical hypertext is defined by the following constructive rules:

- A logical hypertext constituted by a navigation chain over an entity followed by a data unit on such entity is valid.

- The logical hypertext obtained by adding a linked sequence of container units over a relationship or component of the structural schema, from a data unit of a valid hypertext to another data unit (an existing one or a new one) is valid.

Figure illustrates an invalid logical hypertext, made of a contextuall *link* between two data units upon the entities Artist and Album; the hypertext is invalid because the album to be shown after following the *link* is undefined.

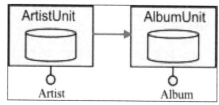

Example of invalid logical hypertext.

A second notion of correctness is based on the definition of valid physical hypertext and checks that the aggregation of units into *pages* produces application screens whose content is well defined. Given a valid logical hypertext, a valid physical hypertext is obtained by grouping units within *pages* and adding non-contextual links between *pages according* to the following rules:

- Reachability: There must not be pages (with the exception of the home page) without any incoming link (contextual or non-contextual).

- Context flow: If a page contains a unit that needs context information, then such context information must be supplied by a contextual link. There are two sub-cases:

  ○ The unit may receive context from another unit in the same *page* that does not require context *information* (e.g., an index unit over an entity).

  ○ If the above case does not hold, the unit must receive its context from all the entry units in the same page, where an entry unit is any unit which is the destination of contextual links coming from outside the page.

- Uniqueness of context: If a unit in the page has more than one path from which it receives context information from another unit inside the same page, then only for one such paths the initial filling option should be enabled.

Note that physical hypertext validity does not restrict the presence of non-contextual links between pages. These can be placed at will, without hampering the site correctness.

Figure (left part) illustrates an invalid physical hypertext: the Album page includes the Artist Info unit, which requires context information to determine the album to display, but is not linked to any other unit. On accessing the page by means of the link into the Album Info unit, the content of the Track Index unit is well defined, but the content of the Artist Info unit is not, because this unit has no incoming contextual link supplying the identifier of the artist to show.

Figure (right part) illustrates a second potentially invalid physical hypertext, in which the Album Info unit has two incoming contextual links, one from the index unit showing all albums of an artist, the other one from the index unit showing only this year's albums. If both indexes specify a non-empty initial filling option, the content of the destination data unit may be not uniquely defined upon accessing the *page*.

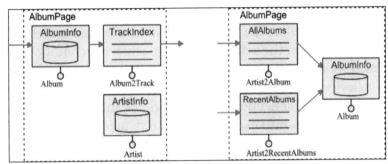

Two examples of invalid physical hypertext.

Other Features of Web ML

We next present briefly the other features of Web ML; for greater *detail*, we refer the reader to and to the W3I3*project*'s documentation available at the site.

Derivation

Derivation is the process of adding redundant *information* to the structure schema, in order to augment its expressiveness. Derivation in Web ML is expressed in a formal query language, which is a restricted version of OQL; it is possible to derive entities, attributes, components, and relationships.

User Modelling

In order to support personalization, Web ML includes an explicit notion of group and user. Groups describe sets of users with common characteristics, whereas users denote individuals. Users always belong to at least one group, possibly the default one (called everyone). Users may belong to *more* than one group, but in this *case* they are required to provide a default group or to indicate one preferred group when accessing the site. Each user or group is *described* by means of specific properties (collectively called profile), modeled as special type of entities in the structure schema. As the normal entities, user and group profiles may be internally sub-structured into attributes and components, classified by means of inheritance, semantically related to other entities, and used for writing derivation queries. Typically, profiles include user- or group-specific data (e.g., the most frequently or recently visited objects, the list of the last purchases), whose content is progressively modified during the Web site evolution as result of user's actions.

Declarative and Procedural Personalization

Personalization is the definition of content or presentation style based on user profile data. In Web ML, units, *pages*, their presentation styles, and site views can be defined so to take user- or group-specific data into account. This can be done in two complementary ways:

- Declarative personalization: The designer defines derived concepts (e.g., entities, attributes, multi-valued components) whose definition depends on user-specific data. In this way, customization is specified declaratively; the system fills in the *information* relative to each user when computing the content of units.

- Procedural personalization: Web ML includes an XML syntax for writing business rules that compute and store user-specific information. A business rule is a triple event-condition-action, which specifies the event to be monitored, the precondition to be checked when the event occurs, and the action to be taken when the condition is found true. Typical tasks performed by business rules are the assignment of users to user groups based on dynamically collected information (e.g., the purchase history, or the access device), the notification of messages to users upon the update of the information base (push technology), the logging of user actions into user-specific data structures (user tracking), and so on.

As an example of declarative personalization, the computation of an album's discounted price could be based on personalized discounts, associated with users or user groups. As an example of procedural personalization, a business rule could assign a customer to the "best buyer" group, based on his/her purchase *history*. Web ML declarative and procedural personalization are *discussed* in greater *details* in.

Presentation Model

Presentation modeling is concerned with the actual look and feel of the pages identified by composition modeling. Web ML pages are rendered according to a style sheet. A style sheet dictates the layout of pages and the content elements to be inserted into such layout, and is independent of the actual language used for page rendition. For better reusability, two categories of style sheets are provided: untyped style sheets (also called models) describe the page layout independently of its content, and thus can be applied regardless of the mapping of the page to a given concept; typed style sheets are specified at a finer granularity and thus apply only to pages describing specific concepts.

Updates and Operations

Web ML is currently being extended to support a new type of pages for performing operations and updating the site content. Write access modeling is achieved by extending the current set of Web ML concepts with the introduction of operation units, a novel type of unit whereby users can invoke operations on the site. An operation unit specifies the operation to be performed, and is linked to other units, which may show the alternative results of performing the operation (e.g., in case of success or failure). A set of generic update operations (such as: insert, delete, modify for entities, and drop, add for relationships) are predefined and need not be declared. Parameters needed to perform the operation either come from the context flowing to the operation unit via an incoming link, or are supplied by the user via forms. Operation units generalize the notion of filter units, which can be regarded as a particular operation unit associated to a search operation over a set of objects. Thanks to the orthogonal nature of Web ML, operation units can be freely combined with the other types of units to compose complex pages, mixing information to be presented to the user and interfaces to perform operations on the site. Operation units are currently being designed by looking at trolleys and online purchase procedures used in the most sophisticated e-commerce sites.

References

- Sedano, Todd; Ralph, Paul; Péraire, Cécile (2016). Proceedings of the 10th ACM/IEEE International Symposium on Empirical Software Engineering and Measurement - ESEM '16. Pp. 1–10. Doi:10.1145/2961111.2962590. ISBN 9781450344272

- Web-development, definition: techterms.com, Retrieved 20 March, 2019

- John Carroll; David Morris (July 29, 2015). Agile Project Management in easy steps, 2nd edition. In Easy Steps. P. 162. ISBN 978-1-84078-703-0

- Web-application-development, definition: searchcloudcomputing.techtarget.com, Retrieved 21 April, 2019

- Johnson, Hillary Louise (January 13, 2011). "scrummaster vs scrum master: What do you think?". Agilelearninglabs.com. Retrieved May 10, 2017

- Cho, L (2009). Adopting an Agile Culture A User Experience Team's Journey. Agile Conference. Pp. 416–421. Doi:10.1109/AGILE.2009.76. ISBN 978-0-7695-3768-9

- Online-CASE-Tool-for-Development-of-Web-Applications: researchgate.net, Retrieved 22 May, 2019

- Poppendieck, Mary (2010). Leading Lean Software Development: Results Are Not the Point. Upper Saddle River, NJ: Addison-Wesley. P. 139. ISBN 978-0-321-62070-5

- Castañeda, J.A Francisco; Muñoz-Leiva, Teodoro Luque (2007). "Web Acceptance Model (WAM): Moderating effects of user experience". Information & Management. 44: 384–396. Doi:10.1016/j.im.2007.02.003

Programming languages are the sets of instructions which are used to command the computer to perform specific tasks. Languages used for performing actions such as content creation, web security, web design, etc. are defined as web development languages. The languages elaborated in this chapter will help in gaining a better perspective about web development.

JAVASCRIPT

JavaScript has stormed the web technology and nowadays small software ventures to fortune 500, all are using node js for web apps. Recently wordpress.com has rewritten its dashboard in javascript, paypal also chose to rewrite some of its components in java script. Be it google/twitter/facebook, javascript is important for everyone. It is used in applications like single page applications, Geolocation APIs, net advertisements etc.

However JavaScript is quirky/dynamic/scripting/ functional oriented language, and it has its own idiosyncrasies. It is not scalable, it is good for some 3000 line of code but for a bigger app, it becomes difficult to manage ,read and debug. Also not everyone is very much familiar to JavaScript.

Working of JavaScript Engines

JavaScript Engines are complicated. But it works on some simple basics:

- The engine reads (parses) the script.

- Then it converts or compiles the script to the machine language.

- After that machine code runs.

Here, JavaScript engine applies optimizations at each step of the process. It reads a compiled script and analyzes the data that passes in JavaScript engine. After that, it applies optimizations to the machine code from that acquired knowledge. When this process is completed, scripts run quite fast.

Functionality of In-browser JavaScript

JavaScript's functionality depends on the environment it's running in. For example, Node.js supports functions which allows JavaScript to read and write arbitrary files, perform network requests, object-oriented, etc. The roles that JavaScript plays in both client-side (front end) and server-side (back end) development of applications can vary wildly.

In-browser JavaScript also allows you to perform webpage manipulation, interaction with the user and with the web server.

Javascript offer advantages like:

- Show dynamic content based on the user profile.

- React to user's operations, like mouse clicks events, key presses or pointer movements.

- Support features like auto-validated form entries and interactive drop-down menus.

- Send requests to remote servers, Upload and download files.

- JavaScript code can also create movement and sound.

- Ask questions to the users, Get and set cookies, show messages, switch browser tabs.

- Allows the data on to be stored in the local storage.

Limitations of In-browser JavaScript

JavaScript's capabilities in the browser are quite limited for the sake of the user's safety. It helps to prevent any unauthorized webpage from accessing private information.

Examples of such limitations are:

- JavaScript on a webpage may not allow you to copy, execute or read/write arbitrary files on the hard disk. It doesn't offer any access to Operating system functions.

- Many browsers allow it to work with files, but the access is very limited and only provided if the user is performing a specific action like, dropping a file into a browser window or selecting using <input> tag.

- JavaScript allows you to communicate over the net to the server where the current page came from. Although, it does not allow you to receive data from other sites/domains.

Uniqueness of JavaScript

Here, are the three most important features which make JavaScript unique:

- It offers full integration with HTML/CSS.

- Simple things are done quickly without any complication or following strict rules.

- Supported by all major browsers and JavaScript is enabled by default.

Alternatives to JavaScript

The syntax of JavaScript not suited for everyone as different project demands different features. However, some modern tool like a Coffee script, Typescript, and Dart allowing developers to code in another language and then auto-convert into the JavaScript code.

Features

The following features are common to all conforming ECMAScript implementations, unless explicitly specified otherwise.

Universal Support

All popular modern Web browsers support JavaScript with built-in interpreters.

Imperative and Structured

JavaScript supports much of the structured programming syntax from C (e.g., if statements, while loops, switch statements, do while loops, etc.). One partial exception is scoping: JavaScript originally had only function scoping with var. ECMAScript 2015 added keywords let and const for block scoping, meaning JavaScript now has both function and block scoping. Like C, JavaScript makes a distinction between expressions and statements. One syntactic difference from C is automatic semicolon insertion, which allows the semicolons that would normally terminate statements to be omitted.

Dynamic

- Typing:

  JavaScript is dynamically typed like most other scripting languages. A type is associated with a value rather than an expression. For example, a variable initially bound to a number may be reassigned to a string. JavaScript supports various ways to test the type of objects, including duck typing.

- Run-time evaluation:

  JavaScript includes an eval function that can execute statements provided as strings at run-time.

Prototype-based (Object-oriented)

JavaScript is almost entirely object-based. In JavaScript, an object is an associative array, augmented with a prototype; each string key provides the name for an object property, and there are two syntactical ways to specify such a name: dot notation (obj.x = 10) and bracket notation (obj['x'] = 10). A property may be added, rebound, or deleted at run-time. Most properties of an object (and any property that belongs to an object's prototype inheritance chain) can be enumerated using a for in loop.

JavaScript has a small number of built-in objects, including Function and Date.

- Prototypes:

  JavaScript uses prototypes where many other object-oriented languages use classes for inheritance. It is possible to simulate many class-based features with prototypes in JavaScript.

- Functions as object constructors:

Functions double as object constructors, along with their typical role. Prefixing a function call with *new* will create an instance of a prototype, inheriting properties and methods from the constructor (including properties from the Object prototype). ECMAScript 5 offers the Object.create method, allowing explicit creation of an instance without automatically inheriting from the Object prototype (older environments can assign the prototype to null). The constructor's prototype property determines the object used for the new object's internal prototype. New methods can be added by modifying the prototype of the function used as a constructor. JavaScript's built-in constructors, such as Array or Object, also have prototypes that can be modified. While it is possible to modify the Object prototype, it is generally considered bad practice because most objects in JavaScript will inherit methods and properties from the Object prototype, and they may not expect the prototype to be modified.

- Functions as methods:

Unlike many object-oriented languages, there is no distinction between a function definition and a method definition. Rather, the distinction occurs during function calling; when a function is called as a method of an object, the function's local *this* keyword is bound to that object for that invocation.

Functional

A function is first-class; a function is considered to be an object. As such, a function may have properties and methods, such as .call() and .bind(). A *nested* function is a function defined within another function. It is created each time the outer function is invoked. In addition, each nested function forms a lexical closure: The lexical scope of the outer function (including any constant, local variable, or argument value) becomes part of the internal state of each inner function object, even after execution of the outer function concludes. JavaScript also supports anonymous functions.

Delegative

JavaScript supports implicit and explicit delegation.

- Functions as roles (Traits and Mixins):

JavaScript natively supports various function-based implementations of Role patterns like Traits and Mixins. Such a function defines additional behavior by at least one method bound to the this keyword within its function body. A Role then has to be delegated explicitly via call or apply to objects that need to feature additional behavior that is not shared via the prototype chain.

- Object composition and inheritance:

Whereas explicit function-based delegation does cover composition in JavaScript, implicit delegation already happens every time the prototype chain is walked in order to, e.g., find a method that might be related to but is not directly owned by an object. Once the method is found it gets called within this object's context. Thus inheritance in JavaScript is covered by a delegation automatism that is bound to the prototype property of constructor functions.

Miscellaneous

- Run-time environment:

  JavaScript typically relies on a run-time environment (e.g., a Web browser) to provide objects and methods by which scripts can interact with the environment (e.g., a webpage DOM). It also relies on the run-time environment to provide the ability to include/import scripts (e.g., HTML <script> elements). This is not a language feature per se, but it is common in most JavaScript implementations. JavaScript processes messages from a queue one at a time. JavaScript calls a function associated with each new message, creating a call stack frame with the function's arguments and local variables. The call stack shrinks and grows based on the function's needs. When the call stack is empty upon function completion, JavaScript proceeds to the next message in the queue. This is called the event loop, described as "run to completion" because each message is fully processed before the next message is considered. However, the language's concurrency model describes the event loop as non-blocking: program input/output is performed using events and callback functions. This means, for instance, that JavaScript can process a mouse click while waiting for a database query to return information.

- Variadic functions:

  An indefinite number of parameters can be passed to a function. The function can access them through formal parameters and also through the local arguments object. Variadic functions can also be created by using the bind method.

- Array and object literals:

  Like many scripting languages, arrays and objects (associative arrays in other languages) can each be created with a succinct shortcut syntax. In fact, these literals form the basis of the JSON data format.

- Regular expressions:

  JavaScript also supports regular expressions in a manner similar to Perl, which provide a concise and powerful syntax for text manipulation that is more sophisticated than the built-in string functions.

Vendor-specific Extensions

JavaScript is officially managed by Mozilla Foundation, and new language features are added periodically. However, only some JavaScript engines support these new features:

- Property getter and setter functions (supported by WebKit, Gecko, Opera, ActionScript, and Rhino).

- Conditional catch clauses.

- Iterator protocol (adopted from Python).

- Shallow generators-coroutines (adopted from Python).

- Array comprehensions and generator expressions (adopted from Python).

- Proper block scope via the let keyword.

- Array and object destructuring (limited form of pattern matching).

- Concise function expressions (function(args) expr).

- ECMAScript for XML (E4X), an extension that adds native XML support to ECMAScript (unsupported in Firefox since version 21).

Syntax

Simple Examples

Variables in JavaScript can be defined using either the var, let or const keywords.

```
let x; // declares the variable x and assigns to it the special value "undefined"
(not to be confused with an undefined value)

let y = 2; // declares the variable y and assigns to it the value 2

let z = "Hello, World!"; // declares the variable z and assigns to it a string
containing "Hello, World!"
```

Note the comments in the example above, all of which were preceded with two forward slashes.

There is no built-in Input/output functionality in JavaScript; the run-time environment provides that. The ECMAScript specification in edition 5.1 mentions:

Indeed, there are no provisions in this specification for input of external data or output of computed results.

However, most runtime environments have a console object that can be used to print output. Here is a minimalist Hello World program in JavaScript:

```
console.log("Hello World!");
```

A simple recursive function:

```
function factorial(n) {
    if (n === 0)
        return 1; // 0! = 1
    return n * factorial(n - 1);
}
factorial(3); // returns 6
```

An anonymous function (or lambda):

```
function counter() {
    let count = 0;
```

```
    return function() {

        return ++count;

    };

}
let closure = counter();
closure(); // returns 1
closure(); // returns 2
closure(); // returns 3
```

This example shows that, in JavaScript, function closures capture their non-local variables by reference.

Arrow functions were first introduced in 6th Edition - ECMAScript 2015 . They shorten the syntax for writing functions in JavaScript. Arrow functions are anonymous in nature; a variable is needed to refer to them in order to invoke them after their creation.

Example of arrow function:

```
// Arrow functions let us omit the `function` keyword. Here `long_example`
// points to an anonymous function value.
const long_example = (input1, input2) => {
    console.log("Hello, World!");
    const output = input1 + input2;
    return output;
};
// Arrow functions also let us automatically return the expression to the right
// of the arrow (here `input + 5`), omitting braces and the `return` keyword.
const short_example = input => input + 5;
long_example(2, 3); // Prints "Hello, World!" and returns 5.
short_example(2); // Returns 7.
```

In JavaScript, objects are created in the same way as functions; this is known as a function object.

Object example:

```
function Ball(r) {
    this.radius = r; // the radius variable is local to the ball object
    this.area = pi * r ** 2;
    this.show = function(){ // objects can contain functions
        drawCircle(r); // references a circle drawing function
```

```
        }
}
let myBall = new Ball(5); // creates a new instance of the ball object with ra-
dius 5

myBall.show(); // this instance of the ball object has the show function per-
formed on it
```

Variadic function demonstration (arguments is a special variable):

```
function sum() {
    let x = 0;
    for (let i = 0; i < arguments.length; ++i)
        x += arguments[i];
    return x;
}
sum(1, 2); // returns 3
sum(1, 2, 3); // returns 6
```

Immediately-invoked function expressions are often used to create modules; before ECMAScript 2015 there was no built-in module construct in the language. Modules allow gathering properties and methods in a namespace and making some of them private:

```
let counter = (function() {
    let i = 0; // private property
    return { // public methods
        get: function() {
            alert(i);
        },
        set: function(value) {
            i = value;
        },
        increment: function() {
            alert(++i);
        }
    };
})(); // module
counter.get(); // shows 0
counter.set(6);
```

```
counter.increment(); // shows 7

counter.increment(); // shows 8
```

Exporting and Importing modules in javascript:

Export example:

```
/* mymodule.js */

// This function remains private, as it is not exported

let sum = (a, b) => {

    return a + b;

}

// Export variables

export let name = 'Alice';

export let age = 23;

// Export named functions

export function add(num1, num2){

 return num1 + num2;

}

// Export class

export class Multiplication {

    constructor(num1, num2) {

        this.num1 = num1;

        this.num2 = num2;

    }

    add() {

        return sum(this.num1, this.num2);

    }

}
```

Import example:

```
// Import one property

import { add } from './mymodule.js';

console.log(add(1, 2)); // 3

// Import multiple properties

import { name, age } from './mymodule.js';

console.log(name, age);
```

```
//> "Alice", 23

// Import all properties from a module

import * from './module.js'

console.log(name, age);

//> "Alice", 23

console.log(add(1,2));

//> 3
```

More Advanced Example

This sample code displays various JavaScript features:

```javascript
/* Finds the lowest common multiple (LCM) of two numbers */

function LCMCalculator(x, y) { // constructor function

    let checkInt = function(x) { // inner function

        if (x % 1 !== 0)

            throw new TypeError(x + "is not an integer"); // var a = mouseX

        return x;

    };


    this.a = checkInt(x)

    // semicolons ^^^^ are optional, a newline is enough

    this.b = checkInt(y);

}

// The prototype of object instances created by a constructor is

// that constructor's "prototype" property.

LCMCalculator.prototype = { // object literal

    constructor: LCMCalculator, // when reassigning a prototype, set the con-
structor property appropriately

    gcd: function() { // method that calculates the greatest common divisor

        // Euclidean algorithm:

        let a = Math.abs(this.a), b = Math.abs(this.b), t;

        if (a < b) {

            // swap variables

            // t = b; b = a; a = t;

            [a, b] = [b, a]; // swap using destructuring assignment (ES6)
```

```
        }
        while (b !== 0) {
            t = b;
            b = a % b;
            a = t;
        }

        // Only need to calculate GCD once, so "redefine" this method.

        // (Actually not redefinition—it's defined on the instance itself,

        // so that this.gcd refers to this "redefinition" instead of LCMCalcula-
tor.prototype.gcd.

        // Note that this leads to a wrong result if the LCMCalculator object
members "a" and/or "b" are altered afterwards.)

        // Also, 'gcd' === "gcd", this['gcd'] === this.gcd

        this['gcd'] = function() {
            return a;
        };

            return a;
    },

    // Object property names can be specified by strings delimited by double (")
or single (') quotes.
    lcm: function() {
        // Variable names do not collide with object properties, e.g., |lcm| is
not |this.lcm|.

        // not using |this.a*this.b| to avoid FP precision issues
        let lcm = this.a / this.gcd() * this.b;


        // Only need to calculate lcm once, so "redefine" this method.
        this.lcm = function() {
            return lcm;
        };
        return lcm;
    },

    toString: function() {
        return "LCMCalculator: a = " + this.a + ", b = " + this.b;
    }
```

```
};
// Define generic output function; this implementation only works for Web brows-
ers
function output(x) {
    document.body.appendChild(document.createTextNode(x));
    document.body.appendChild(document.createElement('br'));
}
// Note: Array's map() and forEach() are defined in JavaScript 1.6.
// They are used here to demonstrate JavaScript's inherent functional nature.
[
    [25, 55],
    [21, 56],
    [22, 58],
    [28, 56]
].map(function(pair) { // array literal + mapping function
    return new LCMCalculator(pair, pair);
}).sort((a, b) => a.lcm() - b.lcm()) // sort with this comparative function; =>
is a shorthand form of a function, called "arrow function"
    .forEach(printResult);
function printResult(obj) {
    output(obj + ", gcd = " + obj.gcd() + ", lcm = " + obj.lcm());
}
```

The following output should be displayed in the browser window:

```
LCMCalculator: a = 28, b = 56, gcd = 28, lcm = 56
LCMCalculator: a = 21, b = 56, gcd = 7, lcm = 168
LCMCalculator: a = 25, b = 55, gcd = 5, lcm = 275
LCMCalculator: a = 22, b = 58, gcd = 2, lcm = 638
```

Use in Web Pages

As of May 2017 94.5% of 10 million most popular web pages used JavaScript. The most common use of JavaScript is to add client-side behavior to HTML pages, also known as Dynamic HTML (DHTML). Scripts are embedded in or included from HTML pages and interact with the Document Object Model (DOM) of the page. Some simple examples of this usage are:

- Loading new page content or submitting data to the server via Ajax without reloading the page (for example, a social network might allow the user to post status updates without leaving the page).

- Animation of page elements, fading them in and out, resizing them, moving them, etc.

- Interactive content, for example games, and playing audio and video.

- Validating input values of a Web form to make sure that they are acceptable before being submitted to the server.

- Transmitting information about the user's reading habits and browsing activities to various websites. Web pages frequently do this for Web analytics, ad tracking, personalization or other purposes.

JavaScript code can run locally in a user's browser (rather than on a remote server), increasing the application's overall responsiveness to user actions. JavaScript code can also detect user actions that HTML alone cannot, such as individual keystrokes. Applications such as Gmail take advantage of this: much of the user-interface logic is written in JavaScript, and JavaScript dispatches requests for information (such as the content of an e-mail message) to the server. The wider trend of Ajax programming similarly exploits this strength.

A JavaScript engine (also known as JavaScript interpreter or JavaScript implementation) is an interpreter that interprets JavaScript source code and executes the script accordingly. The first JavaScript engine was created by Brendan Eich at Netscape, for the Netscape Navigator Web browser. The engine, code-named SpiderMonkey, is implemented in C. It has since been updated (in JavaScript 1.5) to conform to ECMAScript 3. The Rhino engine, created primarily by Norris Boyd (formerly at Netscape, now at Google) is a JavaScript implementation in Java. Rhino, like SpiderMonkey, is ECMAScript 3 compliant.

A Web browser is the most common host environment for JavaScript. However, a Web browser does not have to execute JavaScript code. (For example, text-based browsers have no JavaScript engines; and users of other browsers may disable scripts through a preference or extension).

A Web browser typically creates "host objects" to represent the DOM in JavaScript. The Web server is another common host environment. A JavaScript Web server would typically expose host objects representing HTTP request and response objects, which a JavaScript program could then interrogate and manipulate to dynamically generate Web pages.

JavaScript is the only language that the most popular browsers share support for and has inadvertently become a target language for frameworks in other languages. The increasing speed of JavaScript engines has made the language a feasible compilation target, despite the performance limitations inherent to its dynamic nature.

Example Script

Below is a minimal example of a standards-conforming Web page containing JavaScript (using HTML 5 syntax) and the DOM:

```
<!DOCTYPE html>

<html>

    <head>
```

```
  <title>Example</title>
 </head>
 <body>
  <button id="hellobutton">Hello</button>
  <script>
        document.getElementById('hellobutton').onclick = function() {
              alert('Hello world!'); // Show a dialog

              var myTextNode = document.createTextNode('Some new words.');

              document.body.appendChild(myTextNode); // Append "Some new words"
to the page
          };
   </script>
  </body>
</html>
```

Compatibility Considerations

Because JavaScript runs in widely varying environments, an important part of testing and debugging is to test and verify that the JavaScript works across multiple browsers.

The DOM interfaces are officially defined by the W3C in a standardization effort separate from JavaScript. The implementation of these DOM interfaces differ between web browsers.

JavaScript authors can deal with these differences by writing standards-compliant code that can be executed correctly by most browsers. Failing that, they can write code that behaves differently in the absence of certain browser features. Authors may also find it practical to detect what browser is running, as two browsers may implement the same feature with differing behavior. Libraries and toolkits that take browser differences into account are also useful to programmers.

Furthermore, scripts may not work for some users. For example, a user may:

- Use an old or rare browser with incomplete or unusual DOM support;
- Use a PDA or mobile phone browser that cannot execute JavaScript;
- Have JavaScript execution disabled as a security precaution;
- Use a speech browser due to, for example, a visual disability.

To support these users, Web authors can try to create pages that degrade gracefully on user agents (browsers) that do not support the page's JavaScript. In particular, the page should remain usable albeit without the extra features that the JavaScript would have added. Some sites use the HTML <noscript> tag, which contains alt content if JS is disabled. An alternative approach that many find preferable is to first author content using basic technologies that work in all browsers, then enhance the content for users that have JavaScript enabled. This is known as progressive enhancement.

Security

JavaScript and the DOM provide the potential for malicious authors to deliver scripts to run on a client computer via the Web. Browser authors minimize this risk using two restrictions. First, scripts run in a sandbox in which they can only perform Web-related actions, not general-purpose programming tasks like creating files. Second, scripts are constrained by the same-origin policy: scripts from one Web site do not have access to information such as usernames, passwords, or cookies sent to another site. Most JavaScript-related security bugs are breaches of either the same origin policy or the sandbox.

There are subsets of general JavaScript—ADsafe, Secure ECMAScript (SES)—that provide greater levels of security, especially on code created by third parties (such as advertisements). Caja is another project for safe embedding and isolation of third-party JavaScript and HTML.

Content Security Policy is the main intended method of ensuring that only trusted code is executed on a Web page.

Cross-site Vulnerabilities

A common JavaScript-related security problem is cross-site scripting (XSS), a violation of the same-origin policy. XSS vulnerabilities occur when an attacker is able to cause a target Web site, such as an online banking website, to include a malicious script in the webpage presented to a victim. The script in this example can then access the banking application with the privileges of the victim, potentially disclosing secret information or transferring money without the victim's authorization. A solution to XSS vulnerabilities is to use *HTML escaping* whenever displaying untrusted data.

Some browsers include partial protection against *reflected* XSS attacks, in which the attacker provides a URL including malicious script. However, even users of those browsers are vulnerable to other XSS attacks, such as those where the malicious code is stored in a database. Only correct design of Web applications on the server side can fully prevent XSS.

XSS vulnerabilities can also occur because of implementation mistakes by browser authors.

Another cross-site vulnerability is cross-site request forgery (CSRF). In CSRF, code on an attacker's site tricks the victim's browser into taking actions the user did not intend at a target site (like transferring money at a bank). When target sites rely solely on cookies for request authentication, requests originating from code on the attacker's site can carry the same valid login credentials of the initiating user. In general, the solution to CSRF is to require an authentication value in a hidden form field, and not only in the cookies, to authenticate any request that might have lasting effects. Checking the HTTP Referrer header can also help.

"JavaScript hijacking" is a type of CSRF attack in which a <script> tag on an attacker's site exploits a page on the victim's site that returns private information such as JSON or JavaScript. Possible solutions include:

- Requiring an authentication token in the POST and GET parameters for any response that returns private information.

Misplaced Trust in the Client

Developers of client-server applications must recognize that untrusted clients may be under the control of attackers. The application author cannot assume that their JavaScript code will run as intended (or at all) because any secret embedded in the code could be extracted by a determined adversary. Some implications are:

- Web site authors cannot perfectly conceal how their JavaScript operates because the raw source code must be sent to the client. The code can be obfuscated, but obfuscation can be reverse-engineered.

- JavaScript form validation only provides convenience for users, not security. If a site verifies that the user agreed to its terms of service, or filters invalid characters out of fields that should only contain numbers, it must do so on the server, not only the client.

- Scripts can be selectively disabled, so JavaScript cannot be relied on to prevent operations such as right-clicking on an image to save it.

- It is considered very bad practice to embed sensitive information such as passwords in JavaScript because it can be extracted by an attacker.

Misplaced Trust in Developers

Package management systems such as npm and Bower are popular with JavaScript developers. Such systems allow a developer to easily manage their program's dependencies upon other developer's program libraries. Developers trust that the maintainers of the libraries will keep them secure and up to date, but that is not always the case. A vulnerability has emerged because of this blind trust. Relied-upon libraries can have new releases that cause bugs or vulnerabilities to appear in all programs that rely upon the libraries. Inversely, a library can go unpatched with known vulnerabilities out in the wild. In a study done looking over a sample of 133k websites, researchers found 37% of the websites included a library with at-least one known vulnerability. "The median lag between the oldest library version used on each website and the newest available version of that library is 1,177 days in ALEXA, and development of some libraries still in active use ceased years ago." Another possibility is that the maintainer of a library may remove the library entirely. This occurred in March 2016 when Azer Koçulu removed his repository from npm. This caused all tens of thousands of programs and websites depending upon his libraries to break.

Browser and Plugin Coding Errors

JavaScript provides an interface to a wide range of browser capabilities, some of which may have flaws such as buffer overflows. These flaws can allow attackers to write scripts that would run any code they wish on the user's system. This code is not by any means limited to another JavaScript application. For example, a buffer overrun exploit can allow an attacker to gain access to the operating system's API with superuser privileges.

These flaws have affected major browsers including Firefox, Internet Explorer, and Safari.

Plugins, such as video players, Adobe Flash, and the wide range of ActiveX controls enabled by default in Microsoft Internet Explorer, may also have flaws exploitable via JavaScript (such flaws have been exploited in the past).

In Windows Vista, Microsoft has attempted to contain the risks of bugs such as buffer overflows by running the Internet Explorer process with limited privileges. Google Chrome similarly confines its page renderers to their own "sandbox".

Sandbox Implementation Errors

Web browsers are capable of running JavaScript outside the sandbox, with the privileges necessary to, for example, create or delete files. Such privileges are not intended to be granted to code from the Web.

Incorrectly granting privileges to JavaScript from the Web has played a role in vulnerabilities in both Internet Explorer and Firefox. In Windows XP Service Pack 2, Microsoft demoted JScript's privileges in Internet Explorer.

Microsoft Windows allows JavaScript source files on a computer's hard drive to be launched as general-purpose, non-sandboxed programs. This makes JavaScript (like VBScript) a theoretically viable vector for a Trojan horse, although JavaScript Trojan horses are uncommon in practice.

Hardware Vulnerabilities

In 2015, a JavaScript-based proof-of-concept implementation of a rowhammer attack was described in a paper by security researchers.

In 2017, a JavaScript-based attack via browser was demonstrated that could bypass ASLR. It's called "ASLR⊕Cache" or AnC.

Uses Outside Web Pages

In addition to Web browsers and servers, JavaScript interpreters are embedded in a number of tools. Each of these applications provides its own object model that provides access to the host environment. The core JavaScript language remains mostly the same in each application.

Embedded Scripting Language

- Google's Chrome extensions, Opera's extensions, Apple's Safari 5 extensions, Apple's Dashboard Widgets, Microsoft's Gadgets, Yahoo! Widgets, Google Desktop Gadgets, and Serence Klipfolio are implemented using JavaScript.

- The MongoDB database accepts queries written in JavaScript. MongoDB and NodeJS are the core components of MEAN: a solution stack for creating Web applications using just JavaScript.

- The Clusterpoint database accept queries written in JS/SQL, which is a combination of SQL and JavaScript. Clusterpoint has built-in computing engine that allows execution of JavaScript code right inside the distributed database.

- Adobe's Acrobat and Adobe Reader support JavaScript in PDF files.

- Tools in the Adobe Creative Suite, including Photoshop, Illustrator, After Effects, Dreamweaver, and InDesign, allow scripting through JavaScript.

- LibreOffice, an office application suite, allows JavaScript to be used as a scripting language.

- The visual programming language Max, released by Cycling '74, offers a JavaScript model of its environment for use by developers. It allows users to reduce visual clutter by using an object for a task rather than many.

- Apple's Logic Pro X digital audio workstation (DAW) software can create custom MIDI effects plugins using JavaScript.

- The Unity game engine supported a modified version of JavaScript for scripting via Mono until 2017.

- DX Studio (3D engine) uses the SpiderMonkey implementation of JavaScript for game and simulation logic.

- Maxwell Render (rendering software) provides an ECMA standard based scripting engine for tasks automation.

- Google Apps Script in Google Spreadsheets and Google Sites allows users to create custom formulas, automate repetitive tasks and also interact with other Google products such as Gmail.

- Many IRC clients, like ChatZilla or XChat, use JavaScript for their scripting abilities.

- RPG Maker MV uses JavaScript as its scripting language.

- The text editor UltraEdit uses JavaScript 1.7 as internal scripting language, introduced with version 13 in 2007.

Scripting Engine

- Microsoft's Active Scripting technology supports JScript as a scripting language.

- Java introduced the javax.script package in version 6 that includes a JavaScript implementation based on Mozilla Rhino. Thus, Java applications can host scripts that access the application's variables and objects, much like Web browsers host scripts that access a webpage's Document Object Model (DOM).

- The Qt C++ toolkit includes a QtScript module to interpret JavaScript, analogous to Java's javax.script package.

- OS X Yosemite introduced JavaScript for Automation (JXA), which is built upon JavaScriptCore and the Open Scripting Architecture. It features an Objective-C bridge that enables entire Cocoa applications to be programmed in JavaScript.

- Late Night Software's JavaScript OSA (also known as JavaScript for OSA, or JSOSA) is a freeware alternative to AppleScript for OS X. It is based on the Mozilla JavaScript 1.5 implementation, with the addition of a MacOS object for interaction with the operating system and third-party applications.

Application Platform

- ActionScript, the programming language used in Adobe Flash, is another implementation of the ECMAScript standard.

- Adobe AIR (Adobe Integrated Runtime) is a JavaScript runtime that allows developers to create desktop applications.

- Electron is an open-source framework developed by GitHub.

- CA Technologies AutoShell cross-application scripting environment is built on the SpiderMonkey JavaScript engine. It contains preprocessor-like extensions for command definition, as well as custom classes for various system-related tasks like file I/O, operation system command invocation and redirection, and COM scripting.

- Apache Cordova is a mobile application development framework.

- Cocos2d is an open source software framework. It can be used to build games, apps and other cross platform GUI based interactive programs.

- Chromium Embedded Framework (CEF) is an open source framework for embedding a web browser engine based on the Chromium core.

- RhoMobile Suite is a set of development tools for creating data-centric, cross-platform, native mobile consumer and enterprise applications.

- NW.js call all Node.js modules directly from DOM and enable a new way of writing applications with all Web technologies.

- GNOME Shell, the shell for the GNOME 3 desktop environment, made JavaScript its default programming language in 2013.

- The Mozilla application framework (XPFE) platform, which underlies Firefox, Thunderbird, and some other Web browsers, uses JavaScript to implement the graphical user interface (GUI) of its various products.

- Qt Quick's markup language (available since Qt 4.7) uses JavaScript for its application logic. Its declarative syntax is also similar to JavaScript.

- Ubuntu Touch provides a JavaScript API for its unified usability interface.

- Open webOS is the next generation of web-centric platforms built to run on a wide range of form factors.

- enyo JS is a framework to develop apps for all major platforms, from phones and tablets to PCs and TVs.

- WinJS provides a special Windows Library for JavaScript functionality in Windows 8 that enables the development of Modern style (formerly *Metro style*) applications in HTML5 and JavaScript.

- NativeScript is an open-source framework to develop apps on the Apple iOS and Android platforms.

- Weex is a framework for building Mobile cross-platform UI, created by China Tech giant Alibaba.

- XULRunner is packaged version of the Mozilla platform to enable standalone desktop application development.

Development Tools

Within JavaScript, access to a debugger becomes invaluable when developing large, non-trivial programs. There can be implementation differences between the various browsers (particularly within the DOM), so it is useful to have access to a debugger for each of the browsers that a Web application targets.

Script debuggers are integrated within many mainstream browsers such as Internet Explorer, Firefox, Safari, Google Chrome, Opera and Node.js.

In addition to the native Internet Explorer Developer Tools, three other debuggers are available for Internet Explorer: Microsoft Visual Studio has the most features of the three, closely followed by Microsoft Script Editor (a component of Microsoft Office), and finally the free Microsoft Script Debugger. The free Microsoft Visual Web Developer Express provides a limited version of the JavaScript debugging functionality in Microsoft Visual Studio.

In comparison to Internet Explorer, Firefox has a more comprehensive set of developer tools, which includes a debugger as well. Old versions of Firefox without these tools used a Firefox add-on called Firebug, or the older Venkman debugger. WebKit's Web Inspector includes a JavaScript debugger, which is used in Safari. A modified version called Blink DevTools is used in Google Chrome. Node.js has Node Inspector, an interactive debugger that integrates with the Blink DevTools. Opera includes a set of tools called Dragonfly.

In addition to the native computer software, there are online JavaScript integrated development environment (IDEs), which has debugging aids that are themselves written in JavaScript and built to run on the Web. An example is the program JSLint, developed by Douglas Crockford who has written extensively on the language. JSLint scans JavaScript code for conformance to a set of standards and guidelines. Many libraries for JavaScript, such as three.js, provide links to demonstration code that can be edited by users. Demonstration codes are also used as a pedagogical tool by institutions such as Khan Academy to allow students to experience writing code in an environment where they can see the output of their programs, without needing any setup beyond a Web browser.

Benchmark Tools for Developers

JavaScript's increased usage in web development warrants further considerations about performance. Frontend code has inherited many responsibilities previously handled by the backend. Mobile devices in particular may encounter problems rendering poorly optimized frontend code.

A library for doing benchmarks is benchmark.js. A benchmarking library that supports high-resolution timers and returns statistically significant results.

Another tool is jsben.ch. An online JavaScript benchmarking tool, where code snippets can be tested against each other.

Related Languages and Technologies

- JSON, or JavaScript Object Notation, is a general-purpose data interchange format that is defined as a subset of JavaScript's object literal syntax.

- jQuery is a JavaScript library designed to simplify DOM-oriented client-side HTML scripting along with offering cross-browser compatibility because various browsers respond differently to certain vanilla JavaScript code.

- Underscore.js is a utility JavaScript library for data manipulation that is used in both client-side and server-side network applications.

- Angular and AngularJS are web application frameworks to use for developing single-page applications and also cross-platform mobile apps.

- React is an open source JavaScript library providing views that are rendered using components specified as custom HTML tags.

- Vue.js is an open source JavaScript framework that features an incrementally adoptable architecture focusing on declarative rendering and component composition.

- Mozilla browsers currently support LiveConnect, a feature that allows JavaScript and Java to intercommunicate on the Web. However, Mozilla-specific support for LiveConnect was scheduled to be phased out in the future in favor of passing on the LiveConnect handling via NPAPI to the Java 1.6+ plug-in (not yet supported on the Mac as of March 2010). Most browser inspection tools, such as Firebug in Firefox, include JavaScript interpreters that can act on the visible page's DOM.

- asm.js is a subset of JavaScript that can be run in any JavaScript engine or run faster in an ahead-of-time (AOT) compiling engine.

- JSFuck is an esoteric programming language. Programs are written using only six different characters, but are still valid JavaScript code.

- p5.js is an object oriented JavaScript library designed for artists and designers. It is based on the ideas of the Processing project but is for the web.

- jsben.ch is an online JavaScript benchmarking tool, where different code snippets can be tested against each other.

Use as an Intermediate Language

As JavaScript is the most widely supported client-side language that can run within a Web browser, it has become an intermediate language for other languages (also called *transpilers*) to target. This has included both newly created languages and ports of existing languages. Some of these include:

- ClojureScript, a dialect of Clojure that targets JavaScript. Its compiler is designed to emit JavaScript code that is compatible with the advanced compilation mode of the Google Closure optimizing compiler.

- CoffeeScript, an alternate syntax for JavaScript intended to be more concise and readable. It adds features like array comprehensions (also available in JavaScript since version 1.7) and pattern matching. Like Objective-J, it compiles to JavaScript. Ruby and Python have been cited as influential on CoffeeScript syntax.

- Dart, an all-purpose, open source language that compiles to JavaScript.

- Elm, a pure functional language for web apps. Unlike handwritten JavaScript, Elm-generated JavaScript has zero runtime exceptions, a time-traveling debugger, and enforced semantic versioning.

- Emscripten, a LLVM-backend for porting native libraries to JavaScript, known as asm.js.

- Fantom, a programming language that runs on JVM, .NET and JavaScript.

- Free Pascal, a compiler for Pascal that targets JavaScript.

- Google Web Toolkit, a toolkit that translates a subset of Java to JavaScript.

- Haxe, an open-source high-level multiplatform programming language and compiler that can produce applications and source code for many different platforms including JavaScript.

- OberonScript, a full implementation of the Oberon programming language that compiles to high-level JavaScript.

- Objective-J, a superset of JavaScript that compiles to standard JavaScript. It adds traditional inheritance and Smalltalk/Objective-C style dynamic dispatch and optional pseudo-static typing to JavaScript.

- Processing.js, a JavaScript port of the Processing programming language designed to write visualizations, images, and interactive content. It allows Web browsers to display animations, visual applications, games and other graphical rich content without the need for a Java applet or Flash plugin.

- Pyjs, a port of Google Web Toolkit to Python that translates a subset of Python to JavaScript.

- Scala, an object-oriented and functional programming language, has a Scala-to-JavaScript compiler.

- SqueakJS, a virtual machine and DOM environment for the open-source Squeak implementation of the Smalltalk programming language.

- TypeScript, a free and open-source programming language developed by Microsoft. It is a superset of JavaScript, and essentially adds support for optional type annotations and some other language extensions such as classes, interfaces and modules. A TS-script compiles into plain JavaScript and can be executed in any JS host supporting ECMAScript 3 or higher. The compiler is itself written in TypeScript.

- Whalesong, a Racket-to-JavaScript compiler.

As JavaScript has unusual limitations – such as no explicit integer type, only double-precision binary floating point – languages that compile to JavaScript and do not take care to use the integer-converting shift and bitwise logical operators may have slightly different behavior than in other environments.

JavaScript and Java

A common misconception is that JavaScript is similar or closely related to Java. It is true that both have a C-like syntax (the C language being their most immediate common ancestor language). They also are both typically sandboxed (when used inside a browser), and JavaScript was designed with Java's syntax and standard library in mind. In particular, all Java keywords were reserved in original JavaScript, JavaScript's standard library follows Java's naming conventions, and JavaScript's Math and Date objects are based on classes from Java 1.0, but the similarities end there.

Java and JavaScript both first appeared in 1995, but Java was developed by James Gosling of Sun Microsystems, and JavaScript by Brendan Eich of Netscape Communications.

The differences between the two languages are more prominent than their similarities. Java has static typing, while JavaScript's typing is dynamic. Java is loaded from compiled bytecode, while JavaScript is loaded as human-readable source code. Java's objects are class-based, while JavaScript's are prototype-based. Finally, Java did not support functional programming until Java 8, while JavaScript has done so from the beginning, being influenced by Scheme.

WebAssembly

Starting in 2017, web browsers began supporting WebAssembly, a technology standardized by the W3C. The WebAssembly standard specifies a binary format, which can be produced by a compiler toolchain such as LLVM, to execute in the browser at near native speed. WebAssembly allows programming languages such as C, C++, C# and Java to be used as well as JavaScript to author client-side code for the World Wide Web.

CASCADING STYLE SHEETS

Cascading Style Sheets (CSS) is a style sheet language used for describing the presentation of a document written in a markup language like HTML. CSS is a cornerstone technology of the World Wide Web, alongside HTML and JavaScript.

CSS is designed to enable the separation of presentation and content, including layout, colors, and fonts. This separation can improve content accessibility, provide more flexibility and control in the specification of presentation characteristics, enable multiple web pages to share formatting by specifying the relevant CSS in a separate .css file, and reduce complexity and repetition in the structural content.

Separation of formatting and content also makes it feasible to present the same markup page in different styles for different rendering methods, such as on-screen, in print, by voice (via speech-based browser or screen reader), and on Braille-based tactile devices. CSS also has rules for alternate formatting if the content is accessed on a mobile device.

The name cascading comes from the specified priority scheme to determine which style rule applies if more than one rule matches a particular element. This cascading priority scheme is predictable.

The CSS specifications are maintained by the World Wide Web Consortium (W3C). Internet media type (MIME type) text/css is registered for use with CSS by RFC 2318. The W3C operates a free CSS validation service for CSS documents.

In addition to HTML, other markup languages support the use of CSS including XHTML, plain XML, SVG, and XUL.

Syntax

CSS has a simple syntax and uses a number of English keywords to specify the names of various style properties.

A style sheet consists of a list of rules. Each rule or rule-set consists of one or more selectors, and a declaration block.

Selector

In CSS, *selectors* declare which part of the markup a style applies to by matching tags and attributes in the markup itself.

Selectors may apply to the following:

- All elements of a specific type, e.g. the second-level headers h2.

- Elements specified by attribute, in particular:

  ○ id: An identifier unique within the document.

  ○ Class: An identifier that can annotate multiple elements in a document.

- Elements depending on how they are placed relative to others in the document tree.

Classes and IDs are case-sensitive, start with letters, and can include alphanumeric characters, hyphens and underscores. A class may apply to any number of instances of any elements. An ID may only be applied to a single element.

Pseudo-classes are used in CSS selectors to permit formatting based on information that is not contained in the document tree. One example of a widely used pseudo-class is `:hover`, which identifies content only when the user "points to" the visible element, usually by holding the mouse cursor over it. It is appended to a selector as in `a:hover` or `#elementid:hover`. A pseudo-class classifies document elements, such as `:link` or `:visited`, whereas a *pseudo-element* makes a selection that may consist of partial elements, such as `::first-line or ::first-letter`.

Selectors may be combined in many ways to achieve great specificity and flexibility. Multiple selectors may be joined in a spaced list to specify elements by location, element type, id, class, or any combination thereof. The order of the selectors is important. For example, `div .myClass {color: red;}` applies to all elements of class myClass that are inside div elements, whereas `.myClass div {color: red;}` applies to all div elements that are in elements of class myClass.

The following table provides a summary of selector syntax indicating usage and the version of CSS that introduced it.

Pattern	Matches	First defined in CSS level
E	an element of type E	1
E:link	an E element is the source anchor of a hyperlink of which the target is not yet visited (:link) or already visited (:visited)	1
E:active	an E element during certain user actions	1
E::first-line	the first formatted line of an E element	1
E::first-letter	the first formatted letter of an E element	1
.c	all elements with class="c"	1
#myid	the element with id="myid"	1
E.warning	an E element whose class is "warning" (the document language specifies how class is determined)	1
E#myid	an E element with ID equal to "myid"	1
E F	an F element descendant of an E element	1
*	any element	2
E[foo]	an E element with a "foo" attribute	2
E[foo="bar"]	an E element whose "foo" attribute value is exactly equal to "bar"	2
E[foo~="bar"]	an E element whose "foo" attribute value is a list of whitespace-separated values, one of which is exactly equal to "bar"	2
E[foo|="en"]	an E element whose "foo" attribute has a hyphen-separated list of values beginning (from the left) with "en"	2
E:first-child	an E element, first child of its parent	2
E:lang(fr)	an element of type E in language "fr" (the document language specifies how language is determined)	2
E::before	generated content before an E element's content	2
E::after	generated content after an E element's content	2
E > F	an F element child of an E element	2
E + F	an F element immediately preceded by an E element	2
E[foo^="bar"]	an E element whose "foo" attribute value begins exactly with the string "bar"	3
E[foo$="bar"]	an E element whose "foo" attribute value ends exactly with the string "bar"	3
E[foo*="bar"]	an E element whose "foo" attribute value contains the substring "bar"	3
E:root	an E element, root of the document	3
E:nth-child(n)	an E element, the n-th child of its parent	3
E:nth-last-child(n)	an E element, the n-th child of its parent, counting from the last one	3
E:nth-of-type(n)	an E element, the n-th sibling of its type	3
E:nth-last-of-type(n)	an E element, the n-th sibling of its type, counting from the last one	3

E:last-child	an E element, last child of its parent	3
E:first-of-type	an E element, first sibling of its type	3
E:last-of-type	an E element, last sibling of its type	3
E:only-child	an E element, only child of its parent	3
E:only-of-type	an E element, only sibling of its type	3
E:empty	an E element that has no children (including text nodes)	3
E:target	an E element being the target of the referring URI	3
E:enabled	a user interface element E that is enabled	3
E:disabled	a user interface element E that is disabled	3
E:checked	a user interface element E that is checked (for instance a radio-button or checkbox)	3
E:not(s)	an E element that does not match simple selector s	3
E ~ F	an F element preceded by an E element	3

Declaration Block

A declaration block consists of a list of *declarations* in braces. Each declaration itself consists of a *property*, a colon (:), and a *value*. If there are multiple declarations in a block, a semi-colon (;) must be inserted to separate each declaration.

Properties are specified in the CSS standard. Each property has a set of possible values. Some properties can affect any type of element, and others apply only to particular groups of elements.

Values may be keywords, such as "center" or "inherit", or numerical values, such as 200px (200 pixels), 50vw (50 percent of the viewport width) or 80% (80 percent of the parent element's width). Color values can be specified with keywords (e.g. `red`), hexadecimal values (e.g. #FF0000, also abbreviated as #F00), RGB values on a 0 to 255 scale (e.g. rgb(255, 0, 0)), RGBA values that specify both color and alpha transparency (e.g. rgba(255, 0, 0, 0.8)), or HSL or HSLA values (e.g. hsl(000, 100%, 50%), hsla(000, 100%, 50%, 80%)).

Length Units

Non-zero numeric values representing linear measures must include a length unit, which is either an alphabetic code or abbreviation, as in 200px or 50vw; or a percentage sign, as in 80%. Some units – cm (centimetre); in (inch); mm (millimetre); pc (pica); and pt (point) – are *absolute*, which means that the rendered dimension does not depend upon the structure of the page; others – em (em); ex (ex) and px (pixel) – are *relative*, which means that factors such as the font size of a parent element can affect the rendered measurement. These eight units were a feature of CSS 1 and retained in all subsequent revisions. The proposed CSS Values and Units Module Level 3 will, if adopted as a W3C Recommendation, provide seven further length units: ch; Q; rem; vh; vmax; vmin; and vw.

Use

Before CSS, nearly all presentational attributes of HTML documents were contained within the HTML markup. All font colors, background styles, element alignments, borders and sizes had to be explicitly described, often repeatedly, within the HTML. CSS lets authors move much of that information to another file, the style sheet, resulting in considerably simpler HTML.

For example, headings (h1 elements), sub-headings (h2), sub-sub-headings (h3), etc., are defined structurally using HTML. In print and on the screen, choice of font, size, color and emphasis for these elements is *presentational.*

Before CSS, document authors who wanted to assign such typographic characteristics to, say, all h2 headings had to repeat HTML presentational markup for each occurrence of that heading type. This made documents more complex, larger, and more error-prone and difficult to maintain. CSS allows the separation of presentation from structure. CSS can define color, font, text alignment, size, borders, spacing, layout and many other typographic characteristics, and can do so independently for on-screen and printed views. CSS also defines non-visual styles, such as reading speed and emphasis for aural text readers. The W3C has now deprecated the use of all presentational HTML markup.

For example, under pre-CSS HTML, a heading element defined with red text would be written as:

```
<h1><font color="red"> Chapter 1. </font></h1>
```

Using CSS, the same element can be coded using style properties instead of HTML presentational attributes:

```
<h1 style="color: red;"> Chapter 1. </h1>
```

The advantages of this may not be immediately clear (since the second form is actually more verbose), but the power of CSS becomes more apparent when the style properties are placed in an internal style element or, even better, an external CSS file. For example, suppose the document contains the style element:

```
<style>
h1 {
    color: red;
}
</style>
```

All h1 elements in the document will then automatically become red without requiring any explicit code. If the author later wanted to make h1 elements blue instead, this could be done by changing the style element to:

```
<style>
h1 {
    color: blue;
}
</style>
```

rather than by laboriously going through the document and changing the color for each individual h1 element.

The styles can also be placed in an external CSS file, as described below, and loaded using syntax similar to:

```
<link href="path/to/file.css" rel="stylesheet" type="text/css">
```

This further decouples the styling from the HTML document, and makes it possible to restyle multiple documents by simply editing a shared external CSS file.

Sources

CSS information can be provided from various sources. These sources can be the web browser, the user and the author. The information from the author can be further classified into inline, media type, importance, selector specificity, rule order, inheritance and property definition. CSS style information can be in a separate document or it can be embedded into an HTML document. Multiple style sheets can be imported. Different styles can be applied depending on the output device being used; for example, the screen version can be quite different from the printed version, so that authors can tailor the presentation appropriately for each medium.

The style sheet with the highest priority controls the content display. Declarations not set in the highest priority source are passed on to a source of lower priority, such as the user agent style. The process is called cascading.

One of the goals of CSS is to allow users greater control over presentation. Someone who finds red italic headings difficult to read may apply a different style sheet. Depending on the browser and the web site, a user may choose from various style sheets provided by the designers, or may remove all added styles and view the site using the browser's default styling, or may override just the red italic heading style without altering other attributes.

CSS priority scheme (highest to lowest)		
Priority	CSS source type	Description
1	Importance	The "!important" annotation overwrites the previous priority types.
2	Inline	A style applied to an HTML element via HTML "style" attribute.
3	Media Type	A property definition applies to all media types, unless a media specific CSS is defined.
4	User defined	Most browsers have the accessibility feature: a user defined CSS.
5	Selector specificity	A specific contextual selector (#heading p) overwrites generic definition.
6	Rule order	Last rule declaration has a higher priority.
7	Parent inheritance	If a property is not specified, it is inherited from a parent element.
8	CSS property definition in HTML document	CSS rule or CSS inline style overwrites a default browser value.
9	Browser default	The lowest priority: browser default value is determined by W3C initial value specifications.

Specificity

Specificity refers to the relative weights of various rules. It determines which styles apply to an element when more than one rule could apply. Based on specification, a simple selector (e.g. H1) has a specificity of 1, class selectors have a specificity of 1,0, and ID selectors a specificity of 1,0,0.

Because the specificity values do not carry over as in the decimal system, commas are used to separate the "digits" (a CSS rule having 11 elements and 11 classes would have a specificity of 11,11, not 121).

Thus the following rules selectors result in the indicated specificity:

Selectors	Specificity
`H1 {color: white;}`	0, 0, 0, 1
`P EM {color: green;}`	0, 0, 0, 2
`.grape {color: red;}`	0, 0, 1, 0
`P.bright {color: blue;}`	0, 0, 1, 1
`P.bright EM.dark {color: yellow;}`	0, 0, 2, 2
`#id218 {color: brown;}`	0, 1, 0, 0
`style=" "`	1, 0, 0, 0

Consider this HTML fragment:

```
<!DOCTYPE html>

<html>

  <head>

    <meta charset="utf-8">

    <style>

    #xyz { color: blue; }

    </style>

  </head>

  <body>

    <p id="xyz" style="color: green;"> To demonstrate specificity </p>

  </body>

</html>
```

In the above example, the declaration in the style attribute overrides the one in the <style> element because it has a higher specificity, and thus, the paragraph appears green.

Inheritance

Inheritance is a key feature in CSS; it relies on the ancestor-descendant relationship to operate. Inheritance is the mechanism by which properties are applied not only to a specified element, but also to its descendants. Inheritance relies on the document tree, which is the hierarchy of XHTML elements in a page based on nesting. Descendant elements may inherit CSS property values from any ancestor element enclosing them. In general, descendant elements inherit text-related properties, but their box-related properties are not inherited. Properties that can be inherited are color, font, letter-spacing, line-height, list-style, text-align, text-indent, text-transform, visibility, white-space and word-spacing. Properties that cannot be inherited are background, border, display, float and clear, height, and width, margin, min- and max-height and -width, outline, overflow, padding, position, text-decoration, vertical-align and z-index.

Inheritance can be used to avoid declaring certain properties over and over again in a style sheet, allowing for shorter CSS.

Inheritance in CSS is not the same as inheritance in class-based programming languages, where it is possible to define class B as "like class A, but with modifications". With CSS, it is possible to style an *element* with "class A, but with modifications". However, it is not possible to define a CSS *class* B like that, which could then be used to style multiple elements without having to repeat the modifications.

Given the following style sheet:

```
h1 {

    color: pink;

}
```

Suppose there is an h1 element with an emphasizing element (em) inside:

```
<h1>

    This is to <em>illustrate</em> inheritance

</h1>
```

If no color is assigned to the em element, the emphasized word "illustrate" inherits the color of the parent element, h1. The style sheet h1 has the color pink, hence, the em element is likewise pink.

Whitespace

Whitespace between properties and selectors is ignored. This code snippet:

```
body{overflow:hidden;background:#000000;background-image:url(images/bg.
gif);background-repeat:no-repeat;background-position:left top;}
```

is functionally equivalent to this one:

```
body {

    overflow: hidden;

    background-color: #000000;

    background-image: url(images/bg.gif);

    background-repeat: no-repeat;

    background-position: left top;

}
```

One common way to format CSS for readability is to indent each property and give it its own line. In addition to formatting CSS for readability, shorthand properties can be used to write out the code faster, which also gets processed more quickly when being rendered:

```
body {

    overflow: hidden;

    background: #000 url(images/bg.gif) no-repeat left top;

}
```

Positioning

CSS 2.1 defines three positioning schemes:

- Normal flow:

  Inline items are laid out in the same way as the letters in words in text, one after the other across the available space until there is no more room, then starting a new line below. Block items stack vertically, like paragraphs and like the items in a bulleted list. Normal flow also includes relative positioning of block or inline items, and run-in boxes.

- Floats:

  A floated item is taken out of the normal flow and shifted to the left or right as far as possible in the space available. Other content then flows alongside the floated item.

- Absolute positioning:

  An absolutely positioned item has no place in, and no effect on, the normal flow of other items. It occupies its assigned position in its container independently of other items.

Position Property

There are four possible values of the `position` property. If an item is positioned in any way other than static, then the further properties `top`, `bottom`, `left`, and `right` are used to specify offsets and positions.

- Static:

  The default value places the item in the *normal flow*.

- Relative:

  The item is placed in the normal flow, and then shifted or offset from that position. Subsequent flow items are laid out as if the item had not been moved.

- Absolute:

  Specifies absolute positioning. The element is positioned in relation to its nearest non-static ancestor.

- Fixed:

  The item is absolutely positioned in a fixed position on the screen even as the rest of the document is scrolled.

Float and Clear

The `float` property may have one of three values. *Absolutely* positioned or *fixed* items cannot be floated. Other elements normally flow around floated items, unless they are prevented from doing so by their `clear` property.

- Left:

  The item *floats* to the left of the line that it would have appeared in; other items may flow around its right side.

- Right:

  The item *floats* to the right of the line that it would have appeared in; other items may flow around its left side.

- Clear:

  Forces the element to appear underneath ('clear') floated elements to the left (`clear: left`), right (`clear:right`) or both sides (`clear:both`).

Browser Support

Each web browser uses a layout engine to render web pages, and support for CSS functionality is not consistent between them. Because browsers do not parse CSS perfectly, multiple coding techniques have been developed to target specific browsers with workarounds (commonly known as CSS hacks or CSS filters). Adoption of new functionality in CSS can be hindered by lack of support in major browsers. For example, Internet Explorer was slow to add support for many CSS 3 features, which slowed adoption of those features and damaged the browser's reputation among developers. In order to ensure a consistent experience for their users, web developers often test their sites across multiple operating systems, browsers, and browser versions, increasing development time and complexity. Tools such as BrowserStack have been built to reduce the complexity of maintaining these environments.

In addition to these testing tools, many sites maintain lists of browser support for specific CSS properties, including CanIUse and the Mozilla Developer Network. Additionally, the CSS 3 defines feature queries, which provide an `@supports` directive that will allow developers to target browsers with support for certain functionality directly within their CSS. CSS that is not supported by older browsers can also sometimes be patched in using JavaScript polyfills, which are pieces of JavaScript code designed to make browsers behave consistently. These workarounds—and the need to support fallback functionality—can add complexity to development projects, and consequently, companies frequently define a list of browser versions that they will and will not support.

As websites adopt newer code standards that are incompatible with older browsers, these browsers can be cut off from accessing many of the resources on the web (sometimes intentionally). Many of the most popular sites on the internet are not just visually degraded on older browsers due to poor CSS support, but do not work at all, in large part due to the evolution of JavaScript and other web technologies.

Limitations

Some noted limitations of the current capabilities of CSS include:

- Selectors are unable to ascend:

  CSS currently offers no way to select a *parent* or *ancestor* of an element that satisfies certain criteria. CSS Selectors Level 4, which is still in Working Draft status, proposes such a selector, but only as part of the "complete" selector profile, not the "fast" profile used in dynamic CSS styling. A more advanced selector scheme (such as XPath) would enable more sophisticated style sheets. The major reasons for the CSS Working Group previously rejecting proposals for parent selectors are related to browser performance and incremental rendering issues.

- Cannot explicitly declare new scope independently of position:

  Scoping rules for properties such as z-index look for the closest parent element with a position:absolute or position:relative attribute. This odd coupling has undesired effects. For example, it is impossible to avoid declaring a new scope when one is forced to adjust an element's position, preventing one from using the desired scope of a parent element.

- Pseudo-class dynamic behavior not controllable:

  CSS implements pseudo-classes that allow a degree of user feedback by conditional application of alternate styles. One CSS pseudo-class, "`:hover`", is dynamic (equivalent of JavaScript "onmouseover") and has potential for abuse (e.g., implementing cursor-proximity popups), but CSS has no ability for a client to disable it (no "disable"-like property) or limit its effects (no "nochange"-like values for each property).

- Cannot name rules:

  There is no way to name a CSS rule, which would allow (for example) client-side scripts to refer to the rule even if its selector changes.

- Cannot include styles from a rule into another rule:

  CSS styles often must be duplicated in several rules to achieve a desired effect, causing additional maintenance and requiring more thorough testing. Some new CSS features were proposed to solve this, but are not yet implemented anywhere.

- Cannot target specific text without altering markup:

  Besides the `:first-letter` pseudo-element, one cannot target specific ranges of text without needing to utilize place-holder elements.

Former Issues

Additionally, several more issues were present in prior versions of the CSS standard, but have been alleviated:

- Vertical control limitations:

  Though horizontal placement of elements was always generally easy to control, vertical placement was frequently unintuitive, convoluted, or outright impossible. Simple tasks, such as centering an element vertically or placing a footer no higher than bottom of the viewport required either complicated and unintuitive style rules, or simple but widely unsupported rules. The Flexible Box Module improved the situation considerably and vertical control is much more straightforward and supported in all of the modern browsers. Older browsers still have those issues, but most of those are no longer supported by their vendors.

- Absence of expressions:

  There was no standard ability to specify property values as simple expressions (such as `margin-left: 10% - 3em + 4px;`). This would be useful in a variety of cases, such as calculating the size of columns subject to a constraint on the sum of all columns. Internet Explorer versions 5 to 7 support a proprietary expression() statement, with similar functionality. This proprietary expression() statement is no longer supported from Internet Explorer 8 onwards, except in compatibility modes. This decision was taken for "standards compliance, browser performance, and security reasons". However, a candidate recommendation with a calc() value to address this limitation has been published by the CSS WG and has since been supported in all of the modern browsers.

- Lack of column declaration:

  Although possible in current CSS 3 (using the `column-count` module), layouts with multiple columns can be complex to implement in CSS 2.1. With CSS 2.1, the process is often done using floating elements, which are often rendered differently by different browsers, different computer screen shapes, and different screen ratios set on standard monitors. All of the modern browsers support this CSS 3 feature in one form or another.

Advantages

- Separation of content from presentation:

  CSS facilitates publication of content in multiple presentation formats based on nominal parameters. Nominal parameters include explicit user preferences, different web browsers, the type of device being used to view the content (a desktop computer or mobile device), the geographic location of the user and many other variables.

- Site-wide consistency:

  When CSS is used effectively, in terms of inheritance and "cascading", a global style sheet can be used to affect and style elements site-wide. If the situation arises that the styling of the elements should be changed or adjusted, these changes can be made by editing rules in the global style sheet. Before CSS, this sort of maintenance was more difficult, expensive and time-consuming.

- Bandwidth:

A stylesheet, internal or external, specifies the style once for a range of HTML elements selected by class, type or relationship to others. This is much more efficient than repeating style information inline for each occurrence of the element. An external stylesheet is usually stored in the browser cache, and can therefore be used on multiple pages without being reloaded, further reducing data transfer over a network.

- Page reformatting:

With a simple change of one line, a different style sheet can be used for the same page. This has advantages for accessibility, as well as providing the ability to tailor a page or site to different target devices. Furthermore, devices not able to understand the styling still display the content.

- Accessibility:

Without CSS, web designers must typically lay out their pages with techniques such as HTML tables that hinder accessibility for vision-impaired users.

Standardization

Frameworks

CSS frameworks are pre-prepared libraries that are meant to allow for easier, more standards-compliant styling of web pages using the Cascading Style Sheets language. CSS frameworks include Foundation, Blueprint, Bootstrap, Cascade Framework and Materialize. Like programming and scripting language libraries, CSS frameworks are usually incorporated as external .css sheets referenced in the HTML <head>. They provide a number of ready-made options for designing and laying out the web page. Although many of these frameworks have been published, some authors use them mostly for rapid prototyping, or for learning from, and prefer to 'handcraft' CSS that is appropriate to each published site without the design, maintenance and download overhead of having many unused features in the site's styling.

Design Methodologies

As the size of CSS resources used in a project increases, a development team often needs to decide on a common design methodology to keep them organized. The goals are ease of development, ease of collaboration during development and performance of the deployed stylesheets in the browser. Popular methodologies include OOCSS (object oriented CSS), ACSS (atomic CSS), oCSS (organic Cascade Style Sheet), SMACSS (scalable and modular architecture for CSS), and BEM (block, element, modifier).

HTML

A markup language is a set of markup tags described by HTML tags. Each HTML tag describes different document content. HTML tags are the hidden keywords within a web page. It defines how the browser must format and display the content. Most tags must have two parts, an opening and a closing part: < *tagname* > *content* < /*tagname* > HTML tags normally come in pairs like <

$p >$ and $< /p >$ The first tag in a pair is the start tag while the second tag is the end tag. The end tag is written like the start tag, but with a slash before the tag name. The web page is divided into two main parts Figure :

- The head part: Includes the title of the page and what appears on the head.

- The body: Includes all the elements that should be appear on the webpage. The body area is displayed in the browser.

The first HTML page figure show a small HTML code for a simple page. The code may be explained as follows:

- The DOCTYPE declaration defines the document type to be HTML.

- The text between $< html >$ and $< /html >$ describes an HTML document.

- The text between $< head >$ and $< /head >$ provides information about the document.

- The text between $< title >$ and $< /title >$ provides a title for the document.

- The text between $< body >$ and $< /body >$ describes the visible page content.

- The text between $< h1 >$ and $< /h1 >$ describes a heading.

- The text between $< p >$ and $< /p >$ describes a paragraph.

```
<!DOCTYPE html>
<html>
<head>
<title>Page Title</title>
</head>
<body>

<h1>My First Heading</h1>
<p>My first paragraph.</p>

</body>
</html>
```

HTML code example.

The code may be written in any editor such as notepad or wordpad. The document should be saved as .html and then opened from any web browser such as Internet Explorer, Google Chrome or Firefox.

HTML Headings

HTML headings are defined with the $< h1 >$ to $< h6 >$ tags with different sizes starting with the largest size at $< h1 >$ and ending with the smallest size at $< h6 >$. If we have the following portion of code, then the result will appear.

The webpage created after execturting figure code.

```
<h1>Largest size heading</h1>
<h2>Smaller size heading</h2>
<h3>Smaller size heading</h3>
<h4>Largest size heading</h4>
<h5>Smaller size heading</h5>
<h6>Smallest size heading</h6>
```

Largest size heading

Smaller size heading

Smaller size heading

Largest size heading

Smaller size heading

Smallest size heading

The headeing results.

HTML Paragraphs

HTML paragraphs are defined with the $< p >$ text $< /p >$ tags. The spaces and the new lines are ignored. If you want to force for a new line you should write $< br >$. If you want to have a paragraph with the same formatting like you write, write what you want between $< pre > < /pre >$ tags.

```
<p>This paragraph ignore spacing and new lines </p>
<p>This is another paragraph. <br> here start new line </p>
<pre> Here it appear with the same formatting </pre>
```

This paragraph ignore spacing and new lines

This is another paragraph.
here start new line

```
        Here it appear with the same formatting
```

The paragraph styles.

There are a lot of options that could be used for text formatting such as:

- $< b >$ bold $< /b >$: write in bold style.
- $< I >$ italic $< /I >$: write in italic style.
- $< u >$ underline $< /u >$: put underline.
- $< hr >$ Horizontal line: draw a horizontal line.

```
<p>This paragraph ignore <b> spacing </b> and new lines</p>

<p>This is another paragraph.<br> <I>here start newlIne</I> </p>

<pre> <u>Here it appear with </u> the same formatting </pre> <hr >
```

HTML Links

Links are a text that when clicked will open another page or do certain action. To make a hyperlink, you have to specify:

- The text that will appear on the screen.

This paragraph ignor **spacing** and new lines

This is another paragraph.
here start new line

~~Here it appear with~~   the same formatting

The formatting results.

- The page that will be opened when the text is clicked.

  The HTML tag $< a >< /a >$ is used to specify the HTML code for the hyperlink as follows:

  ```
  <a href="url">link text</a>
  ```

The previous code can be dissected as follows:

- href="url: Here you specify the webpage or HTML page that should be opened when the text is clicked.

- link text: The text that will appear on the webpage and that when clicked the url will open.

  For example, the following code is used to open Google web page when the text *Open Google* is clicked.

  ```
  <a href="google.com"> Open google </a>
  ```

HTML Images

HTML allows you to put an image inside your webpage. You have to specify the path of the image that should appear as well as an alternative text that might appear if the image is not found. The HTML tag for image is written as follows:

```
<img src ="url"    alt= some text">
```

The previous code can be dissected as follows:

- ¡img is the HTML tag for putting an image inside the webpage.

- src ="url": Specify the url (the path) of the image that should appear.

- alt="some text": will appear if HTML failed to show the image for any reason.

If we want to put an image called flower.jpg located at the same folder with the webpage, the following code should be written:

```
<img src ="flower.jpg" alt= Flower picture">
```

The flower picture will appear on the webpage, if not the word Flower picture will appear instead.

Images as Links

Images can be used instead of text as hyperlink. The same $< a >$ tag is used but the image tag is inserted instead of the link text. The HTML tag to use image as hyperlink is as follows:

```
<a href="url"><img src ="url"  alt=  some_text"></a>
```

Now, we want to make the flower image a link that when clicked the Google website is opened. The following code can be used to open Google website using the flower image:

```
<a href="google.com"><img src ="flower.jpg"

alt= Flower picture"></a>
```

HTML Tables

The tables could be created in HTML using the tag $< table >< /table >$ as follows:

- Start with $< table >$ and end with $< /table >$

- $< tr >< /tr >$ for each row:

- $< th > text < /th >$: the header of the columns

- $< td >< /td >$ for table data (column)

- $< caption >$ Monthly savings $< /caption >$ to define th etitle of the table

```
<table style="width:100%">

<tr>

<th>Header 1</th>
```

```html
<th>Header 2</th>
</tr>
<tr>
<td>Data 1</td>
<td>Data 2</td>
</tr>
<tr>
<td>Data 1</td>
<td>Data 2</td>
</tr>
</table>
```

The table using HTML:

Header 1	Header 2
Data 1	Data 2
Data 1	Data 2

The table has no borders and enlraged on the whole page as we used width =100%. If you want to make borders around each row and column, you can use the following code:

```html
<table border="3" style="width:100%">
<tr>
<th>Name</th>
<th>Grades</th>
</tr>
<tr>
  <td>Ahmed</td>
<td>50</td>
</tr>
<tr>
  <td>Mohamed</td>
  <td>60</td>
</tr>
</table>
```

Here, the border thickness is specified at the header of the table (border="3") and the width of the table is specified as 100%. There are a lot of options at the designing of the tables. For example, if you want to expand the row or the column you can use:

- colspan = 2: To expand the column into two column. Expand the column into two cells.

- rowspan = 2: To expand this row into two rows.

The table with border using HTML:

Name	Grades	
Ahmed	50	
Mohammed	60	

```
<table border="1" style="width:100%">
<tr>
<th> Name</th>
<th colspan=2>Grades</th>
</tr>
<tr>
    <td >Ahmed</td>
<td >50</td>
<td >40</td>
</tr>
<tr>
    <td >Mohamed</td>
    <td >60</td>
<td >80</td>
</tr>
</table>
```

Here, the grade column is expanded into two columns and the thickness of the border is reduced to 1 10.

The table with column expanded:

Name	Grades	
Ahmed	50	40
Mohammed	60	80

HTML Lists

HTML can generate either ordered or unordered list.

Unordered List

The unordered list is generated using the< *ul* >< */ul* > tags. Moreover, each item in the unordered list is generated using the< *li* >< */li* > tag. The following code is used to generate 3 items unordered list. The result of the code is shown at 10.

```
Three items unordered list:

<ul>
  <li>Coffee</li>
  <li>Tea</li>
  <li>Milk</li>
</ul>
```

```
Three items unordered list:

  • Coffee
  • Tea
  • Milk
```

Unordered list.

The type of the item symbol could be specified at the header of the list. The unordered list has four different types of the item symbol 1. The following code use the square symbol instead of the default bullet at the previous code.

Table: The list marks table.

Style	Description
list-style-type:disc:	The list items will be marked with bullets (default)
list-style-type:circle	The list items will be marked with circles
list-style-type:square	The list items will be marked with squares
list-style-type:none	The list items will not be marked

Three items unordered list with rectangle symbol:

```
<ul style=list-style-type:square>
  <li>Coffee</li>
  <li>Tea</li>
  <li>Milk</li>
</ul>
```

Three items unordered list with rectangle symbol:

- Coffee
- Tea
- Milk

Unordered list with square symbol.

Ordered List

The unordered list is generated using the < *ol* >< */ol* > tags. Moreover, each item in the unordered list is generated using the < *li* >< */li* > tag. The following code is used to generate 3 items ordered list. The result of the code is shown.

Three items ordered list:

```
<ol>
  <li>Coffee</li>
  <li>Tea</li>
  <li>Milk</li>
</ol>
```

The type of the item numbering could be specified at the header of the list. The ordered list has five different types of the item symbol 2. The following code use the *I* numbering instead of the default numbering at the previous code.

Three items unordered list with rectangle symbol:

```
<ol type="I">
  <li>Coffee</li>
  <li>Tea</li>
  <li>Milk</li>
</ol>
```

Three items ordered list:

1. Coffee
2. Tea
3. Milk

Ordered list.

Table: The list marks table.

Style	Description
type="1"	Numbered with numbers (default)
type="A"	Numbered with uppercase letters

type="a"	Numbered with lowercase letters
type="I"	Numbered with uppercase roman numbers
type="i"	Numbered with lowercase roman numbers

The result of the code is presented:

```
Three items unordered list with rectangle symbol:

    I.  Coffee
   II.  Tea
  III.  Milk
```

Ordered list with *I* symbol.

Description List

A description list is a list of terms, with a description of each term. < *dl* > tag defines the description list, < *dt* > tag defines the term (name), and < *dd* > tag describes each term. The following code use the description list to describe each item and the result of executing the code is shown.

```
<dl >

<dt >Coffee </dt >

<dd> black hot drink </dd>

<dt >Milk </dt >

<dd> white cold drink </dd>

</dl>
```

```
Coffee
        black hot drink
Milk
        white cold drink
```

Description list.

Nested List

Any type of the previous list could be used inside another type. You can use ordered list inside unordered or vica versa. The following code is used to explain a nested unordered list. The results of the code is shown in Figure.

```
<ul >

<li >Coffee </li >

<li >Tea
```

```
<ul>
    <li>Black tea</li>
    <li>Green tea</li>
</ul>
</li>
<li>Milk</li>
</ul>
```

The following code reused the previous code with changing the inside unordered list to ordered list. The result of the code is shown in Figure.

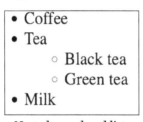

- Coffee
- Tea
  - Black tea
  - Green tea
- Milk

Nested unordered list.

```
<ul>
<li>Coffee</li>
<li>Tea
    <ol>
    <li>Black tea</li>
    <li>Green tea</li>
</ol>
</li>
<li>Milk</li>
</ul>
```

Cascade Style Sheet - CSS

CSS is a style that makes the elements of the HTML web page appears in better way. You can assign fonts, color, size to the text at the web page. The style could be assigned in one of three different locations: inline, internal and external style.

Inline Style

At this style, you have to assign any style at the tag of the element. However, the effect of the style is performed only on this element. You have to write *style = "properiety : value;"*, and change the properiety and the value. For example, *style = "color : blue;"* is used to make the color of the text blue. The compelete list of the CSS properieties could be found at this link http://www.w3schools.com/cssref/. The following code is used to clarify the inline style .

```
• Coffee
• Tea
     1. Black tea
     2. Green tea
• Milk
```

Nested list.

```
<h1 style ="color:blue;">This is a Blue Heading </h1>

<h1 style ="color:red;">This is a red Heading </h1>

<h1 >This is a default Heading </h1>
```

```
This is a Blue Heading

This is a Red Heading

This is a Default Heading
```

Inline style.

The results of the code is presented in figure. As you can see, the effect of the inline style is only on the element that the style specified at. The blue color is applied on the first one only, while the red on the second heading and the one without style has the default color.

Internal Style

In this style, a part of the HTML file started with < *style* > tag and ended with < */style* > tag is used to specify the style of the current page. The effect of the style assigned to any element will be applied on all the elements iniside the current page. If you specify the color of < *h1* > as red at the style part, the effect of the style will be applied on each occurrence of < *h1* > at the current file. The following code is used to specify some properties of heading and paragraphs.

```
<style >

body {background –color:lightgrey;}

h1 {

     color: blue;

     font family: verdana;
```

```
        font size:300%;

        border:2px solid black;

        margin:50px;

        padding:10px;

}

p      color:      red;

background:yelllow

        font-family: verdana;

        font size:300%;

        border:5px solid black;

        margin:50px;

        padding:10px;

}

#p1   {

color:      blue;

}

}

</style>

<h1>This is heading one </h1>

<h1>This is heading two </h1>

<p>This is paragraph one </p>

<p>This is paragraph two </p>

<p id=" p1"> I am different </p>
```

The code start with the style part where the proprieties of the heading and the paragraphs are stated. The color, the font, the font size, the border width, the margin and the padding are specified. You can see that the border width at the paragraph is heavier than the heading (5 for paragraph and 2 for heading). You can specify the proprieties you want in the same way. The results of the code could be seen If you want to make one element different, you have to give it an ID. Hence, the element with the id will have the propriety assigned for the id at the style part. Thereore, the paragraph with *id = p1* has a blue color because the this id is assigned to has blue color in style part.

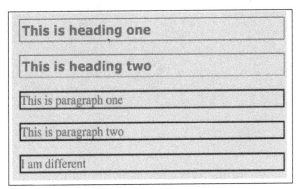

Internal style.

External Style

In external style, you have to create a separate file with .css extension. In this file, all the required styles are specified. This file could be linked to any HTML file you want.Therefore, the effect of the external file may be extended to more than one file. The link is written in the head part of the HTML page as follows:

< head >

< linkrel = "stylesheet"href = "styles.css" >

< /head >

The css file is specified after the href part.

References

- Severance, Charles (February 2012). "JavaScript: Designing a Language in 10 Days". Computer. IEEE Computer Society. 45 (2): 7–8. doi:10.1109/MC.2012.57. Retrieved 23 March2013

- how-to-be-a-javascript-developer-without-knowing-javascript: geeksforgeeks.org, Retrieved 23 June, 2019

- Payment, S. (2007). Marc Andreessen and Jim Clark: The Founders of Netscape. Rosen Publishing Group. ISBN 978-1-4042-0719-6

- interactive-javascript-tutorials: guru99.com, Retrieved 24 July, 2019

- "JavaScript". Collins English Dictionary – Complete & Unabridged 2012 Digital Edition. William Collins Sons & Co. 2012. Retrieved 21 August 2015

- Hyper-Text-Markup-Language-HTML-A-Tutorial: researchgate.net, Retrieved 25 August, 2019

- "W3C CSS2.1 specification for pseudo-elements and pseudo-classes". World Wide Web Consortium. 7 June 2011. Retrieved 30 April 2012

- Meyer, Eric A. (2006). Cascading Style Sheets: The Definitive Guide (3rd ed.). O'Reilly Media, Inc. ISBN 0-596-52733-0

Web Protocols

World Wide Web depends upon numerous protocols for maintaining the efficiency in its functioning. A few of such protocols are hypertext transfer protocol, common gateway interface, web services for remote portlets, websocket, etc. This chapter has been carefully written to provide an easy understanding of these different web protocols.

HYPERTEXT TRANSFER PROTOCOL

HTTP (Hypertext Transfer Protocol) is the set of rules for transferring files, such as text, graphic images, sound, video, and other multimedia files, on the World Wide Web. As soon as a Web user opens their Web browser, the user is indirectly making use of HTTP. HTTP is an application protocol that runs on top of the TCP/IP suite of protocols (the foundation protocols for the Internet). The latest version of HTTP is HTTP/2, which was published in May 2015. It is an alternative to its predecessor, HTTP 1.1, but does not it make obsolete.

How HTTP Works

As the Hypertext part of the name implies, HTTP concepts include the idea that files can contain references to other files whose selection will elicit additional transfer requests. In addition to the Web page files it can serve, any Web server machine contains an HTTP daemon, a program that is designed to wait for HTTP requests and handle them when they arrive. A Web browser is an HTTP client, sending requests to server machines. When the browser user enters file requests by either "opening" a Web file (typing in a URL) or clicking on a hypertext link, the browser builds an HTTP request and sends it to the Internet Protocol address (IP address) indicated by the URL. The HTTP daemon in the destination server machine receives the request and sends back the requested file or files associated with the request. As a note, a Web page often consists of more than one file.

To further expound this example, a user wants to visit TechTarget.com. The user types in the Web address, and the computer sends a "GET" request to a server that hosts that address. That GET request is sent using HTTP and it is telling the TechTarget server that the user is looking for the HTML (Hypertext Markup Language) code used to structure and give it the login page its look and feel. The text of that login page is included in the HTML response, but other parts of the page, particularly its images and videos, are requested by separate HTTP requests and responses. The more requests that must be made -- for example, to call a page that has numerous images -- the longer it will take the server to respond to those requests and for the user's system to load the page.

When these requests and responses are being sent, they use TCP/IP to reduce and transport information in small packets of binary sequences of ones and zeros that are physically sent through electric wires, fiber optic cables and wireless networks.

HTTP vs. HTTPS

HTTPS (HTTP over SSL or HTTP Secure) is the use of Secure Sockets Layer (SSL) or Transport Layer Security (TLS) as a sublayer under regular HTTP application layering. HTTPS encrypts and decrypts user HTTP page requests as well as the pages that are returned by the Web server. The use of HTTPS protects against eavesdropping and man-in-the-middle (MitM) attacks. HTTPS was developed by Netscape.

Types of Status Codes

In response to HTTP requests, servers often issue response codes, indicating the request is being processed, that there was an error in the request or that the request is being redirected. Common response codes include:

- 200 OK: This means that the request, such as GET or POST, worked and is being acted upon.

- 300 Moved Permanently: This response code means that the URI of the requested resource has been changed permanently.

- 401 Unauthorized: The client - the user making the request of the server - has not been authenticated.

- 403 Forbidden: The client's identity is known but has not been given access authorization.

- 404 Not Found: This is the most frequent and most recognized error code. It means that the URL is nor recognized or the resource at the location does not exist.

- 500 Internal Server Error: The server has encountered a situation it doesn't know how to handle.

HTTP functions as a request–response protocol in the client–server computing model. A web browser, for example, may be the *client* and an application running on a computer hosting a website may be the *server*. The client submits an HTTP *request* message to the server. The server, which provides *resources* such as HTML files and other content, or performs other functions on behalf of the client, returns a *response* message to the client. The response contains completion status information about the request and may also contain requested content in its message body.

A web browser is an example of a *user agent* (UA). Other types of user agent include the indexing software used by search providers (web crawlers), voice browsers, mobile apps, and other software that accesses, consumes, or displays web content.

HTTP is designed to permit intermediate network elements to improve or enable communications between clients and servers. High-traffic websites often benefit from web cache servers that deliver content on behalf of upstream servers to improve response time. Web browsers cache previously accessed web resources and reuse them, when possible, to reduce network traffic. HTTP proxy servers at private network boundaries can facilitate communication for clients without a globally routable address, by relaying messages with external servers.

HTTP is an application layer protocol designed within the framework of the Internet protocol suite. Its definition presumes an underlying and reliable transport layer protocol, and Transmission Control Protocol (TCP) is commonly used. However, HTTP can be adapted to use unreliable protocols such as the User Datagram Protocol (UDP), for example in HTTPU and Simple Service Discovery Protocol (SSDP).

HTTP resources are identified and located on the network by Uniform Resource Locators (URLs), using the Uniform Resource Identifiers (URI's) schemes *http* and *https*. For example, including all optional components:

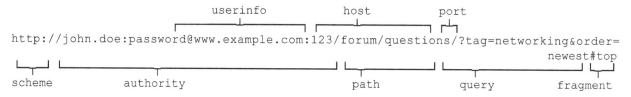

URIs are encoded as hyperlinks in HTML documents, so as to form interlinked hypertext documents.

HTTP/1.1 is a revision of the original HTTP (HTTP/1.0). In HTTP/1.0 a separate connection to the same server is made for every resource request. HTTP/1.1 can reuse a connection multiple times to download images, scripts, stylesheets, *etc* after the page has been delivered. HTTP/1.1 communications therefore experience less latency as the establishment of TCP connections presents considerable overhead.

HTTP Session

An HTTP session is a sequence of network request-response transactions. An HTTP client initiates a request by establishing a Transmission Control Protocol (TCP) connection to a particular port on a server (typically port 80, occasionally port 8080. An HTTP server listening on that port waits for a client's request message. Upon receiving the request, the server sends back a status line, such as "HTTP/1.1 200 OK", and a message of its own. The body of this message is typically the requested resource, although an error message or other information may also be returned.

Persistent Connections

In HTTP/0.9 and 1.0, the connection is closed after a single request/response pair. In HTTP/1.1 a keep-alive-mechanism was introduced, where a connection could be reused for more than one request. Such *persistent connections* reduce request latency perceptibly, because the client does not need to re-negotiate the TCP 3-Way-Handshake connection after the first request has been sent. Another positive side effect is that, in general, the connection becomes faster with time due to TCP's slow-start-mechanism.

Version 1.1 of the protocol also made bandwidth optimization improvements to HTTP/1.0. For example, HTTP/1.1 introduced chunked transfer encoding to allow content on persistent connections to be streamed rather than buffered. HTTP pipelining further reduces lag time, allowing clients to send multiple requests before waiting for each response. Another addition to the protocol was byte serving, where a server transmits just the portion of a resource explicitly requested by a client.

HTTP Session State

HTTP is a stateless protocol. A stateless protocol does not require the HTTP server to retain information or status about each user for the duration of multiple requests. However, some web applications implement states or server side sessions using for instance HTTP cookies or hidden variables within web forms.

HTTP Authentication

HTTP provides multiple authentication schemes such as basic access authentication and digest access authentication which operate via a challenge-response mechanism whereby the server identifies and issues a challenge before serving the requested content.

HTTP provides a general framework for access control and authentication, via an extensible set of challenge-response authentication schemes, which can be used by a server to challenge a client request and by a client to provide authentication information.

Authentication Realms

The HTTP Authentication specification also provides an arbitrary, implementation-specific construct for further dividing resources common to a given root URI. The realm value string, if present, is combined with the canonical root URI to form the protection space component of the challenge. This in effect allows the server to define separate authentication scopes under one root URI.

Message Format

The client sends requests to the server and the server sends responses.

Request Message

The request message consists of the following:

- A request line (e.g., *GET /images/logo.png HTTP/1.1*, which requests a resource called / `images/logo.png` from the server).

- Request header fields (e.g., *Accept-Language: en*).

- An empty line.

- An optional message body.

The request line and other header fields must each end with <CR><LF> (that is, a carriage return character followed by a line feed character). The empty line must consist of only <CR><LF> and no other whitespace. In the HTTP/1.1 protocol, all header fields except *Host* are optional.

A request line containing only the path name is accepted by servers to maintain compatibility with HTTP clients before the HTTP/1.0 specification in RFC 1945.

Request Methods

An HTTP 1.1 request made using telnet. The request message,
response header section, and response body are highlighted.

HTTP defines methods (sometimes referred to as verbs, but nowhere in the specification does it mention verb, nor is OPTIONS or HEAD a verb) to indicate the desired action to be performed on the identified resource. What this resource represents, whether pre-existing data or data that is generated dynamically, depends on the implementation of the server. Often, the resource corresponds to a file or the output of an executable residing on the server. The HTTP/1.0 specification defined the GET, HEAD and POST methods and the HTTP/1.1 specification added five new methods: OPTIONS, PUT, DELETE, TRACE and CONNECT. By being specified in these documents, their semantics are well-known and can be depended on. Any client can use any method and the server can be configured to support any combination of methods. If a method is unknown to an intermediate, it will be treated as an unsafe and non-idempotent method. There is no limit to the number of methods that can be defined and this allows for future methods to be specified without breaking existing infrastructure. For example, WebDAV defined 7 new methods and RFC 5789 specified the PATCH method.

Method names are case sensitive. This is in contrast to HTTP header field names which are case-insensitive.

- GET:

  The GET method requests a representation of the specified resource. Requests using GET should only retrieve data and should have no other effect. (This is also true of some other

HTTP methods.) The W3C has published guidance principles on this distinction, saying, "Web application design should be informed by the above principles, but also by the relevant limitations."

- HEAD:

  The HEAD method asks for a response identical to that of a GET request, but without the response body. This is useful for retrieving meta-information written in response headers, without having to transport the entire content.

- POST:

  The POST method requests that the server accept the entity enclosed in the request as a new subordinate of the web resource identified by the URI. The data POSTed might be, for example, an annotation for existing resources; a message for a bulletin board, newsgroup, mailing list, or comment thread; a block of data that is the result of submitting a web form to a data-handling process; or an item to add to a database.

- PUT:

  The PUT method requests that the enclosed entity be stored under the supplied URI. If the URI refers to an already existing resource, it is modified; if the URI does not point to an existing resource, then the server can create the resource with that URI.

- DELETE:

  The DELETE method deletes the specified resource.

- TRACE:

  The TRACE method echoes the received request so that a client can see what (if any) changes or additions have been made by intermediate servers.

- OPTIONS:

  The OPTIONS method returns the HTTP methods that the server supports for the specified URL. This can be used to check the functionality of a web server by requesting '*' instead of a specific resource.

- CONNECT:

  The CONNECT method converts the request connection to a transparent TCP/IP tunnel, usually to facilitate SSL-encrypted communication (HTTPS) through an unencrypted HTTP proxy.

- PATCH:

  The PATCH method applies partial modifications to a resource.

All general-purpose HTTP servers are required to implement at least the GET and HEAD methods, and all other methods are considered optional by the specification.

Safe Methods

Some of the methods (for example, GET, HEAD, OPTIONS and TRACE) are, by convention, defined as *safe*, which means they are intended only for information retrieval and should not change the state of the server. In other words, they should not have side effects, beyond relatively harmless effects such as logging, web caching, the serving of banner advertisements or incrementing a web counter. Making arbitrary GET requests without regard to the context of the application's state should therefore be considered safe. However, this is not mandated by the standard, and it is explicitly acknowledged that it cannot be guaranteed.

By contrast, methods such as POST, PUT, DELETE and PATCH are intended for actions that may cause side effects either on the server, or external side effects such as financial transactions or transmission of email. Such methods are therefore not usually used by conforming web robots or web crawlers; some that do not conform tend to make requests without regard to context or consequences.

Despite the prescribed safety of *GET* requests, in practice their handling by the server is not technically limited in any way. Therefore, careless or deliberate programming can cause non-trivial changes on the server. This is discouraged, because it can cause problems for web caching, search engines and other automated agents, which can make unintended changes on the server. For example, a website might allow deletion of a resource through a URL, which, if arbitrarily fetched, even using *GET*, would simply delete the article.

One example of this occurring in practice was during the short-lived Google Web Accelerator beta, which prefetched arbitrary URLs on the page a user was viewing, causing records to be automatically altered or deleted *en masse*. The beta was suspended only weeks after its first release, following widespread criticism.

Idempotent Methods and Web Applications

Methods PUT and DELETE are defined to be idempotent, meaning that multiple identical requests should have the same effect as a single request (note that idempotence refers to the state of the system after the request has completed, so while the action the server takes (e.g. deleting a record) or the response code it returns may be different on subsequent requests, the system state will be the same every time). Methods GET, HEAD, OPTIONS and TRACE, being prescribed as safe, should also be idempotent, as HTTP is a stateless protocol.

In contrast, the POST method is not necessarily idempotent, and therefore sending an identical POST request multiple times may further affect state or cause further side effects (such as financial transactions). In some cases this may be desirable, but in other cases this could be due to an accident, such as when a user does not realize that their action will result in sending another request, or they did not receive adequate feedback that their first request was successful. While web browsers may show alert dialog boxes to warn users in some cases where reloading a page may re-submit a POST request, it is generally up to the web application to handle cases where a POST request should not be submitted more than once.

Note that whether a method is idempotent is not enforced by the protocol or web server. It is perfectly possible to write a web application in which (for example) a database insert or other non-idempotent action is triggered by a GET or other request. Ignoring this recommendation, however, may result in undesirable consequences, if a user agent assumes that repeating the same request is safe when it is not.

Security

The TRACE method can be used as part of a class of attacks known as cross-site tracing; for that reason, common security advice is for it to be disabled in the server configuration. Microsoft IIS supports a proprietary "TRACK" method, which behaves similarly, and which is likewise recommended to be disabled.

HTTP method	RFC	Request has Body	Response has Body	Safe	Idempotent	Cacheable
GET	RFC 7231	Optional	Yes	Yes	Yes	Yes
HEAD	RFC 7231	Optional	No	Yes	Yes	Yes
POST	RFC 7231	Yes	Yes	No	No	Yes
PUT	RFC 7231	Yes	Yes	No	Yes	No
DELETE	RFC 7231	Optional	Yes	No	Yes	No
CONNECT	RFC 7231	Optional	Yes	No	No	No
OPTIONS	RFC 7231	Optional	Yes	Yes	Yes	No
TRACE	RFC 7231	No	Yes	Yes	Yes	No
PATCH	RFC 5789	Yes	Yes	No	No	No

Response Message

The response message consists of the following:

- A status line which includes the status code and reason message (e.g., *HTTP/1.1 200 OK*, which indicates that the client's request succeeded).

- Response header fields (e.g., *Content-Type: text/html*).

- An empty line.

- An optional message body.

The status line and other header fields must all end with <CR><LF>. The empty line must consist of only <CR><LF> and no other whitespace. This strict requirement for <CR><LF> is relaxed somewhat within message bodies for consistent use of other system linebreaks such as <CR> or <LF> alone.

Status Codes

In HTTP/1.0 and since, the first line of the HTTP response is called the status line and includes a numeric status code (such as "404") and a textual reason phrase (such as "Not Found"). The way the user agent handles the response depends primarily on the code, and secondarily on the other response header fields. Custom status codes can be used, for if the user agent encounters a code it does not recognize, it can use the first digit of the code to determine the general class of the response.

The standard reason phrases are only recommendations, and can be replaced with "local equivalents" at the web developer's discretion. If the status code indicated a problem, the user agent might display the reason phrase to the user to provide further information about the nature of the problem. The standard also allows the user agent to attempt to interpret the reason phrase, though this might be unwise since the standard explicitly specifies that status codes are machine-readable and reason phrases are human-readable. HTTP status code is primarily divided into five groups for better explanation of request and responses between client and server as named:

- Informational 1XX,

- Successful 2XX,

- Redirection 3XX,

- Client Error 4XX,

- Server Error 5XX.

Encrypted Connections

The most popular way of establishing an encrypted HTTP connection is HTTPS. Two other methods for establishing an encrypted HTTP connection also exist: Secure Hypertext Transfer Protocol, and using the HTTP/1.1 Upgrade header to specify an upgrade to TLS. Browser support for these two is, however, nearly non-existent.

Example Session

Below is a sample conversation between an HTTP client and an HTTP server running on www.example.com, port 80.

Client Request

```
GET / HTTP/1.1

Host: www.example.com
```

A client request (consisting in this case of the request line and only one header field) is followed by a blank line, so that the request ends with a double newline, each in the form of a carriage return followed by a line feed. The "Host" field distinguishes between various DNS names sharing a single IP address, allowing name-based virtual hosting. While optional in HTTP/1.0, it is mandatory in HTTP/1.1. (The "/" means /index.html if there is one).

Server Response

```
HTTP/1.1 200 OK

Date: Mon, 23 May 2005 22:38:34 GMT

Content-Type: text/html; charset=UTF-8
```

```
Content-Length: 138

Last-Modified: Wed, 08 Jan 2003 23:11:55 GMT

Server: Apache/1.3.3.7 (Unix) (Red-Hat/Linux)

ETag: "3f80f-1b6-3e1cb03b"

Accept-Ranges: bytes

Connection: close

<html>

  <head>

    <title>An Example Page</title>

  </head>

  <body>

    <p>Hello World, this is a very simple HTML document.</p>

  </body>

</html>
```

The ETag (entity tag) header field is used to determine if a cached version of the requested resource is identical to the current version of the resource on the server. *Content-Type* specifies the Internet media type of the data conveyed by the HTTP message, while *Content-Length* indicates its length in bytes. The HTTP/1.1 webserver publishes its ability to respond to requests for certain byte ranges of the document by setting the field *Accept-Ranges: bytes*. This is useful, if the client needs to have only certain portions of a resource sent by the server, which is called byte serving. When *Connection: close* is sent, it means that the web server will close the TCP connection immediately after the transfer of this response.

Most of the header lines are optional. When *Content-Length* is missing the length is determined in other ways. Chunked transfer encoding uses a chunk size of 0 to mark the end of the content. *Identity* encoding without *Content-Length* reads content until the socket is closed.

A *Content-Encoding* like *gzip* can be used to compress the transmitted data.

Similar Protocols

The Gopher protocol is a content delivery protocol that was displaced by HTTP in the early 1990s. The SPDY protocol is an alternative to HTTP developed at Google, it is superseded by the new HTTP protocol, HTTP/2.

COMMON GATEWAY INTERFACE

In computing, Common Gateway Interface (CGI) offers a standard protocol for web servers to execute programs that execute like console applications (also called command-line interface programs) running on a server that generates web pages dynamically. Such programs are known as *CGI scripts* or simply as *CGIs*. The specifics of how the script is executed by the server are determined by the server. In the common case, a CGI script executes at the time a request is made and generates HTML.

In brief, an HTTP POST request from the client will send the HTML form data to the CGI program via standard input. Other data, such as URL paths, and HTTP header data, are presented as process environment variables.

Purpose of the CGI Standard

Each web server runs HTTP server software, which responds to requests from web browsers. Generally, the HTTP server has a directory (folder), which is designated as a document collection — files that can be sent to Web browsers connected to this server. For example, if the Web server has the domain name `example.com,` and its document collection is stored at `/usr/local/apache/htdocs` in the local file system, then the Web server will respond to a request for `http://example.com/index.html` by sending to the browser the (pre-written) file `/usr/local/apache/htdocs/index.html.`

For pages constructed on the fly, the server software may defer requests to separate programs and relay the results to the requesting client (usually, a web browser that displays the page to the end user). In the early days of the web, such programs were usually small and written in a scripting language; hence, they were known as *scripts*.

Such programs usually require some additional information to be specified with the request. For instance, if Wikipedia were implemented as a script, one thing the script would need to know is whether the user is logged in and, if logged in, under which name.

HTTP provides ways for browsers to pass such information to the web server, e.g. as part of the URL. The server software must then pass this information through to the script somehow.

Conversely, upon returning, the script must provide all the information required by HTTP for a response to the request: the HTTP status of the request, the document content (if available), the document type (e.g. HTML, PDF, or plain text), et cetera.

Initially, different server software would use different ways to exchange this information with scripts. As a result, it wasn't possible to write scripts that would work unmodified for different server software, even though the information being exchanged was the same. Therefore, it was decided to establish a standard way for exchanging this information: CGI (the Common Gateway Interface, as it defines a common way for server software to interface with scripts). Webpage generating programs invoked by server software that operate according to the CGI standard are known as CGI scripts.

This standard was quickly adopted and is still supported by all well-known server software, such as Apache, IIS, and (with an extension) node.js-based servers.

An early use of CGI scripts was to process forms. In the beginning of HTML, HTML forms typically had an "action" attribute and a button designated as the "submit" button. When the submit button is pushed the URI specified in the "action" attribute would be sent to the server with the data from the form sent as a query string. If the "action" specifies a CGI script then the CGI script would be executed and it then produces an HTML page.

Using CGI Scripts

A web server allows its owner to configure which URLs shall be handled by which CGI scripts.

This is usually done by marking a new directory within the document collection as containing CGI scripts — its name is often `cgi-bin`. For example, `/usr/local/apache/htdocs/cgi-bin` could be designated as a CGI directory on the web server. When a Web browser requests a URL that points to a file within the CGI directory (e.g., `http://example.com/cgi-bin/printenv.pl/with/additional/path?and=a&query=string`), then, instead of simply sending that file (`/usr/local/apache/htdocs/cgi-bin/printenv.pl`) to the Web browser, the HTTP server runs the specified script and passes the output of the script to the Web browser. That is, anything that the script sends to standard output is passed to the Web client instead of being shown on-screen in a terminal window.

As remarked above, the CGI standard defines how additional information passed with the request is passed to the script. For instance, if a slash and additional directory name(s) are appended to the URL immediately after the name of the script (in this example, `/with/additional/path`), then that path is stored in the PATH_INFO environment variable before the script is called. If parameters are sent to the script via an HTTP GET request (a question mark appended to the URL, followed by param=value pairs; in the example, `?and=a&query=string`), then those parameters are stored in the QUERY_STRING environment variable before the script is called. If parameters are sent to the script via an HTTP POST request, they are passed to the script's standard input. The script can then read these environment variables or data from standard input and adapt to the Web browser's request.

The following Perl program shows all the environment variables passed by the Web server:

```perl
#!/usr/bin/perl
=head1 DESCRIPTION
printenv — a CGI program that just prints its environment
=cut
print "Content-type: text/plain\n\n";
for my $var ( sort keys %ENV ) {
  printf "%s = \"%s\"\n", $var, $ENV{$var};
}
```

If a Web browser issues a request for the environment variables at `http://example.com/cgi-bin/printenv.pl/foo/bar?var1=value1&var2=with%20percent%20encoding`, a 64-bit Windows 7 web server running cygwin returns the following information:

```
COMSPEC="C:\Windows\system32\cmd.exe"
DOCUMENT_ROOT="C:/Program Files (x86)/Apache Software Foundation/Apache2.4/htdocs"
```

```
GATEWAY_INTERFACE="CGI/1.1"

HOME="/home/SYSTEM"

HTTP_ACCEPT="text/html,application/xhtml+xml,application/xml;q=0.9,*/*;q=0.8"

HTTP_ACCEPT_CHARSET="ISO-8859-1,utf-8;q=0.7,*;q=0.7"

HTTP_ACCEPT_ENCODING="gzip, deflate, br"

HTTP_ACCEPT_LANGUAGE="en-us,en;q=0.5"

HTTP_CONNECTION="keep-alive"

HTTP_HOST="example.com"

HTTP_USER_AGENT="Mozilla/5.0 (Windows NT 6.1; WOW64; rv:67.0) Gecko/20100101
Firefox/67.0"

PATH="/home/SYSTEM/bin:/bin:/cygdrive/c/progra~2/php:/cygdrive/c/windows/sys-
tem32:..."

PATHEXT=".COM;.EXE;.BAT;.CMD;.VBS;.VBE;.JS;.JSE;.WSF;.WSH;.MSC"

PATH_INFO="/foo/bar"

PATH_TRANSLATED="C:\Program Files (x86)\Apache Software Foundation\Apache2.4\
htdocs\foo\bar"

QUERY_STRING="var1=value1&var2=with%20percent%20encoding"

REMOTE_ADDR="127.0.0.1"

REMOTE_PORT="63555"

REQUEST_METHOD="GET"

REQUEST_URI="/cgi-bin/printenv.pl/foo/bar?var1=value1&var2=with%20percent%20
encoding"

SCRIPT_FILENAME="C:/Program Files (x86)/Apache Software Foundation/Apache2.4/
cgi-bin/printenv.pl"

SCRIPT_NAME="/cgi-bin/printenv.pl"

SERVER_ADDR="127.0.0.1"

SERVER_ADMIN="(server admin's email address)"

SERVER_NAME="127.0.0.1"

SERVER_PORT="80"

SERVER_PROTOCOL="HTTP/1.1"

SERVER_SIGNATURE=""

SERVER_SOFTWARE="Apache/2.4.39 (Win32) PHP/7.3.7"

SYSTEMROOT="C:\Windows"

TERM="cygwin"

WINDIR="C:\Windows"
```

Some, but not all, of these variables are defined by the CGI standard. Some, such as PATH_INFO, QUERY_STRING, and the ones starting with HTTP_, pass information along from the HTTP request.

From the environment, it can be seen that the Web browser is Firefox running on a Windows 7 PC, the Web server is Apache running on a system that emulates Unix, and the CGI script is named cgi-bin/printenv.pl.

The program could then generate any content, write that to standard output, and the Web server will transmit it to the browser.

The following are environment variables passed to CGI programs:

- Server specific variables:

  ◦ SERVER_SOFTWARE: *name/version* of HTTP server.

  ◦ SERVER_NAME: host name of the server, may be dot-decimal IP address.

  ◦ GATEWAY_INTERFACE: CGI/*version.*

- Request specific variables:

  ◦ SERVER_PROTOCOL: HTTP/*version.*

  ◦ SERVER_PORT: TCP port (decimal).

  ◦ REQUEST_METHOD: name of HTTP method.

  ◦ PATH_INFO: path suffix, if appended to URL after program name and a slash.

  ◦ PATH_TRANSLATED: Corresponding full path as supposed by server, if PATH_INFO is present.

  ◦ SCRIPT_NAME: Relative path to the program, like /cgi-bin/script.cgi.

  ◦ QUERY_STRING: The part of URL after ? character. The query string may be composed of *name=value* pairs separated with ampersands (such as *var1=val1&var2=val2...*) when used to submit form data transferred via GET method as defined by HTML application/x-www-form-urlencoded.

  ◦ REMOTE_HOST: Host name of the client, unset if server did not perform such lookup.

  ◦ REMOTE_ADDR: IP address of the client (dot-decimal).

  ◦ AUTH_TYPE: Identification type, if applicable.

  ◦ REMOTE_USER used for certain AUTH_TYPEs.

  ◦ REMOTE_IDENT: Only if server performed such lookup.

  ◦ CONTENT_TYPE: Internet media type of input data if PUT or POST method are used, as provided via HTTP header.

- ◦ CONTENT_LENGTH: Similarly, size of input data (decimal, in octets) if provided via HTTP header.

- ◦ Variables passed by user agent (HTTP_ACCEPT, HTTP_ACCEPT_LANGUAGE, HTTP_USER_AGENT, HTTP_COOKIE and possibly others) contain values of corresponding HTTP headers and therefore have the same sense.

The program returns the result to the Web server in the form of standard output, beginning with a header and a blank line.

The header is encoded in the same way as an HTTP header and must include the MIME type of the document returned. The headers, supplemented by the Web server, are generally forwarded with the response back to the user.

Here is a simple CGI program written in Python 3 along with the HTML that handles a simple addition problem.

```
<!DOCTYPE html>

<html>

 <body>

  <form action="add.cgi" method="POST">

   <fieldset>

    <legend>Enter two numbers to add</legend>

    <label>First Number: <input type="number" name="num1"></label><br>

    <label>Second Number: <input type="number" name="num2"></label><br>

   </fieldset>

   <button>Add</button>

  </form>

 </body>

</html>
```

```
#!/usr/bin/env python3

import cgi

import cgitb

cgitb.enable()

input_data = cgi.FieldStorage()

print('Content-Type:text/html') # HTML is following

print() # Leave a blank line

print('<h1>Addition Results</h1>')

try:

  num1 = int(input_data["num1"].value)
```

```
 num2 = int(input_data["num2"].value)
except:
 print('<output>Sorry, we cannot turn your inputs into numbers (integers).</
output>')
 raise SystemExit(1)
print('<output>{0} + {1} = {2}</output>'.format(num1, num2, num1 + num2))
```

This Python 3 CGI gets the inputs from the HTML and adds the two numbers together.

Deployment

A Web server that supports CGI can be configured to interpret a URL that it serves as a reference to a CGI script. A common convention is to have a `cgi-bin/` directory at the base of the directory tree and treat all executable files within this directory (and no other, for security) as CGI scripts. Another popular convention is to use filename extensions; for instance, if CGI scripts are consistently given the extension `.cgi`, the web server can be configured to interpret all such files as CGI scripts. While convenient, and required by many prepackaged scripts, it opens the server to attack if a remote user can upload executable code with the proper extension.

In the case of HTTP PUT or POSTs, the user-submitted data are provided to the program via the standard input. The Web server creates a subset of the environment variables passed to it and adds details pertinent to the HTTP environment.

Uses

CGI is often used to process inputs information from the user and produce the appropriate output. An example of a CGI program is one implementing a Wiki. The user agent requests the name of an entry; the Web server executes the CGI; the CGI program retrieves the source of that entry's page (if one exists), transforms it into HTML, and prints the result. The web server receives the input from the CGI and transmits it to the user agent. If the "Edit this page" link is clicked, the CGI populates an HTML `text area` or other editing control with the page's contents, and saves it back to the server when the user submits the form in it.

Alternatives

Calling a command generally means the invocation of a newly created process on the server. Starting the process can consume much more time and memory than the actual work of generating the output, especially when the program still needs to be interpreted or compiled. If the command is called often, the resulting workload can quickly overwhelm the server.

The overhead involved in process creation can be reduced by techniques such as FastCGI that "prefork" interpreter processes, or by running the application code entirely within the web server, using extension modules such as mod_perl or mod_php. Another way to reduce the overhead is to use precompiled CGI programs, e.g. by writing them in languages such as C or C++, rather than interpreted or compiled-on-the-fly languages such as Perl or PHP, or by implementing the page generating software as a custom webserver module.

Alternative approaches include:

- Extensions such as Apache modules, NSAPI plugins, and ISAPI plugins allow third-party software to run on the web server. Web 2.0 allows to transfer data from the client to the server without using HTML forms and without the user noticing.

- FastCGI reduces overhead by allowing a single, long-running process to handle more than one user request. Unlike converting an application to a web server plug-in, FastCGI applications remain independent of the web server.

- Simple Common Gateway Interface or SCGI is designed to be easier to implement, yet it reduces latency in some operations compared to CGI.

- Replacement of the architecture for dynamic websites can also be used. This is the approach taken by Java EE, which runs Java code in a Java servlet container in order to serve dynamic content and optionally static content. This approach replaces the overhead of generating and destroying processes with the much lower overhead of generating and destroying threads, and also exposes the programmer to the library that comes with Java Platform, Standard Edition on which the version of Java EE in use is based.

The optimal configuration for any Web application depends on application-specific details, amount of traffic, and complexity of the transaction; these tradeoffs need to be analyzed to determine the best implementation for a given task and time budget. Web Frameworks offer an alternative to using CGI scripts to interact with user agents.

SIMPLE COMMON GATEWAY INTERFACE

The Simple Common Gateway Interface (SCGI) is a protocol for applications to interface with HTTP servers, as an alternative to the CGI protocol. It is similar to FastCGI but is designed to be easier to parse. Unlike CGI, it permits a long-running service process to continue serving requests, thus avoiding delays in responding to requests due to setup overhead (such as connecting to a database).

SCGI is a protocol which defines communication between a webserver and an application server. This is in contrast to CGI, which is an earlier application (gateway) interface designed to let the application programmer avoid the complexity of sockets and long-running service processes when poor scalability and high overhead are acceptable.

The SCGI protocol leverages the fact that the client has already parsed and validated the HTTP request, and canonically communicates the request to the SCGI server while letting the application programmer avoid parsing ambiguities and protocol edge cases. This avoids the complicated header-parsing and header-combining rules from RFC2616, saving significant complexity in the SCGI server process.

Specification

The client connects to a SCGI server over a reliable stream protocol allowing transmission of 8-bit bytes. The client begins by sending a request. When the SCGI server sees the end of the request it sends back a response and closes the connection. The format of the response is not specifically specified by this protocol, although CGI-equivalent HTTP responses are generally used.

Request Format

A SCGI request is the concatenation of netstring-encoded headers and a body. A SCGI response is a normal HTTP response.

Each header consists of a name-value pair, where both the name and the value are null-terminated strings (C strings). The value can be an empty string, in which case the terminating null still remains. Neither name nor value can contain any embedded null bytes. These considerations are standard for C strings, but are often confusing for programmers used to other standards for string-handling.

All provided headers are concatenated to form a single byte sequence, then netstring-encoded. The raw body, if any, is then appended.

Duplicate names are not allowed in the request headers; RFC2616-compliant header combining must already have taken place. The first request header must have the name "CONTENT_LENGTH" and a value that is the length of the body in decimal. The "CONTENT_LENGTH" request header must always be present, even if its value is "0". There must also always be a request header with the name "SCGI" and a value of "1". Standard CGI environment variables should be provided in SCGI headers for compatibility when converting older CGI programs to SCGI. The body (if any) provided in the request follows the headers; its length is specified by the "CONTENT_LENGTH" request header.

While the SCGI protocol insulates the service programmer from some HTTP considerations, various details (such as interpreting the octets of the message body as per the Transfer-Encoding header, the CONTENT_LENGTH being the number of octets after the body has been encoded for transmission, etc) still require knowledge of the HTTP protocol specification.

Example:

The web server (a SCGI client) opens a connection and sends the concatenation of the following strings to the service process (a SCGI server):

```
"70:"
    "CONTENT_LENGTH" <00> "27" <00>
    "SCGI" <00> "1" <00>
    "REQUEST_METHOD" <00> "POST" <00>
    "REQUEST_URI" <00> "/deepthought" <00>
","
"What is the answer to life?"
```

The SCGI server sends the following response back to the web server:

```
"Status: 200 OK" <0d 0a>
"Content-Type: text/plain" <0d 0a>
```

```
"" <0d 0a>
"42"
```

The SCGI server closes the connection.

Web Servers that Implement SCGI

- Apache HTTP Server,
- Cherokee,
- Lighttpd,
- Microsoft Internet Information Services with ISAPI SCGI extension,
- nginx.

Language Bindings for the SCGI API

SCGI can be implemented in any language that supports network sockets and netstrings. The following is a partial list of languages with known SCGI bindings:

- Cobra,
- Haskell,
- Java, with the SCGI connector,
- Lisp,
- Perl, with the SCGI package,
- PHP,
- Python,
- Racket, with the scgi library,
- Ruby,
- Rust, with the tokio-scgi crate,
- Scheme,
- Tcl,
- Nim.

FASTCGI

FastCGI is a binary protocol for interfacing interactive programs with a web server. It is a variation on the earlier Common Gateway Interface (CGI). FastCGI's main aim is to reduce the overhead related to interfacing between web server and CGI programs, allowing a server to handle more web page requests per unit of time.

Implementation Details

Instead of creating a new process for each request, FastCGI uses persistent processes to handle a series of requests. These processes are owned by the FastCGI server, not the web server.

To service an incoming request, the web server sends environment variable information and the page request to a FastCGI process over either a Unix domain socket, a named pipe, or a Transmission Control Protocol (TCP) connection. Responses are returned from the process to the web server over the same connection, and the web server then delivers that response to the end user. The connection may be closed at the end of a response, but both web server and FastCGI service processes persist.

Each individual FastCGI process can handle many requests over its lifetime, thereby avoiding the overhead of per-request process creation and termination. Processing multiple requests concurrently can be done in several ways: by using one connection with internal multiplexing (i.e., multiple requests over one connection); by using multiple connections; or by a mix of these methods. Multiple FastCGI servers can be configured, increasing stability and scalability.

Web site administrators and programmers can find that separating web applications from the web server in FastCGI has many advantages over embedded interpreters (mod_perl, mod_php, etc.). This separation allows server and application processes to be restarted independently – an important consideration for busy web sites. It also enables the implementation of per-application, hosting service security policies, which is an important requirement for ISPs and web hosting companies. Different types of incoming requests can be distributed to specific FastCGI servers which have been equipped to handle those types of requests efficiently.

Web Servers that Implement FastCGI

Unless stated, completeness of FastCGI implementation is unknown.

- Apache HTTP Server *(partial):*
  - Implemented by mod_fcgid. This module used to be third-party, but was granted to The Apache Software Foundation (ASF) as an Apache Server subproject in 2009, shepherded by Chris Darroch. It only supports Unix domain sockets, no TCP sockets.
  - A third-party module mod_fastcgi is also being used. For a while, this module no longer compiled properly under Apache 2.4.x, although that problem has been solved with a fork of the original project.
  - Multiplexing of requests through one connection is prohibited by Apache 1.x design, so this isn't supported
  - In Apache 2.4, mod_proxy_fcgi was added, supporting TCP FastCGI servers.
- Caddy,
- Cherokee,

- H2O,
- Hiawatha,
  - ◦ Loadbalancing FastCGI support,
  - ◦ Supports chrooted FastCGI servers.
- Jetty,
- Kerio WebSTAR,
- Lighttpd,
- LiteSpeed Web Server,
- Microsoft IIS,
- Nginx,
- NaviServer,
- Oracle iPlanet Web Server,
- OpenBSD's httpd(8),
- Open Market web server,
- Resin web and application server,
- Roxen web server,
- ShimmerCat web server,
- Zeus Web Server.

Language Bindings for its API

FastCGI can be implemented in any language that supports network sockets. Since "FastCGI is a protocol, not an implementation," it is not tightly bound to any one language. Application programming interfaces (APIs) exist for:

- Ada,
- Delphi, Lazarus Free Pascal,
- C, C++,
- Chicken Scheme,
- Common Lisp,
- D,
- Eiffel,
- Erlang,
- GnuCOBOL,

- Go,

- Guile Scheme,

- Haskell,

- HP BASIC for OpenVMS,

- Java,

- Lua,

- node.js,

- OCaml,

- Perl,

- PHP (via php-fpm, or HipHop for PHP),

- Python,

- Ruby,

- Rust,

- SmallEiffel,

- Smalltalk: FasTalk and Dolphin Smalltalk,

- Tcl,

- WebDNA,

- Vala (via C bindings),

- Xojo (formerly Realbasic, REAL Studio).

Recent frameworks such as Ruby on Rails, Catalyst, Django, Kepler and Plack allow use with either the embedded interpreters (mod_ruby, mod_perl, mod_python or mod_lua, for example), or FastCGI.

WEB SERVICES FOR REMOTE PORTLETS

Web Services for Remote Portlets (WSRP) is an OASIS-approved network protocol standard designed for communications with remote portlets.

The WSRP specification defines a web service interface for interacting with presentation-oriented web services. Initial work was produced through the joint efforts of the Web Services for Interactive Applications (WSIA) and Web Services for Remote Portlets (WSRP) OASIS Technical Committees. With the approval of WSRP v1 as an OASIS standard in September, 2003, these two technical committees merged and continued the work as the Web Services for Remote Portlets (WSRP) OASIS Technical Committee.

Scenarios that motivate WSRP functionality include:

- Content hosts, such as portal servers, providing portlets as presentation-oriented web services that can be used by aggregation engines.

- Content aggregators, such as portal servers, consuming presentation-oriented web services provided by portal or non-portal content providers and integrating them into a portal framework.

Implementation

The WSRP specification does not make any statements as to implementation. Java's portlet specification, JSR 168, and WSRP are not competing technologies. JSR 168 may be used to define a portlet, and WSRP may be used to define a portlet's operations to remote containers. JSR 168 portlets and WSRP may be used together to define a portlet and to provide remote operations. Similarly, .NET portlets may be created for use with WSRP. Interoperability between JSR 168 and .NET WSRP implementations has been demonstrated.

There are several WSRP implementations to assist developers:

- The Oracle WebCenter provides a standards based implementation of WSRP 1.0 and 2.0 producer and consumers.

- The IBM WebSphere Portal provides an implementation of WSRP 1.0 and 2.0 producer and consumers.

- The Liferay Enterprise Portal provides an implementation of WSRP 1.0 and 2.0 producer and consumers available in both its commercial Enterprise Edition and open source Community Edition.

- Microsoft provides a WSRP producer and consumer WebPart for SharePoint 2007, but only a WSRP consumer WebPart for SharePoint 2010 and SharePoint 2013.

- The OpenPortal WSRP project's goal is to create a high quality, enterprise-class WSRP v1 and v2 producer and consumer with an associated developer community.

- The GateIn Portal project (JBoss & eXo Platform), provides an implementation of both WSRP v1 and v2 (as of GateIn 3.1.0), producer and consumer using GateIn and GateIn Portlet Container.

- Apache WSRP4J was an Apache Incubator subproject spearheaded by IBM with the stated goal of "kick starting the broad adoption" of WSRP. WSRP4J was designed to assist in the development and deployment of WSRP v1 services. WSRP4J was in incubator status, primarily due to patent concerns revolving around the WSRP specification. Given WSRP4J's incubator status, the project did not produce formal releases. The project has been terminated in 2010.

The first release, WSRP v1, provided a limited interoperability platform. Further versions of WSRP v1 were abandoned so that effort could be concentrated on WSRP v2. WSRP v2 augments the initial standard with cross-portlet coordination and access management features. This major update to the standard permits a more useful integration of multiple content sources, regardless of whether they are local or remote, into a new web application. In addition, WSRP v2 supports Web 2.0 technologies, such as AJAX and REST, without requiring them. WSRP v2 was approved by OASIS on April 1, 2008.

WEBSOCKET

The WebSocket Protocol enables two-way communication between a client running untrusted code in a controlled environment to a remote host that has opted-in to communications from that code.

WebSocket is especially great for services that require continuous data exchange, e.g. online games, real-time trading systems and so on.

A simple example:

To open a websocket connection, we need to create new WebSocket using the special protocol ws in the url:

```
let socket = new WebSocket("ws://javascript.info");
```

There's also encrypted `wss://`protocol. It's like HTTPS for websockets.

Always prefer `wss://`

The `wss://`protocol not only encrypted, but also more reliable.

That's because `wss://`data is not encrypted, visible for any intermediary. Old proxy servers do not know about WebSocket, they may see "strange" headers and abort the connection.

On the other hand, `wss://`is WebSocket over TLS, (same as HTTPS is HTTP over TLS), the transport security layer encrypts the data at sender and decrypts at the receiver. So data packets are passed encrypted through proxies. They can't see what's inside and let them through.

Once the socket is created, we should listen to events on it. There are totally 4 events:

- Open – connection established,
- Message – data received,
- Error – websocket error,
- Close – connection closed.

And if we'd like to send something, then socket.send(data) will do that.

Here's an example:

```
let socket = new WebSocket("wss://javascript.info/article/websocket/demo/hello");
socket.onopen = function(e) {
  alert("[open] Connection established");
```

```
    alert("Sending to server");

    socket.send("My name is John");

};

socket.onmessage = function(event) {

  alert(`[message] Data received from server: ${event.data}`);

};

socket.onclose = function(event) {

  if (event.wasClean) {

    alert(`[close] Connection closed cleanly, code=${event.code} reason=${event.
reason}`);

  } else {

    // e.g. server process killed or network down

    // event.code is usually 1006 in this case

    alert('[close] Connection died');

  }

};

socket.onerror = function(error) {

  alert(`[error] ${error.message}`);

};
```

For demo purposes, there's a small server server.js written in Node.js, for the example above, running. It responds with "Hello from server, John", then waits 5 seconds and closes the connection.

So you'll see events open → message → close.

Opening a Websocket

When new WebSocket(url) is created, it starts connecting immediately.

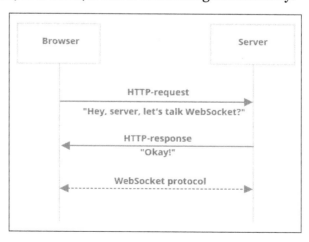

During the connection the browser (using headers) asks the server: "Do you support Websocket?" And if the server replies "yes", then the talk continues in WebSocket protocol, which is not HTTP at all.

Here's an example of browser headers for request made by new WebSocket("wss://javascript. info/chat").

```
GET /chat

Host: javascript.info

Origin: https://javascript.info

Connection: Upgrade

Upgrade: websocket

Sec-WebSocket-Key: Iv8io/9s+lYFgZWcXczP8Q==

Sec-WebSocket-Version: 13
```

- Origin – The origin of the client page, e.g. https://javascript.info. WebSocket objects are cross-origin by nature. There are no special headers or other limitations. Old servers are unable to handle WebSocket anyway, so there are no compabitility issues. But Origin header is important, as it allows the server to decide whether or not to talk WebSocket with this website.

- Connection: Upgrade – signals that the client would like to change the protocol.

- Upgrade: Websocket – the requested protocol is "websocket".

- Sec-WebSocket-Key – a random browser-generated key for security.

- Sec-WebSocket-Version – WebSocket protocol version, 13 is the current one.

WebSocket Handshake can't be Emulated

We can't use XMLHttpRequest or fetch to make this kind of HTTP-request, because JavaScript is not allowed to set these headers.

If the server agrees to switch to WebSocket, it should send code 101 response:

```
101 Switching Protocols

Upgrade: websocket

Connection: Upgrade

Sec-WebSocket-Accept: hsBlbuDTkk24srzEOTBUlZAlC2g=
```

Here Sec-WebSocket-Accept is Sec-WebSocket-Key, recoded using a special algorithm. The browser uses it to make sure that the response corresponds to the request.

Afterwards, the data is transfered using WebSocket protocol, we'll see its structure ("frames") soon. And that's not HTTP at all.

Extensions and Subprotocols

There may be additional headers Sec-WebSocket-Extensions and Sec-WebSocket-Protocol that describe extensions and subprotocols.

For instance:

- Sec-WebSocket-Extensions: Deflate-frame means that the browser supports data compression. An extension is something related to transferring the data, functionality that extends WebSocket protocol. The header Sec-WebSocket-Extensions is sent automatically by the browser, with the list of all extenions it supports.

- Sec-WebSocket-Protocol: Soap, wamp means that we'd like to transfer not just any data, but the data in SOAP or WAMP ("The WebSocket Application Messaging Protocol") protocols.

This optional header is set by us, to tell the server which subprotocols our code supports, using the second (optional) parameter of new WebSocket. That's the array of subprotocols, e.g. if we'd like to use SOAP or WAMP:

```
let socket = new WebSocket("wss://javascript.info/chat", ["soap", "wamp"]);
```

The server should respond with a list of protocols and extensions that it agrees to use.

For example, the request:

```
GET /chat

Host: javascript.info

Upgrade: websocket

Connection: Upgrade

Origin: https://javascript.info

Sec-WebSocket-Key: Iv8io/9s+lYFgZWcXczP8Q==

Sec-WebSocket-Version: 13

Sec-WebSocket-Extensions: deflate-frame

Sec-WebSocket-Protocol: soap, wamp
```

Response:

```
101 Switching Protocols

Upgrade: websocket

Connection: Upgrade

Sec-WebSocket-Accept: hsBlbuDTkk24srzEOTBUlZAlC2g=

Sec-WebSocket-Extensions: deflate-frame

Sec-WebSocket-Protocol: soap
```

Data Transfer

WebSocket communication consists of "frames" – data fragments, that can be sent from either side, and can be of several kinds:

- "Text frames" – contain text data that parties send to each other.

- "Binary data frames" – contain binary data that parties send to each other.

- "Ping/pong frames" are used to check the connection, sent from the server, the browser responds to these automatically.

- There's also "connection close frame" and a few other service frames.

In the browser, we directly work only with text or binary frames.

WebSocket.send() method can send either text or binary data.

A call socket.send(body) allows body in string or a binary format, including Blob, ArrayBuffer, etc. No settings required: just send it out in any format.

When we receive the data, text always comes as string. And for binary data, we can choose between Bloband ArrayBuffer formats.

That's set by socket.bufferType property, it's "blob" by default, so binary data comes as Blob objects.

Blob is a high-level binary object, it directly integrates with <a>, <img> and other tags, so that's a sane default. But for binary processing, to access individual data bytes, we can change it to "arraybuffer":

```
socket.bufferType = "arraybuffer";

socket.onmessage = (event) => {

  // event.data is either a string (if text) or arraybuffer (if binary)

};
```

Rate Limiting

Imagine, our app is generating a lot of data to send. But the user has a slow network connection, maybe on a mobile internet, outside of a city.

We can call socket.send(data) again and again. But the data will be buffered (stored) in memory and sent out only as fast as network speed allows.

The socket.bufferedAmount property stores how many bytes are buffered at this moment, waiting to be sent over the network.

We can examine it to see whether the socket is actually available for transmission.

```
// every 100ms examine the socket and send more data

// only if all the existing data was sent out
```

```
setInterval(() => {
  if (socket.bufferedAmount == 0) {
    socket.send(moreData());
  }
}, 100);
```

Connection Close

Normally, when a party wants to close the connection (both browser and server have equal rights), they send a "connection close frame" with a numeric code and a textual reason.

The method for that is:

```
socket.close([code], [reason]);
```

- Code is a special WebSocket closing code (optional).

- Reason is a string that describes the reason of closing (optional).

Then the other party in close event handler gets the code and the reason, e.g.:

```
// closing party:
socket.close(1000, "Work complete");
// the other party
socket.onclose = event => {
  // event.code === 1000
  // event.reason === "Work complete"
  // event.wasClean === true (clean close)
};
```

Most common code values:

- 1000 – the default, normal closure (used if no code supplied),

- 1006 – no way to such code manually, indicates that the connection was lost (no close frame).

There are other codes like:

- 1001 – the party is going away, e.g. server is shutting down, or a browser leaves the page,

- 1009 – the message is too big to process,

- 1011 – unexpected error on server and so on.

WebSocket codes are somewhat like HTTP codes, but different. In particular, any codes less than 1000 are reserved, there'll be an error if we try to set such a code.

```
// in case connection is broken
```

```
socket.onclose = event => {
  // event.code === 1006
  // event.reason === ""
  // event.wasClean === false (no closing frame)
};
```

Connection State

To get connection state, additionally there's socket.readyState property with values:

- 0 – "CONNECTING": The connection has not yet been established,

- 1 – "OPEN": Communicating,

- 2 – "CLOSING": The connection is closing,

- 3 – "CLOSED": The connection is closed.

Chat Example

Following is a HTML: we need a <form> to send messages and a <div> for incoming messages:

```
<!-- message form -->
<form name="publish">
  <input type="text" name="message">
  <input type="submit" value="Send">
</form>
<!-- div with messages -->
<div id="messages"></div>
```

From JavaScript we want three things:

- Open the connection,

- On form submission – socket.send(message) for the message,

- On incoming message – append it to div#messages.

Here's the code:

```
let socket = new WebSocket("wss://javascript.info/article/websocket/chat/ws");
// send message from the form
document.forms.publish.onsubmit = function() {
  let outgoingMessage = this.message.value;
  socket.send(outgoingMessage);
```

```
  return false;
};
// message received - show the message in div#messages
socket.onmessage = function(event) {
 let message = event.data;
 let messageElem = document.createElement('div');
 messageElem.textContent = message;
 document.getElementById('messages').prepend(messageElem);
}
```

Server-side code is a little bit beyond our scope. Here we'll use Node.js, but you don't have to. Other platforms also have their means to work with WebSocket.

The server-side algorithm will be:

- Create clients = new Set() – a set of sockets.

- For each accepted websocket, add it to the set clients.add(socket) and setup message event listener to get its messages.

- When a message received: iterate over clients and send it to everyone.

- When a connection is closed: clients.delete(socket).

- `const ws = new require('ws');`

- `const wss = new ws.Server({noServer: true});`

- `const clients = new Set();`

- `http.createServer((req, res) => {`

- `  // here we only handle websocket connections`

- `  // in real project we'd have some other code here to handle non-websocket requests`

- `  wss.handleUpgrade(req, req.socket, Buffer.alloc(0), onSocketConnect);`

- `});`

- `function onSocketConnect(ws) {`

- `  clients.add(ws);`

- `  ws.on('message', function(message) {`

- `    message = message.slice(0, 50); // max message length will be 50`

```
for(let client of clients) {

client.send(message);

}

});

ws.on('close', function() {

clients.delete(ws);

});

}
```

References

- Bishop, Mike (July 9, 2019). Draft-ietf-quic-http-22 Hypertext Transfer Protocol Version 3 (HTTP/3) "Hypertext Transfer Protocol Version 3 (HTTP/3)" Check |url= value (help). Tools.ietf.org. Retrieved 2019-08-16

- HTTP-Hypertext-Transfer-Protocol, definition: whatis.techtarget.com, Retrieved 26 January, 2019

- Fielding, Roy T.; Reschke, Julian F. (June 2014). Hypertext Transfer Protocol (HTTP/1.1): Authentication. IETF. Doi:10.17487/RFC7235. RFC 7235

- Websocket: javascript.info, Retrieved 27 February, 2019

- Canavan, John (2001). Fundamentals of Networking Security. Norwood, MA: Artech House. Pp. 82–83. ISBN 9781580531764

- "fastcgi Directives – Configure – H2O – the optimized HTTP/2 server". H2O.example.net. Dena Co., Ltd. Et al. Retrieved 19 March 2019

Web Application Programming Interface

API is a set of functions that allows user to access specific functions, OS and other services. Web API is a concept that allows it to be accessed over the internet via HTTP, HTML5 audio, Cross-Origin Resource Sharing, W3C Geolocation API, HTML5 Video, WebRTC, etc. are some of its components. The diverse applications of Web API have been thoroughly discussed in this chapter.

HTML5 AUDIO

Since the release of HTML5, audios can be added to webpages using the "audio" tag. Previously audios could be only played on webpages using web plugins like Flash. The "audio" tag is an inline element which is used to embed sound files into a web page. It is a very useful tag if you want to add audio such as songs, interviews, etc on your webpage.

Syntax:

```
<audio>
 <source src="sample.mp3" type="audio/mpeg">
</audio>
```

Attributes:

The various attributes that can be used with the "audio" tag are listed below :

- Controls: Designates what controls to display with the audio player.
- Autoplay: Designates that the audio file will play immediately after it loads controls.
- Loop: Designates that the audio file should continuously repeat.
- src: Designates the URL of the audio file.
- muted: Designates that the audio file should be muted

<audio> Element

The <audio> element represents a sound, or an audio stream. It is commonly used to play back a single audio file within a web page, showing a GUI widget with play/pause/volume controls.

The <audio> element has these attributes:

- Global attributes (accesskey; class; contenteditable; contextmenu; dir; draggable; dropzone; hidden; id; lang; spellcheck; style; tabindex; title; translate).

- autoplay = "autoplay" or "" (empty string) or empty.

  Instructs the User-Agent to automatically begin playback of the audio stream as soon as it can do so without stopping.

- preload = "none" or "metadata" or "auto" or "" (empty string) or empty.

  Represents a hint to the User-Agent about whether optimistic downloading of the audio stream itself or its metadata is considered worthwhile.

  - "none": Hints to the User-Agent that the user is not expected to need the audio stream, or that minimizing unnecessary traffic is desirable.

  - "metadata": Hints to the User-Agent that the user is not expected to need the audio stream, but that fetching its metadata (duration and so on) is desirable.

  - "auto": Hints to the User-Agent that optimistically downloading the entire audio stream is considered desirable.

- controls = "controls" or "" (empty string) or empty.

  Instructs the User-Agent to expose a user interface for controlling playback of the audio stream.

- loop = "loop" or "" (empty string) or empty.

  Instructs the User-Agent to seek back to the start of the audio stream upon reaching the end.

- mediagroup = string.

  Instructs the User-Agent to link multiple videos and/or audio streams together.

- muted = "muted" or "" (empty string) or empty.

  Represents the default state of the audio stream, potentially overriding user preferences.

- src = non-empty [URL] potentially surrounded by spaces.

  The URL for the audio stream.

Example:

```
<audio controls>
    <source   src="http://media.w3.org/2010/07/bunny/04-Death_Becomes_Fur.mp4"
type='audio/mp4' />
    <source   src="http://media.w3.org/2010/07/bunny/04-Death_Becomes_Fur.oga"
type='audio/ogg; codecs=vorbis' />
 <p>Your user agent does not support the HTML5 Audio element.</p>
</audio>
```

Supporting Browsers

On PC:

- Google Chrome,

- Internet Explorer 9,

- Firefox 3.5,

- Opera 10.5,

- Safari 3.1.

On mobile devices:

- Android Browser 2.3,

- Blackberry Browser,

- Google Chrome,

- Internet Explorer Mobile 9,

- Safari 4,

- Firefox,

- Opera Mobile 11.

Supported Audio Coding Formats

The adoption of HTML5 audio, as with HTML5 video, has become polarized between proponents of free and patent-encumbered formats. In 2007, the recommendation to use Vorbis was retracted from the specification by the W3C together with that to use Ogg Theora, citing the lack of a format accepted by all the major browser vendors.

Apple and Microsoft support the ISO/IEC-defined formats AAC and the older MP3. Mozilla and Opera support the free and open, royalty-free Vorbis format in Ogg and WebM containers, and criticize the patent-encumbered nature of MP3 and AAC, which are guaranteed to be "non-free". Google has so far provided support for all common formats.

Most AAC files with finite length are wrapped in an MPEG-4 container (.mp4, .m4a), which is supported natively in Internet Explorer, Safari, and Chrome, and supported by the OS in Firefox and Opera. Most AAC live streams with infinite length are wrapped in an Audio Data Transport Stream container (.aac, .adts), which is supported by Chrome, Safari, Firefox and Edge.

Many browsers also support uncompressed PCM audio in a WAVE container.

In 2012, the free and open royalty-free Opus format was released and standardized by IETF. It is supported by Mozilla, Google, Opera and Edge.

This table documents the current support for audio coding formats by the <audio> element.

Formats supported by different web browsers								
Format	Container	MIME type	Chrome	Internet Explorer	Edge	Firefox	Opera	Safari
PCM	WAV	audio/wav	Yes	No	Yes	Yes, in v3.5	Yes, in v11.00	Yes, in v3.1
MP3	MP3	audio/mpeg	Yes	Yes, in IE9	Yes	From OS[a]	Yes	Yes, in v3.1
AAC	MP4	audio/mp4	Yes	Yes, in IE9	Yes	From OS[a]	Yes	Yes
	ADTS[b]	audio/aac audio/aacp	Yes	No	Yes	From OS, in v45.0	Yes	Yes
Vorbis	Ogg	audio/ogg	Yes, in v9	No	In v17, with Web Media Extensions	Yes, in v3.5	Yes, in v10.50	With Xiph QuickTime Components (macOS 10.11 and earlier)
	WebM	audio/webm	Yes	No	In v17, with Web Media Extensions	Yes, in v4.0	Yes, in v10.60	No
Opus	Ogg	audio/ogg	Yes, in v25 (in v31 for Windows)	No	In v17, with Web Media Extensions	Yes, in v15.0	Yes, in v14	No
	WebM	audio/webm	Yes	No	In v14, only via MSE In v17, supports <audio> tag with Web Media Extensions	Yes, in v28.0	Yes	No
FLAC	FLAC	audio/flac	Yes, in v56	No	Yes, in v16	Yes, in v51	Yes	Yes, in v11
	Ogg	audio/ogg	Yes, in v56	No	In v17, with Web Media Extensions	Yes, in v51	Yes	No

Web Audio API and MediaStream Processing API

The Web Audio API specification developed by W3C describes a high-level JavaScript API for processing and synthesizing audio in web applications. The primary paradigm is of an audio routing graph, where a number of AudioNode objects are connected together to define the overall audio rendering. The actual processing will primarily take place in the underlying implementation (typically optimized Assembly / C / C++ code), but direct JavaScript processing and synthesis is also supported.

Mozilla's Firefox browser implements a similar Audio Data API extension since version 4, implemented in 2010 and released in 2011, but Mozilla warns it is non-standard and deprecated, and recommends the Web Audio API instead. Some JavaScript audio processing and synthesis libraries such as Audiolet support both APIs.

The W3C Audio Working Group is also considering the MediaStream Processing API specification developed by Mozilla. In addition to audio mixing and processing, it covers more general media streaming, including synchronization with HTML elements, capture of audio and video streams, and peer-to-peer routing of such media streams.

Supporting Browsers

On PC:

- Google Chrome 10 (Enabled by default since 14),

- Firefox 23 (Enabled by default since 25),

- Opera 15,

- Safari 6,

- Microsoft Edge 12.

On mobile devices:

- Google Chrome for Android 28 (Enabled by default since 29),

- Safari 6 (Has restrictions on use (Muted unless user called)),

- Firefox 23 (Enabled by default since 25),

- Tizen.

Web Speech API

The Web Speech API aims to provide an alternative input method for web applications (without using a keyboard). With this API, developers can give web apps the ability to transcribe voice to text, from the computer's microphone. The recorded audio is sent to speech servers for transcription, after which the text is typed out for the user. The API itself is agnostic of the underlying speech recognition implementation and can support both server based as well as embedded recognizers. The HTML Speech Incubator group has proposed the implementation of audio-speech technology in browsers in the form of uniform, cross-platform APIs. The API contains both:

- Speech Input API,

- Text to Speech API.

Google integrated this feature into Google Chrome on March 2011. Letting its users search the web with their voice with code like:

```
<script type="application/javascript">

    function startSearch(event) {

        event.target.form.submit();

    }
```

```
</script>
<form action="http://www.google.com/search">

    <input type="search" name="q" speech required onspeechchange="startSearch">
</form>
```

Supporting Browsers

- Safari 6.1 and up [PARTIAL: speech synthesis only; no recognition].

- Google Chrome 25 and up.

- Firefox Desktop 44.0 and up (Linux and Mac) / 45.0 and up (Windows) [PARTIAL: speech synthesis only; no recognition; currently requires "media.webspeech.recognition.enable" about:config option to be manually changed to "true"].

CANVAS ELEMENT

The canvas element is part of HTML5 and allows for dynamic, scriptable rendering of 2D shapes and bitmap images. It is a low level, procedural model that updates a bitmap and does not have a built-in scene graph; however through WebGL it allows 3D shapes and images and so-on. HTML5 Canvas also helps in making 2D games.

Usage

Canvas consists of a drawable region defined in HTML code with height and width attributes. JavaScript code may access the area through a full set of drawing functions similar to those of other common 2D APIs, thus allowing for dynamically generated graphics. Some anticipated uses of canvas include building graphs, animations, games, and image composition.

Example:

The following code creates a Canvas element in an HTML page:

```
<canvas id="example" width="200" height="200">
This text is displayed if your browser does not support HTML5 Canvas.
</canvas>
```

Using JavaScript, you can draw on the canvas:

```
var example = document.getElementById('example');
var context = example.getContext('2d');
context.fillStyle = 'red';
context.fillRect(30, 30, 50, 50);
```

This code draws a red rectangle on the screen.

The Canvas API also provides save() and restore(), for saving and restoring all the canvas context's attributes.

Canvas Element Size versus Drawing Surface Size

A canvas actually has two sizes: the size of the element itself and the size of the element's drawing surface. Setting the element's width and height attributes sets both of these sizes; CSS attributes affect only the element's size and not the drawing surface.

By default, both the canvas element's size and the size of its drawing surface is 300 screen pixels wide and 150 screen pixels high. In the listing shown in the example, which uses CSS to set the canvas element's size, the size of the element is 600 pixels wide and 300 pixels high, but the size of the drawing surface remains unchanged at the default value of 300 pixels × 150 pixels. When a canvas element's size does not match the size of its drawing surface, the browser scales the drawing surface to fit the element (which may result in surprising and unwanted effects).

Example on setting element size and drawing surface size to different values:

```
<!DOCTYPE html>

<html>

    <head>

    <title>Canvas element size: 600 x 300,

    Canvas drawing surface size: 300 x 150</title>

    <style>

        body {

            background: #dddddd;

        }

        #canvas {

            margin: 20px;

            padding: 20px;

            background: #ffffff;

            border: thin inset #aaaaaa;

            width: 600px;

            height: 300px;

        }

    </style>

    </head>

    <body>

        <canvas id="canvas">
```

```
    Canvas not supported
    </canvas>
  </body>
</html>
```

Canvas versus Scalable Vector Graphics (SVG)

SVG is an earlier standard for drawing shapes in browsers. However, unlike canvas, which is raster-based, SVG is vector-based, so that each drawn shape is remembered as an object in a scene graph or Document Object Model, which is subsequently rendered to a bitmap. This means that if attributes of an SVG object are changed, the browser can automatically re-render the scene.

Canvas objects, on the other hand, are drawn in immediate mode. In the canvas example above, once the rectangle is drawn the model it was drawn from is forgotten by the system. If its position were to be changed, the entire scene would need to be redrawn, including any objects that might have been covered by the rectangle. But in the equivalent SVG case, one could simply change the position attributes of the rectangle and the browser would determine how to repaint it. There are additional JavaScript libraries that add scene-graph capabilities to the canvas element. It is also possible to paint a canvas in layers and then recreate specific layers.

SVG images are represented in XML, and complex scenes can be created and maintained with XML editing tools.

The SVG scene graph enables event handlers to be associated with objects, so a rectangle may respond to an onClick event. To get the same functionality with canvas, one must manually match the coordinates of the mouse click with the coordinates of the drawn rectangle to determine whether it was clicked.

Conceptually, canvas is a lower-level API upon which an engine, supporting for example SVG, might be built. There are JavaScript libraries that provide partial SVG implementations using canvas for browsers that do not provide SVG but support canvas, such as the browsers in Android 2.x. However, this is not normally the case—they are independent standards. The situation is complicated because there are scene graph libraries for canvas, and SVG has some bitmap manipulation functionality.

Reactions

At the time of its introduction the canvas element was met with mixed reactions from the web standards community. There have been arguments against Apple's decision to create a new proprietary element instead of supporting the SVG standard. There are other concerns about syntax, such as the absence of a namespace.

Intellectual Property over Canvas

On March 14, 2007, WebKit developer Dave Hyatt forwarded an email from Apple's Senior Patent Counsel, Helene Plotka Workman, which stated that Apple reserved all intellectual property rights relative to WHATWG's Web Applications 1.0 Working Draft, entitled "Graphics: The bit-map canvas", but left the door open to licensing the patents should the specification be trans-ferred to a standards body with a formal patent policy. This caused considerable discussion among web developers, and raised questions concerning the WHATWG's lack of a policy on patents in comparison to the World Wide Web Consortium (W3C)'s explicit favoring of royal-ty-free licenses. Apple later disclosed the patents under the W3C's royalty-free patent licensing terms. The disclosure means that Apple is required to provide royalty-free licensing for the pat-ent whenever the Canvas element becomes part of a future W3C recommendation created by the HTML working group.

Privacy Concerns

Canvas fingerprinting is one of a number of browser fingerprinting techniques of tracking online users that allow websites to identify and track visitors using HTML5 canvas element. The tech-nique received wide media coverage in 2014 after researchers from Princeton University and KU Leuven University described it in their paper *The Web never forgets*. The privacy concerns regard-ing canvas fingerprinting centre around the fact that even deleting cookies and clearing the cache will not be sufficient for users to avoid online tracking.

Browser Support

The element is supported by the current versions of Mozilla Firefox, Google Chrome, Internet Ex-plorer, Safari, Konqueror, Opera and Microsoft Edge.

CROSS-ORIGIN RESOURCE SHARING

Cross-origin resource sharing (CORS) is a mechanism that allows restricted resources on a web page to be requested from another domain outside the domain from which the first resource was served. A web page may freely embed cross-origin images, stylesheets, scripts, iframes, and videos. Certain "cross-domain" requests, notably Ajax requests, are forbidden by default by the same-or-igin security policy.

CORS defines a way in which a browser and server can interact to determine whether it is safe to allow the cross-origin request. It allows for more freedom and functionality than purely same-or-igin requests, but is more secure than simply allowing all cross-origin requests. The specification for CORS was originally published as a W3C Recommendation but that document is obsolete. The current actively-maintained specification that defines CORS is WHATWG's Fetch Living Standard.

Working Principle of CORS

The CORS standard describes new HTTP headers which provide browsers a way to request re-mote URLs only when they have permission. Although some validation and authorization can be performed by the server, it is generally the browser's responsibility to support these headers and honor the restrictions they impose.

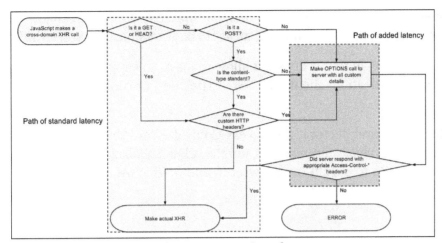

Parts of an HTML container element.

For Ajax and HTTP request methods that can modify data (usually HTTP methods other than GET, or for POST usage with certain MIME types), the specification mandates that browsers "pre-flight" the request, soliciting supported methods from the server with an HTTP OPTIONS request method, and then, upon "approval" from the server, sending the actual request with the actual HTTP request method. Servers can also notify clients whether "credentials" (including Cookies and HTTP Authentication data) should be sent with requests.

Simple Example

Suppose a user visits http://www.example.com and the page attempts a cross-origin request to fetch the user's data from http://service.example.com. A CORS-compatible browser will attempt to make a cross-origin request to service.example.com as follows:

- The browser sends the OPTIONS request with an Origin HTTP header to service.example.com containing the domain that served the parent page:

  ```
  Origin: http://www.example.com
  ```

- The server at service.example.com may respond with:

  - An `Access-Control-Allow-Origin` (ACAO) header in its response indicating which origin sites are allowed. For example:

    ```
    Access-Control-Allow-Origin: http://www.example.com
    ```

    Since www.example.com matches the parent page, the browser then performs the cross-origin request.

  - An Access-Control-Allow-Origin (ACAO) header with a wildcard that allows all domains:

    ```
    Access-Control-Allow-Origin: *
    ```

  - An error page if the server does not allow a cross-origin request.

A wildcard same-origin policy is appropriate when a page or API response is considered complete-ly public content and it is intended to be accessible to everyone, including any code on any site. For example, a freely-available web font on a public hosting service like Google Fonts.

A wildcard same-origin policy is also widely and appropriately used in the object-capability model, where pages have unguessable URLs and are meant to be accessible to anyone who knows the secret.

The value of "*" is special in that it does not allow requests to supply credentials, meaning it does not allow HTTP authentication, client-side SSL certificates, or cookies to be sent in the cross-domain request.

Note that in the CORS architecture, the Access-Control-Allow-Origin header is being set by the external web service (service.example.com), not the original web application server. Here, service.example.com uses CORS to permit the browser to authorize www.example.com to make requests to service.example.com.

Preflight Example

When performing certain types of cross-domain Ajax requests, modern browsers that support CORS will insert an extra "preflight" request to determine whether they have permission to perform the action.

```
OPTIONS /

Host: service.example.com

Origin: http://www.example.com
```

If service.example.com is willing to accept the action, it may respond with the following headers:

```
Access-Control-Allow-Origin: http://www.example.com

Access-Control-Allow-Methods: PUT, DELETE
```

Headers

The HTTP headers that relate to CORS are

Request headers:

- Origin.
- Access-Control-Request-Method.
- Access-Control-Request-Headers.

Response headers:

- Access-Control-Allow-Origin.
- Access-Control-Allow-Credentials.
- Access-Control-Expose-Headers.
- Access-Control-Max-Age.
- Access-Control-Allow-Methods.
- Access-Control-Allow-Headers.

Browser Support

CORS is supported by all browsers based on the following layout engines:

- Blink- and Chromium-based browsers (Chrome 28+, Opera 15+, Amazon Silk, Android's 4.4+ WebView and Qt's WebEngine).

- Gecko 1.9.1 (Firefox 3.5, SeaMonkey 2.0) and above.

- MSHTML/Trident 6.0 (Internet Explorer 10) has native support. MSHTML/Trident 4.0 & 5.0 (Internet Explorer 8 & 9) provide partial support via the XDomainRequest object.

- Presto-based browsers (Opera) implement CORS as of Opera 12.00 and Opera Mobile 12, but not Opera Mini.

- WebKit (Initial revision uncertain, Safari 4 and above, Google Chrome 3 and above, possibly earlier).

- Microsoft Edge All versions.

Cross-origin support was originally proposed by Matt Oshry, Brad Porter, and Michael Bodell of Tellme Networks in March 2004 for inclusion in VoiceXML 2.1 to allow safe cross-origin data requests by VoiceXML browsers. The mechanism was deemed general in nature and not specific to VoiceXML and was subsequently separated into an implementation NOTE. The WebApps Working Group of the W3C with participation from the major browser vendors began to formalize the NOTE into a W3C Working Draft on track toward formal W3C Recommendation status.

In May 2006 the first W3C Working Draft was submitted. In March 2009 the draft was renamed to "Cross-Origin Resource Sharing" and in January 2014 it was accepted as a W3C Recommendation.

CORS vs. JSONP

CORS can be used as a modern alternative to the JSONP pattern. While JSONP supports only the GET request method, CORS also supports other types of HTTP requests. Using CORS enables a web programmer to use regular XMLHttpRequest, which supports better error handling than JSONP. On the other hand, JSONP works on legacy browsers which predate CORS support. CORS is supported by most modern web browsers. Also, while JSONP can cause cross-site scripting (XSS) issues when the external site is compromised, CORS allows websites to manually parse responses to increase security.

DOCUMENT OBJECT MODEL

The Document Object Model (DOM) is a cross-platform and language-independent interface that treats an XML or HTML document as a tree structure wherein each node is an object representing a part of the document. The DOM represents a document with a logical tree. Each branch of the tree ends in a node, and each node contains objects. DOM methods allow programmatic access to the tree; with them one can change the structure, style or content of a document. Nodes can have event handlers attached to them. Once an event is triggered, the event handlers get executed.

The principal standardization of the DOM was handled by the World Wide Web Consortium, which last developed a recommendation in 2004. WHATWG took over development of the standard, publishing it as a living document. The W3C now publishes stable snapshots of the WHATWG standard.

Standards

The W3C DOM Working Group published its final recommendation and subsequently disbanded in 2004. Development efforts migrated to the WHATWG, which continues to maintain a living standard. In 2009, the Web Applications group reorganized DOM activities at the W3C. In 2013, due to a lack of progress and the impending release of HTML5, the DOM Level 4 specification was reassigned to the HTML Working Group to expedite its completion. Meanwhile, in 2015, the Web Applications group was disbanded and DOM stewardship passed to the Web Platform group. Beginning with the publication of DOM Level 4 in 2015, the W3C creates new recommendations based on snapshots of the WHATWG standard.

- DOM Level 1 provided a complete model for an entire HTML or XML document, including the means to change any portion of the document.

- DOM Level 2 was published in late 2000. It introduced the getElementById function as well as an event model and support for XML namespaces and CSS.

- DOM Level 3, published in April 2004, added support for XPath and keyboard event handling, as well as an interface for serializing documents as XML.

- DOM Level 4 was published in 2015. It is a snapshot of the WHATWG living standard.

Applications

Web Browsers

To render a document such as a HTML page, most web browsers use an internal model similar to the DOM. The nodes of every document are organized in a tree structure, called the *DOM tree*, with the topmost node named as "Document object". When an HTML page is rendered in browsers, the browser downloads the HTML into local memory and automatically parses it to display the page on screen.

JavaScript

When a web page is loaded, the browser creates a Document Object Model of the page, which is an object oriented representation of an HTML document that acts as an interface between JavaScript and the document itself. This allows the creation of dynamic web pages, because within a page JavaScript can:

- Add, change, and remove any of the HTML elements and attributes.

- Change any of the CSS styles.

- React to all the existing events.

- Create new events.

Implementations

Because the DOM supports navigation in any direction (e.g., parent and previous sibling) and allows for arbitrary modifications, an implementation must at least buffer the document that has been read so far (or some parsed form of it).

Layout Engines

Web browsers rely on layout engines to parse HTML into a DOM. Some layout engines, such as Trident/MSHTML, are associated primarily or exclusively with a particular browser, such as Internet Explorer. Others, including Blink, WebKit, and Gecko, are shared by a number of browsers, such as Google Chrome, Opera, Safari, and Firefox. The different layout engines implement the DOM standards to varying degrees of compliance.

Libraries

DOM Implementations:

- libxml2
- MSXML
- Xerces is a collection of DOM implementations written in C++, Java and Perl.
- XML for <SCRIPT> is a JavaScript-based DOM implementation.
- PHP.Gt DOM is a server-side DOM implementation based on libxml2 and brings DOM level 4 compatibility to the PHP programming language.
- Domino is a Server-side (Node.js) DOM implementation based on Mozilla's dom.js. Domino is used in the MediaWiki stack with Visual Editor.

APIs that Expose DOM Implementations:

- JAXP (Java API for XML Processing) is an API for accessing DOM providers.
- Lazarus (Free Pascal IDE) contains two variants of the DOM - with UTF-8 and ANSI format.

Inspection Tools:

- DOM Inspector is a web developer tool.

ENCRYPTED MEDIA EXTENSIONS

Encrypted Media Extensions (EME) is a W3C specification for providing a communication channel between web browsers and digital rights management (DRM) agent software. This allows the use of HTML5 video to play back DRM-wrapped content such as streaming video services without the use of heavy third-party media plugins like Adobe Flash or Microsoft Silverlight. The use of a third-party key management system may be required, depending on whether the publisher chooses to scramble the keys.

EME is based on the HTML5 Media Source Extensions specification, which enables adaptive bitrate streaming in HTML5 using e.g. MPEG-DASH with MPEG-CENC protected content.

EME has been highly controversial because it places a necessarily proprietary, closed component into what might otherwise be an entirely open and free software ecosystem. On July 6th, 2017, W3C publicly announced its intention to publish EME web standard, and did so on September 18th. On the same day, the Electronic Frontier Foundation published an open letter resigning from W3C.

Support

In April 2013, on the Samsung Chromebook, Netflix became the first company to offer HTML5 video using EME.

As of 2016, the Encrypted Media Extensions interface has been implemented in the Google Chrome, Internet Explorer, Safari, Firefox, and Microsoft Edge browsers.

While backers and the developers of the Firefox web browser were hesitant in implementing the protocol for ethical reasons due to its dependency on proprietary code, Firefox introduced EME support on Windows platforms in May 2015. Firefox's implementation of EME uses an open-source sandbox to load the proprietary DRM modules, which are treated as plug-ins that are loaded when EME-encrypted content is requested. The sandbox was also designed to frustrate the ability for services and the DRM to uniquely track and identify devices. Additionally, it is always possible to disable DRM in Firefox, which then not only disables EME, but also uninstalls the CDM Widevine.

Netflix supports HTML5 video using EME with a supported web browser: Chrome, Firefox, Microsoft Edge, Internet Explorer (on Windows 8.1 or newer), or Safari (on OS X Yosemite or newer). YouTube supports the HTML5 MSE. Available players supporting MPEG-DASH using the HTML5 MSE and EME are NexPlayer, THEOplayer by OpenTelly, the bitdash MPEG-DASH player, dash.js by DASH-IF or rx-player.

Version 4.3 and subsequent versions of Android support EME.

Content Decryption Modules

- Adobe Primetime CDM (used by old Firefox versions 47 to 51).
- Widevine (used in Chrome, Firefox, and Opera among others).
- PlayReady (used in Microsoft Edge or Internet Explorer 11 for Windows 8.1).
- FairPlay (used in Safari in OS X Yosemite).

HTML5 FILE API

HTML5 File API aspect provides an API for representing file objects in web applications and programmatic selection and accessing their data. In addition, this specification defines objects to be used within threaded web applications for the synchronous reading of files. The File API describes how interactions with files are handled, for reading information about them and their data as well, to be able to upload it. Despite the name, the File API is not part of HTML5.

W3C GEOLOCATION API

The W3C Geolocation API is an effort by the World Wide Web Consortium (W3C) to standardize an interface to retrieve the geographical location information for a client-side device. It defines a set of objects, ECMAScript standard compliant, that executing in the client application give the client's device location through the consulting of Location Information Servers, which are transparent for the application programming interface (API). The most common sources of location information are IP address, Wi-Fi and Bluetooth MAC address, radio-frequency identification (RFID), Wi-Fi connection location, or device Global Positioning System (GPS) and GSM/CDMA cell IDs. The location is returned with a given accuracy depending on the best location information source available.

Deployment in Web Browsers

Web pages can use the Geolocation API directly if the web browser implements it. Historically, some browsers could gain support via the Google Gears plugin, but this was discontinued in 2010 and the server-side API it depended on stopped responding in 2012.

The Geolocation API is ideally suited to web applications for mobile devices such as personal digital assistants (PDA) and smartphones. On desktop computers, the W3C Geolocation API works in Firefox since version 3.5, Google Chrome, Opera 10.6, Internet Explorer 9.0, and Safari 5. On mobile devices, it works on Android (firmware 2.0+), iOS, Windows Phone and Maemo. The W3C Geolocation API is also supported by Opera Mobile 10.1 — available for Android and Symbian devices (S60 generations 3 & 5) since November 24, 2010.

Google Gears provided geolocation support for older and non-compliant browsers, including Internet Explorer 7.0+ as a Gears plugin, and Google Chrome which implemented Gears natively. It also supported geolocation on mobile devices as a plugin for the Android browser (pre version 2.0) and Opera Mobile for Windows Mobile. However, the Google Gears Geolocation API is incompatible with the W3C Geolocation API and is no longer supported.

Features

The result of W3C Geolocation API will usually give 4 location properties, including latitude and longitude (coordinates), altitude (height), and [accuracy of the position gathered], which all depend on the location sources. In some queries, altitude may yield or return no value.

Location Sources

The Geolocation API does not provide the location information. The location information is obtained by a device (such as a smartphone, PC or modem), which is then served by the API to be brought in browser. Usually geolocation will try to determine a device's position using one of these several methods:

- GPS (Global Positioning System):

  This happens for any device which has GPS capabilities. A smartphone with GPS capabilities and set to high accuracy mode will be likely to obtain the location data from this. GPS calculate location information from the satellite signal. It has the highest accuracy; in most Android smartphones, the accuracy can be up to 10 metres.

- Mobile Network Location:

  Mobile phone tracking is used if a cellphone or wireless modem is used without a GPS chip built in.

- WiFi Positioning System:

  If WiFi is used indoors, a Wi-Fi positioning system is the likeliest source. Some WiFi spots have location services capabilities.

- IP Address Location:

  Location is detected based on nearest Public IP Address on a device (which can be a computer, the router it is connected to, or the ISP the router uses). The location depends on the IP information available, but in many cases where the IP is hidden behind Internet Service Provider NAT, the accuracy is only to the level of a city, region or even country.

Implementation

Though the implementation is not specified, W3C Geolocation API is built on extant technologies, and is heavily influenced by Google Gears Geolocation API. Example: Firefox's Geolocation implementation uses Google's network location provider.

Google Gears Geolocation works by sending a set of parameters that could give a hint as to where the user's physical location is to a network location provider server, which is by default the one provided by Google. Some of the parameters are lists of sensed mobile cell towers and Wi-Fi networks, all with sensed signal strengths. These parameters are encapsulated into a JavaScript Object Notation (JSON) message and sent to the network location provider via HTTP POST. Based on these parameters, the network location provider can calculate the location. Common uses for this location information include enforcing access controls, localizing and customizing content, analyzing traffic, contextual advertising and preventing identity theft.

Example Code

Simple JavaScript code that checks if the browser has the Geolocation API implemented and then uses it to get the current position of the device. this code creates a function which can be called on HTML using `<body onload="geoFindMe()">`:

```
const geoFindMe = () => {

    if (navigator.geolocation) {
```

```
        navigator.geolocation.getCurrentPosition(success, error, geoOptions);
    } else {
        console.log("Geolocation services are not supported by your web brows-
er.");
    }
}
const success = (position) => {
    const latitude = position.coords.latitude;
    const longitude = position.coords.longitude;
    const altitude = position.coords.altitude;
    const accuracy = position.coords.accuracy;
    console.log(`lat: ${latitude} long: ${longitude}`);
}
const error = (error) => {
    console.log(`Unable to retrieve your location due to ${error.code}: ${error.
message}`);
}
const geoOptions = {
    enableHighAccuracy: true,
    maximumAge: 30000,
    timeout: 27000
};
```

INDEXED DATABASE API

IndexedDB is a large-scale, NoSQL storage system. It lets you store just about anything in the user's browser. In addition to the usual search, get, and put actions, IndexedDB also supports transactions. Here is the definition of IndexedDB on MDN:

> "IndexedDB is a low-level API for client-side storage of significant amounts of structured data, including files/blobs. This API uses indexes to enable high performance searches of this data. While DOM Storage is useful for storing smaller amounts of data, it is less useful for storing larger amounts of structured data. IndexedDB provides a solution."

Each IndexedDB database is unique to an origin (typically, this is the site domain or subdomain), meaning it cannot access or be accessed by any other origin. Data storage limits are usually quite large, if they exist at all, but different browsers handle limits and data eviction differently.

MEDIA SOURCE EXTENSIONS

Media Source Extensions (MSE) is a W3C specification that allows JavaScript to send byte streams to media codecs within Web browsers that support HTML 5 video and audio. Among other possible uses, this allows the implementation of client-side prefetching and buffering code for streaming media entirely in JavaScript. It is compatible with, but should not be confused with, the Encrypted Media Extensions specification, and neither requires the use of the other.

Netflix announced experimental support in June 2014 for the use of MSE playback on the Safari browser on the OS X Yosemite beta release.

YouTube started using MSE with its HTML 5 player in September 2013.

Browser Support

- Firefox 42 with support for all sites since 3 November 2015, with a subset of the functionality available for use with only YouTube in Firefox 37 on Windows Vista or later only. Firefox added the same subset of MSE for YouTube playback support to Mac OS X starting in Firefox 38.

- Google Chrome since early 2013, also on Android.

- Internet Explorer from version 11 on Windows 8.1.

- Microsoft Edge since its launch in November 2015.

- Opera since 9 June 2015.

- Pale Moon from version 27.0, since 22 November 2016.

- Safari 8 on OS X.

Players

- NexPlayer for HTML5 MSE and EME supporting HLS and DASH.

- castLabs PRESTOplay video player for HMTL5 MSE and EME supporting DASH and HLS.

- Akamai Media Player as a contributor to the Dash Industry Forum and DASH.js (DASH IF reference client). AMP includes Dash.js, HLS.js and advanced QUIC protocol playback from Akamai Edge Servers.

- Shaka Player, an open source javascript player library for HTML5 MSE and EME video with DASH and HLS support.

- The Video Player by Comcast Technology Solutions.

- THEOplayer by OpenTelly: HLS and MPEG-DASH player for cross-platform HTML5 support without the need for Flash fallback.

- Viblast Player: HLS and MPEG-DASH player for HTML5 MSE and EME, with Flash fallback.

- bitmovin's bitdash MPEG-DASH player for HTML5 MSE and EME, with Flash fallback.

- dash-js for HTML5 MSE.

- dash.js for HTML5 MSE and EME.

- rx-player for HTML5 MSE and EME (Live and On Demand).

- hls.js for HTML5 MSE.

- hasplayer.js for HTML5 MSE and EME, supporting DASH, Smooth Streaming and HLS.

- JW Player 7 and later for MPEG-DASH using HTML5 MSE and EME.

- SLDP HTML5 Player supports SLDP via MSE playback.

- Azure Media Player supports MSE, EME, DASH, HLS, Flash, and Silverlight. Streaming URLs are published in an ism/manifest.

- Unreal HTML5 player uses MSE for low latency (sub-second) live playback of streams sent via WebSockets by Unreal Media Server.

SERVER SENT EVENTS

Server-Sent Events (SSE) is a server push technology enabling a client to receive automatic updates from a server via HTTP connection. The Server-Sent Events EventSource API is standardized as part of HTML5 by the W3C.

The WHATWG Web Applications 1.0 proposal included a mechanism to push content to the client. On September 1, 2006, the Opera web browser implemented this new experimental technology in a feature called "Server-Sent Events".

Server-Sent Events is a standard describing how servers can initiate data transmission towards clients once an initial client connection has been established. They are commonly used to send message updates or continuous data streams to a browser client and designed to enhance native, cross-browser streaming through a JavaScript API called EventSource, through which a client requests a particular URL in order to receive an event stream.

Web Browsers

Web browser support for Server-Sent Events		
Browser	Supported	Notes
Internet Explorer	No	
Mozilla Firefox	Yes	Starting with Firefox 6.0
Google Chrome	Yes	Starting with Chrome 6

Opera	Yes	Starting with Opera 11
Safari	Yes	Starting with Safari 5.0
Microsoft Edge	Yes	Starting with Edge 75

Libraries

.NET

- Service Stack EventSource library with both server and client implementations.

ASP.NET

- SignalR - Transparent implementation for ASP.NET.

C

- HaSSEs Asynchronous server-side SSE daemon written in C (It uses one thread for all connected clients).

Erlang

- Lasse EventSource server handler for Erlang's cowboy.

- Shotgun EventSource client in Erlang.

Go

- eventsource EventSource library for Go.

Java

- jEaSSE - Server-side asynchronous implementation for Java servlets and Vert.x.

- Akka HTTP has SSE support since version 10.0.8.

- alpakka Event Source Connector EventSource library for alpakka which supports reconnection.

- Spring WebFlux Server and client side Java implementation built on reactive streams and non-blocking servers.

- Jersey has a full implementation of JAX-RS support for Server Sent Events as defined in JSR-370.

- Micronaut HTTP server supports emitting Server Sent Events.

- JeSSE - Server-side library with user/session management, group broadcast, and authentication.

- Armeria has server and client-side asynchronous SSE implementation built on top of Netty and Reactive Streams.

Node.js

- sse-stream - Node.js/Browserify implementation (client and server).
- total.js - web application framework for Node.js - example + supports WebSockets (RFC 6455).
- eventsource-node - EventSource client for Node.js.

Objective C

- TRVSEventSource - EventSource implementation in Objective-C for iOS and macOS using NSURLSession.

Perl

- Mojolicious - Perl real-time web framework.

PHP

- Hoa\Eventsource - Server implementation.

Python

- Python SSE Client - EventSource client library for Python using Requests library.
- Server Side Events (SSE) client for Python - EventSource client library for Python using Requests or urllib3 library.
- django-eventstream - Server-Sent Events for Django.
- flask-sse - A simple Flask extension powered by Redis.
- sse - Implementation on python2 and python3 in the same codebase.
- event-source-library - Implementation in python2 with Tornado. Client and server implementations.

Scala

- Akka HTTP has SSE support since version 10.0.8.
- alpakka Event Source Connector EventSource library for alpakka which supports reconnection.

Swift

- EventSource - EventSource implementation using NSURLSession.

SCALABLE VECTOR GRAPHICS

Scalable Vector Graphics (SVG) is an XML-based vector image format for two-dimensional graphics with support for interactivity and animation. The SVG specification is an open standard developed by the World Wide Web Consortium (W3C) since 1999.

SVG images and their behaviors are defined in XML text files. This means that they can be searched, indexed, scripted, and compressed. As XML files, SVG images can be created and edited with any text editor, as well as with drawing software.

All major modern web browsers—including Mozilla Firefox, Internet Explorer, Google Chrome, Opera, Safari, and Microsoft Edge—have SVG rendering support.

This image illustrates the difference between bitmap and vector images. The bitmap image is composed of a fixed set of pixels, while the vector image is composed of a fixed set of shapes. In the picture, scaling the bitmap reveals the pixels while scaling the vector image preserves the shapes.

SVG has been in development within the World Wide Web Consortium (W3C) since 1999 after six competing proposals for vector graphics languages had been submitted to the consortium during 1998. The early SVG Working Group decided not to develop any of the commercial submissions, but to create a new markup language that was informed by but not really based on any of them.

SVG allows three types of graphic objects: vector graphic shapes such as paths and outlines consisting of straight lines and curves, bitmap images, and text. Graphical objects can be grouped, styled, transformed and composited into previously rendered objects. The feature set includes nested transformations, clipping paths, alpha masks, filter effects and template objects. SVG drawings can be interactive and can include animation, defined in the SVG XML elements or via scripting that accesses the SVG Document Object Model (DOM). SVG uses CSS for styling and JavaScript for scripting. Text, including internationalization and localization, appearing in plain text within the SVG DOM enhances the accessibility of SVG graphics.

The SVG specification was updated to version 1.1 in 2011. There are two 'Mobile SVG Profiles,' SVG Tiny and SVG Basic, meant for mobile devices with reduced computational and display capabilities. Scalable Vector Graphics 2 became a W3C Candidate Recommendation on 15 September 2016. SVG 2 incorporates several new features in addition to those of SVG 1.1 and SVG Tiny 1.2.

Printing

Though the SVG Specification primarily focuses on vector graphics markup language, its design includes the basic capabilities of a page description language like Adobe's PDF. It contains provisions for rich graphics, and is compatible with CSS for styling purposes. SVG has the information needed to place each glyph and image in a chosen location on a printed page.

Scripting and Animation

SVG drawings can be dynamic and interactive. Time-based modifications to the elements can be described in SMIL, or can be programmed in a scripting language (e.g. ECMAScript or JavaScript). The W3C explicitly recommends SMIL as the standard for animation in SVG.

A rich set of event handlers such as *onmouseover* and *onclick* can be assigned to any SVG graphical object.

Compression

SVG images, being XML, contain many repeated fragments of text, so they are well suited for lossless data compression algorithms. When an SVG image has been compressed with the industry standard gzip algorithm, it is referred to as an "SVGZ" image and uses the corresponding .svgz filename extension. Conforming SVG 1.1 viewers will display compressed images. An SVGZ file is typically 20 to 50 percent of the original size. W3C provides SVGZ files to test for conformance.

SVG was developed by the W3C SVG Working Group starting in 1998, after six competing vector graphics submissions were received that year:

- Web Schematics, from CCLRC.

- PGML, from Adobe Systems, IBM, Netscape and Sun Microsystems.

- VML, by Autodesk, Hewlett-Packard, Macromedia, Microsoft, and Vision.

- Hyper Graphics Markup Language (HGML), by Orange UK and PRP.

- WebCGM, from Boeing, InterCAP Graphics Systems, Inso Corporation, CCLRC, and Xerox

- DrawML, from Excosoft AB.

The working group was chaired at the time by Chris Lilley of the W3C.

Version 1.x

- SVG 1.0 became a W3C Recommendation on 4 September 2001.

- SVG 1.1 became a W3C Recommendation on 14 January 2003. The SVG 1.1 specification is modularized in order to allow subsets to be defined as profiles. Apart from this, there is very little difference between SVG 1.1 and SVG 1.0.

  ○ SVG Tiny and SVG Basic (the Mobile SVG Profiles) became W3C Recommendations on 14 January 2003. These are described as profiles of SVG 1.1.

- SVG Tiny 1.2 became a W3C Recommendation on 22 December 2008. It was initially drafted as a profile of the planned SVG Full 1.2 (which has since been dropped in favor of SVG 2), but was later refactored as a standalone specification.

- SVG 1.1 Second Edition, which includes all the errata and clarifications, but no new features to the original SVG 1.1 was released on 16 August 2011.

Version 2.x

SVG 2.0 removes or deprecates some features of SVG 1.1 and incorporates new features from HTML5 and Web Open Font Format:

- For example, SVG 2.0 removes several font elements such as glyph and altGlyph (replaced by the WOFF font format).

- The xml:space attribute is deprecated in favor of CSS.

- HTML5 features such as `translate` and `data-*` attributes have been added.

It reached Candidate Recommendation stage on 15 September 2016. The latest draft was released on 23 September 2019.

Mobile Profiles

Because of industry demand, two mobile profiles were introduced with SVG 1.1: *SVG Tiny* (SVGT) and *SVG Basic* (SVGB).

These are subsets of the full SVG standard, mainly intended for user agents with limited capabilities. In particular, SVG Tiny was defined for highly restricted mobile devices such as cellphones; it does not support styling or scripting. SVG Basic was defined for higher-level mobile devices, such as smartphones.

In 2003, the 3GPP, an international telecommunications standards group, adopted SVG Tiny as the mandatory vector graphics media format for next-generation phones. SVGT is the required vector graphics format and support of SVGB is optional for Multimedia Messaging Service (MMS) and Packet-switched Streaming Service. It was later added as required format for vector graphics in 3GPP IP Multimedia Subsystem (IMS).

Differences from Non-mobile SVG

Neither mobile profile includes support for the full Document Object Model (DOM), while only SVG Basic has optional support for scripting, but because they are fully compatible subsets of the full standard, most SVG graphics can still be rendered by devices which only support the mobile profiles.

SVGT 1.2 adds a microDOM (μDOM), styling and scripting.

Related Work

The MPEG-4 Part 20 standard - Lightweight Application Scene Representation (LASeR) and Simple Aggregation Format (SAF) is based on SVG Tiny. It was developed by MPEG (ISO/IEC JTC1/SC29/WG11) and published as ISO/IEC 14496-20:2006. SVG capabilities are enhanced in MPEG-4 Part 20 with key features for mobile services, such as dynamic updates, binary encoding, state-of-art font representation. SVG was also accommodated in MPEG-4 Part 11, in the Extensible MPEG-4 Textual (XMT) format - a textual representation of the MPEG-4 multimedia content using XML.

Functionality

The SVG 1.1 specification defines 14 functional areas or feature sets:

- Paths:

  Simple or compound shape outlines are drawn with curved or straight lines that can be filled in, outlined, or used as a clipping path. Paths have a compact coding.

  For example, M (for "move to") precedes initial numeric x and y coordinates, and L (for "line to") precedes a point to which a line should be drawn. Further command letters (C, S, Q, T, and A) precede data that is used to draw various Bézier and elliptical curves. Z is used to close a path.

  In all cases, absolute coordinates follow capital letter commands and relative coordinates are used after the equivalent lower-case letters.

- Basic shapes:

  Straight-line paths and paths made up of a series of connected straight-line segments (polylines), as well as closed polygons, circles, and ellipses can be drawn. Rectangles and round-cornered rectangles are also standard elements.

- Text:

  Unicode character text included in an SVG file is expressed as XML character data. Many visual effects are possible, and the SVG specification automatically handles bidirectional text (for composing a combination of English and Arabic text, for example), vertical text (as Chinese was historically written) and characters along a curved path (such as the text around the edge of the Great Seal of the United States).

- Painting:

  SVG shapes can be filled and/or outlined (painted with a color, a gradient, or a pattern). Fills may be opaque, or have any degree of transparency.

  "Markers" are line-end features, such as arrowheads, or symbols that can appear at the vertices of a polygon.

- Color:

  Colors can be applied to all visible SVG elements, either directly or via `fill`, `stroke`, and other properties. Colors are specified in the same way as in CSS2, i.e. using names like `black` or `blue`, in hexadecimal such as `#2f0` or `#22ff00`, in decimal like `rgb(255,255,127)`, or as percentages of the form `rgb(100%,100%,50%)`.

- Gradients and patterns:

  SVG shapes can be filled or outlined with solid colors as above, or with color gradients or with repeating patterns. Color gradients can be linear or radial (circular), and can involve any number of colors as well as repeats. Opacity gradients can also be specified. Patterns are based on predefined raster or vector graphic objects, which can be repeated in x and/or y directions. Gradients and patterns can be animated and scripted.

Since 2008, there has been discussion among professional users of SVG that either gradient meshes or preferably diffusion curves could usefully be added to the SVG specification. It is said that a "simple representation [using diffusion curves] is capable of representing even very subtle shading effects" and that "Diffusion curve images are comparable both in quality and coding efficiency with gradient meshes, but are simpler to create (according to several artists who have used both tools), and can be captured from bitmaps fully automatically." The current draft of SVG 2 includes gradient meshes.

- Clipping, masking and compositing:

Graphic elements, including text, paths, basic shapes and combinations of these, can be used as outlines to define both inside and outside regions that can be painted (with colors, gradients and patterns) independently. Fully opaque clipping paths and semi-transparent masks are composited together to calculate the color and opacity of every pixel of the final image, using alpha blending.

- Filter effects:

A filter effect consists of a series of graphics operations that are applied to a given source vector graphic to produce a modified bitmapped result.

- Interactivity:

SVG images can interact with users in many ways. In addition to hyperlinks as mentioned below, any part of an SVG image can be made receptive to user interface events such as changes in focus, mouse clicks, scrolling or zooming the image and other pointer, keyboard and document events. Event handlers may start, stop or alter animations as well as trigger scripts in response to such events.

- Linking:

SVG images can contain hyperlinks to other documents, using XLink. Through the use of the `<view>` element or a fragment identifier, URLs can link to SVG files that change the visible area of the document. This allows for creating specific view states that are used to zoom in/out of a specific area or to limit the view to a specific element. This is helpful when creating sprites. XLink support in combination with the `<use>` element also allow linking to and re-using internal and external elements. This allows coders to do more with less markup and makes for cleaner code.

- Scripting:

All aspects of an SVG document can be accessed and manipulated using scripts in a similar way to HTML. The default scripting language is ECMAScript (closely related to JavaScript) and there are defined Document Object Model (DOM) objects for every SVG element and attribute. Scripts are enclosed in `<script>` elements. They can run in response to pointer events, keyboard events and document events as required.

- Animation:

  SVG content can be animated using the built-in animation elements such as `<animate>`, `<animateMotion>` and `<animateColor>`. Content can be animated by manipulating the DOM using ECMAScript and the scripting language's built-in timers. SVG animation has been designed to be compatible with current and future versions of Synchronized Multimedia Integration Language (SMIL). Animations can be continuous, they can loop and repeat, and they can respond to user events.

- Fonts:

  As with HTML and CSS, text in SVG may reference external font files, such as system fonts. If the required font files do not exist on the machine where the SVG file is rendered, the text may not appear as intended. To overcome this limitation, text can be displayed in an *SVG font*, where the required glyphs are defined in SVG as a font that is then referenced from the `<text>` element.

- Metadata:

  In accord with the W3C's Semantic Web initiative, SVG allows authors to provide metadata about SVG content. The main facility is the `<metadata>` element, where the document can be described using Dublin Core metadata properties (e.g. title, creator/author, subject, description, etc.). Other metadata schemas may also be used. In addition, SVG defines `<title>` and `<desc>` elements where authors may also provide plain-text descriptive material within an SVG image to help indexing, searching and retrieval by a number of means.

An SVG document can define components including shapes, gradients etc., and use them repeatedly. SVG images can also contain raster graphics, such as PNG and JPEG images, and further SVG images.

Example:

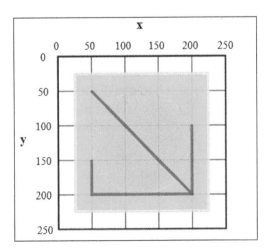

This code will produce the shapes shown in the image (excluding the grid and labels):

```
<?xml version="1.0" encoding="UTF-8" ?>

<svg width="391" height="391" viewBox="-70.5 -70.5 391 391" xmlns="http://www.
w3.org/2000/svg">
```

```
  <rect  x="25"  y="25"  width="200"  height="200"  fill="lime"  stroke-width="4"
stroke="pink" />

  <circle cx="125" cy="125" r="75" fill="black" />

  <polyline points="50,150 50,200 200,200 200,100" stroke="red" stroke-width="4"
fill="none" />

  <line x1="50" y1="50" x2="200" y2="200" stroke="blue" stroke-width="4" />

</svg>
```

SVG on the Web

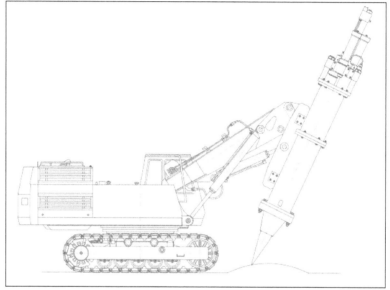

SVG exported from KOMPAS-Graphic.

The use of SVG on the web was limited by the lack of support in older versions of Internet Explorer (IE). Many web sites that serve SVG images, such as Wikipedia, also provide the images in a raster format, either automatically by HTTP content negotiation or by allowing the user directly to choose the file.

Google announced on 31 August 2010 that it had started to index SVG content on the web, whether it is in standalone files or embedded in HTML, and that users would begin to see such content listed among their search results. It was announced on 8 December 2010 that Google Image Search would also begin indexing SVG files. The site announced an option to restrict image searches to SVG files on 11 February 2011.

Native Browser Support

Konqueror was the first browser to support SVG in release version 3.2 in February 2004. As of 2011, all major desktop browsers, and many minor ones, have some level of SVG support. Other browsers' implementations are not yet complete.

Some earlier versions of Firefox (e.g. versions between 1.5 and 3.6), as well as a smattering of other now-outdated web browsers capable of displaying SVG graphics, needed them embedded in <object> or <iframe> elements to display them integrated as parts of an HTML webpage instead of using the standard way of integrating images with <img>. However, SVG images may be included in XHTML pages using XML namespaces.

Tim Berners-Lee, the inventor of the World Wide Web, has been critical of (earlier versions of) Internet Explorer for its failure to support SVG.

- Opera (since 8.0) has support for the SVG 1.1 Tiny specification while Opera 9 includes SVG 1.1 Basic support and some of SVG 1.1 Full. Opera 9.5 has partial SVG Tiny 1.2 support. It also supports SVGZ (compressed SVG).

- Browsers based on the Gecko layout engine (such as Firefox, Flock, Camino, and SeaMonkey) all have had incomplete support for the SVG 1.1 Full specification since 2005. The Mozilla site has an overview of the modules which are supported in Firefox and of the modules which are in progress in the development. Gecko 1.9, included in Firefox 3.0, adds support for more of the SVG specification (including filters).

- Pale Moon, which uses the Goanna layout engine (a fork of the Gecko engine), supports SVG.

- Browsers based on WebKit (such as Apple's Safari, Google Chrome, and The Omni Group's OmniWeb) have had incomplete support for the SVG 1.1 Full specification since 2006.

- Amaya has partial SVG support.

- Internet Explorer 8 and older versions do not support SVG. IE9 (released 14 March 2011) supports the basic SVG feature set. IE10 extended SVG support by adding SVG 1.1 filters.

- Microsoft Edge supports much of SVG 1.1.

- The Maxthon Cloud Browser also supports SVG.

There are several advantages to native and full support: plugins are not needed, SVG can be freely mixed with other content in a single document, and rendering and scripting become considerably more reliable.

Mobile Support

SVG Tiny (SVGT) 1.1 and 1.2 are mobile profiles for SVG. SVGT 1.2 includes some features not found in SVG 1.1, including non-scaling strokes, which are supported by some SVG 1.1 implementations, such as Opera, Firefox and WebKit. As shared code bases between desktop and mobile browsers increased, the use of SVG 1.1 over SVGT 1.2 also increased.

Support for SVG may be limited to SVGT on older or more limited smart phones or may be primarily limited by their respective operating system. Adobe Flash Lite has optionally supported SVG Tiny since version 1.1. At the SVG Open 2005 conference, Sun demonstrated a mobile implementation of SVG Tiny 1.1 for the Connected Limited Device Configuration (CLDC) platform.

Mobiles that use Opera Mobile, as well as the iPhone's built in browser, also include SVG support. However, even though it used the WebKit engine, the Android built-in browser did not support SVG prior to v3.0 (Honeycomb). Prior to v3.0, Firefox Mobile 4.0b2 (beta) for Android was the first browser running under Android to support SVG by default.

The level of SVG Tiny support available varies from mobile to mobile, depending on the SVG engine installed. Many newer mobile products support additional features beyond SVG Tiny 1.1, like gradient and opacity; this is sometimes referred to as "SVGT 1.1+", though there is no such standard.

RIM's BlackBerry has built-in support for SVG Tiny 1.1 since version 5.0. Support continues for WebKit-based BlackBerry Torch browser in OS 6 and 7.

Nokia's S60 platform has built-in support for SVG. For example, icons are generally rendered using the platform's SVG engine. Nokia has also led the JSR 226: Scalable 2D Vector Graphics API expert group that defines Java ME API for SVG presentation and manipulation. This API has been implemented in S60 Platform 3rd Edition Feature Pack 1 and onward. Some Series 40 phones also support SVG (such as Nokia 6280).

Most Sony Ericsson phones beginning with K700 (by release date) support SVG Tiny 1.1. Phones beginning with K750 also support such features as opacity and gradients. Phones with Sony Ericsson Java Platform-8 have support for JSR 226.

Windows Phone has supported SVG since version 7.5

SVG is also supported on various mobile devices from Motorola, Samsung, LG, and Siemens mobile/BenQ-Siemens. eSVG, an SVG rendering library mainly written for embedded devices, is available on some mobile platforms.

Online SVG Converters

This is an incomplete list of web applications that can convert SVG files to raster image formats (this process is known as rasterization), or raster images to SVG (this process is known as image tracing or vectorization) - without the need of installing a desktop software or browser plug-in.

- Autotracer.org - Online raster image vectorizer using the AutoTrace library. BMP, GIF, JPEG, or PNG to DXF, EPS, PDF, or SVG. Upload limit: 1MB.

- FileFormat.info - Converts SVG to PNG, JPEG, TIFF. Output resolution can be specified. No batch processing. Upload limit: 5MB.

- Online-Convert - Converts to/from BMP, EPS, GIF, HDR, ICO, JPEG, PNG, SVG, TGA, TIFF, WBMP, WebP. No batch processing. The output (e. g. image size) is customizable; the conversion to SVG is handled by Potrace.

- SVGConv - Converts SVG to JPEG, PNG, GIF, BMP, TGA, TIFF, PDF, PS, EPS. Allows the user to customize the output (like image size, background color) and has batch processing features (converting multiple files in a single step). Upload limit: 10MB.

- SVG2Android - Converts SVG to an Android VectorDrawable (introduced in API 21).

- Free Online Converter - Converts most raster images to SVG via tracing. When converting from raster images such as PNG to SVG or JPG to SVG, converter will convert the forms and objects in black-and-white images in vector graphics form. The conversion to SVG is handled by Potrace.

- iLoveIMG - Converts a single or multiple SVG to JPG online.

- Photopea - Full online image editor. Converts SVG to/from PSD, PNG, JPEG, GIF, PDF, EMF, WEBP, BMP, PPM, TIFF, ICO, DDS. Also converts to SVG from XCF, Sketch, XD, PXD, CDR, EPS, WMF, IFF, TGA, DNG, NEF, CR2, ARW.

Application Support

SVG images can be produced by the use of a vector graphics editor, such as Inkscape, Adobe Illustrator, Adobe Flash Professional, or CorelDRAW, and rendered to common raster image formats such as PNG using the same software. Inkscape uses a (built-in) potrace to import raster image formats.

Software can be programmed to render SVG images by using a library such as librsvg used by GNOME since 2000, or Batik. SVG images can also be rendered to any desired popular image format by using ImageMagick, a free command-line utility (which also uses librsvg under the hood).

Other uses for SVG include embedding for use in word processing (e.g. with LibreOffice) and desktop publishing (e.g. Scribus), plotting graphs (e.g. gnuplot), and importing paths (e.g. for use in GIMP or Blender). Microsoft Office 365 and Microsoft Office 2019 support for importing and editing SVG images. The Uniform Type Identifier for SVG used by Apple is `public.svg-image` and conforms to `public.image and public.xml`.

DOCTYPE

The DOCTYPE for SVG 1.0 is:

```
<!DOCTYPE svg PUBLIC "-//W3C//DTD SVG 1.0//EN" "http://www.w3.org/TR/2001/REC-
SVG-20010904/DTD/svg10.dtd">
```

and that for SVG 1.1 is:

```
<!DOCTYPE svg PUBLIC "-//W3C//DTD SVG 1.1//EN" "http://www.w3.org/Graphics/
SVG/1.1/DTD/svg11.dtd">
```

but for various reasons, a DOCTYPE should not be included in SVG files.

HTML5 VIDEO

The HTML5 specification introduced the video element for the purpose of playing videos, partially replacing the object element. HTML5 video is intended by its creators to become the new standard way to show video on the web, instead of the previous de facto standard of using the proprietary Adobe Flash plugin, though early adoption was hampered by lack of agreement as to which video coding formats and audio coding formats should be supported in web browsers.

The <video> element started being discussed by the WHATWG in October 2006. The <video> element was proposed by Opera Software in February 2007. Opera also released a preview build that was showcased the same day, and a manifesto that called for video to become a first-class citizen of the web.

\<video\> Element Examples

The following HTML5 code fragment will embed a WebM video into a web page:

```
<video src="movie.webm" poster="movie.jpg" controls>

    This is fallback content to display for user agents that do not support
the video tag.

</video>
```

The "controls" attribute enables the browser's own user interface for controlling playback. Alternatively, playback can be controlled with JavaScript, which the web designer can use to create a custom user interface. The optional "poster" attribute specifies an image to show in the video's place before playback is started. Its purpose is to be representative of the video.

Multiple Sources

Video format support varies among browsers, so a web page can provide video in multiple formats. For other features, browser sniffing is used sometimes, which may be error-prone: any web developer's knowledge of browsers will inevitably be incomplete or not up-to-date. The browser in question "knows best" what formats it can use. The "video" element supports fallback through specification of multiple sources. Using any number of \<source\> elements, as shown below, the browser will choose automatically which file to download. Alternatively, the JavaScript canPlayType() function can be used to achieve the same. The "type" attribute specifies the MIME type and possibly a list of codecs, which helps the browser to determine whether it can decode the file. Even with only one choice, such hints may be necessary to a browser for querying its multimedia framework for third party codecs.

```
<video poster="movie.jpg" controls>

    <source src="movie.webm" type='video/webm; codecs="vp8.0, vorbis"'>

    <source src="movie.ogv" type='video/ogg; codecs="theora, vorbis"'>

    <source src="movie.mp4" type='video/mp4; codecs="avc1.4D401E, mp4a.40.2"'>

    <p>This is fallback content to display for user agents that do not support
the video tag.</p>

</video>
```

Supported Video and Audio Formats

The HTML5 specification does not specify which video and audio formats browsers should support. User agents are free to support any video formats they feel are appropriate, but content authors cannot assume that any video will be accessible by all complying user agents, since user agents have no minimal set of video and audio formats to support.

The HTML5 Working Group considered it desirable to specify at least one video format which all user agents (browsers) should support. The ideal format in this regard would:

- Have good compression, good image quality, and low decode processor use.

- Be royalty-free.

- In addition to software decoders, a hardware video decoder should exist for the format, as many embedded processors do not have the performance to decode video.

Initially, Ogg Theora was the recommended standard video format in HTML5, because it was not affected by any known patents. But on 10 December 2007, the HTML5 specification was updated, replacing the reference to concrete formats:

User agents should support Theora video and Vorbis audio, as well as the Ogg container format.

With a placeholder:

It would be helpful for interoperability if all browsers could support the same codecs. However, there are no known codecs that satisfy all the current players: we need a codec that is known to not require per-unit or per-distributor licensing, that is compatible with the open source development model, that is of sufficient quality as to be usable, and that is not an additional submarine patent risk for large companies.

The result has been the polarisation of HTML5 video between industry-standard, ISO-defined but patented formats, and free, open formats.

Free Formats

Although Theora is not affected by known non-free patents, Apple has expressed concern about unknown patents that might affect it, whose owners might be waiting for a corporation with extensive financial resources to use the format before suing. Formats like H.264 might also be subject to unknown patents in principle, but they have been deployed much more widely and so it is presumed that any patent-holders would have already made themselves known. Apple has also opposed requiring Ogg format support in the HTML standard (even as a "should" requirement) on the grounds that some devices might support other formats much more easily, and that HTML has historically not required particular formats for anything.

Some web developers criticized the removal of the Ogg formats from the specification.

Mozilla and Opera support only the open formats of Theora and WebM. Google stated its intention to remove support for H.264 in 2011, specifically for the HTML5 video tag. Although it has been removed from Chromium, as of November 2016 it has yet to be removed from Google Chrome five years later.

MPEG-DASH Support via the HTML5 Media Source Extensions (MSE)

The adaptive bitrate streaming standard MPEG-DASH can be used in Web browsers via the HTML5 Media Source Extensions (MSE) and JavaScript-based DASH players. Such players are, e.g., the open-source project dash.js of the DASH Industry Forum, but there are also products such as bitdash of bitmovin (using HTML5 with JavaScript, but also a Flash-based DASH players for legacy Web browsers not supporting the HTML5 MSE).

Google's Purchase of On2

Google's acquisition of On2 in 2010 resulted in its acquisition of the VP8 video format. Google has provided a royalty-free license to use VP8. Google also started WebM, which combines the standardized open source VP8 video codec with Vorbis audio in a Matroska based container. The opening of VP8 was welcomed by the Free Software Foundation.

When Google announced in January 2011 that it would end native support of H.264 in Chrome, criticism came from many quarters including Peter Bright of Ars Technica and Microsoft web evangelist Tim Sneath, who compared Google's move to declaring Esperanto the official language of the United States. However, Haavard Moen of Opera Software strongly criticized the Ars Technica article and Google responded to the reaction by clarifying its intent to promote WebM in its products on the basis of openness.

After the launch of WebM, Mozilla and Opera have called for the inclusion of VP8 in HTML.

On 7 March 2013, Google Inc. and MPEG LA, LLC announced agreements covering techniques that "may be essential" to VP8, with Google receiving a license from MPEG LA and 11 patent holders, and MPEG LA ending its efforts to form a VP8 patent pool.

In 2012, VP9 was released by Google as a successor to VP8, also open and royalty free.

At the end of 2017 the new AV1 format developed by the Alliance for Open Media (AOMedia) as the evolution of VP9 has reached the feature freeze, and the bitstream freeze is expected for January 2018. Firefox nightly builds already include support for AV1.

Non-free Formats

H.264/MPEG-4 AVC is widely used, and has good speed, compression, hardware decoders, and video quality, but is patent-encumbered. Users of H.264 need licenses either from the individual patent holders, or from the MPEG LA, a group of patent holders including Microsoft and Apple, except for some Internet broadcast video uses. H.264 is usually used in the MP4 container format, together with Advanced Audio Coding (AAC) audio. AAC is also patented in itself, so users of MP4 will have to license both H.264 and AAC.

In June 2009, the WHATWG concluded that no existing format was suitable as a specified requirement.

Apple still only supports H.264, but Microsoft now supports VP9 and WebM, and has pledged support for AV1.

Cisco Makes a Licensed H.264 Binary module Available for Free

On 30 October 2013, Cisco announced that it was making a binary H.264 module available for download. Cisco will pay the costs of patent licensing for those binary modules when downloaded by the using software while it is being installed, making H.264 free to use in that specific case.

In the announcement, Cisco cited its desire of furthering the use of the WebRTC project as the reason, since WebRTC's video chat feature will benefit from having a video format supported in all browsers. The H.264 module will be available on "all popular or feasibly supportable platforms, which can be loaded into any application".

Cisco is also planning to publish source code for those modules under BSD license, but without paying the royalties, so the code will practically be free software only in countries without H.264 software patents, which has already been true about other existing implementations.

Also on 30 October 2013, Mozilla's Brendan Eich announced that Firefox would automatically download Cisco's H.264 module when needed by default. He also noted that the binary module is not a perfect solution, since users do not have full free software rights to "modify, recompile, and redistribute without license agreements or fees". Thus Xiph and Mozilla continue the development of Daala.

OpenH264 only supports the baseline profile of H.264, and does not by itself address the need for an AAC decoder. Therefore, it is not considered sufficient for typical MP4 web video, which is typically in the high profile with AAC audio. However, for use in WebRTC, the omission of AAC was justified in the release announcement: "the standards bodies have aligned on Opus and G.711 as the common audio codecs for WebRTC". There is doubt as to whether a capped global licensing of AAC, like Cisco's for H.264, is feasible after AAC's licensing bureau removed the price cap shortly after the release of OpenH264.

WEBAUTHN

WebAuthn (Web Authentication) is a web standard published by the World Wide Web Consortium (W3C). WebAuthn is a core component of the FIDO2 Project under the guidance of the FIDO Alliance. The goal of the project is to standardize an interface for authenticating users to web-based applications and services using public-key cryptography.

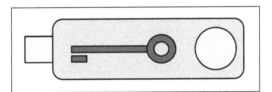

A roaming cryptographic hardware
authenticator with a USB interface.

On the client side, support for WebAuthn can be implemented in a variety of ways. The underlying cryptographic operations are performed by an authenticator, which is an abstract functional model that is mostly agnostic with respect to how the key material is managed. This makes it possible to implement support for WebAuthn purely in software, making use of a processor's trusted execution environment or a Trusted Platform Module (TPM). Sensitive cryptographic operations can also be offloaded to a roaming hardware authenticator that can in turn be accessed via USB, Bluetooth Low Energy, or near-field communications (NFC). A roaming hardware authenticator conforms to the FIDO Client to Authenticator Protocol (CTAP), making WebAuthn effectively backward compatible with the FIDO Universal 2nd Factor (U2F) standard.

Similar to legacy U2F, Web Authentication is resilient to verifier impersonation, that is, it is resistant to active man-in-the-middle-attacks, but unlike U2F, WebAuthn does not require a traditional password. Moreover, a roaming hardware authenticator is resistant to malware since the private key material is at no time accessible to software running on the host machine.

The WebAuthn Level 1 standard was published as a W3C Recommendation on 4 March 2019. A Level 2 specification is under development.

FIDO2 is the successor of the FIDO Universal 2nd Factor (U2F) legacy protocol. FIDO2 authentication has all the advantages of U2F—the primary difference is that a FIDO2 authenticator can also be a multi-factor authenticator.

A FIDO2 authenticator may be used in either single-factor mode or multi-factor mode. In single-factor mode, the authenticator is activated by a test of user presence, which usually consists of a simple button push. In multi-factor mode, the authenticator (*something you have*) performs user verification. Depending on the authenticator capabilities, this can be:

- Something you know: a secret such as a PIN, passcode or swipe pattern.

- Something you are: a biometric such as fingerprint, iris or voice.

In any case, the authenticator performs user verification locally on the device. A secret or biometric stored on the authenticator is not shared with the website. Moreover, a single secret or biometric works with all websites, as the authenticator will select the correct cryptographic key material to use for the service requesting authentication after user verification was completed successfully.

A secret and biometric on the authenticator can be used together, similarly to how they would be used on a smartphone. For example, a fingerprint is used to provide convenient access to your smartphone but occasionally fingerprint access fails, in which case a PIN can be used.

Like its predecessor FIDO U2F, W3C Web Authentication (WebAuthn) involves a website, a web browser, and an authenticator:

- The website is a conforming WebAuthn Relying Party.

- The browser is a conforming WebAuthn Client.

- The authenticator is a FIDO2 authenticator, that is, it is assumed to be compatible with the WebAuthn Client.

WebAuthn specifies how a claimant demonstrates possession and control of a FIDO2 authenticator to a verifier called the WebAuthn Relying Party. The authentication process is mediated by an entity called the WebAuthn Client, which is little more than a conforming web browser.

Authentication

For the purposes of illustration, we assume the authenticator is a roaming hardware authenticator. In any case, the authenticator is a multi-factor cryptographic authenticator that uses public-key cryptography to sign an authentication assertion targeted at the WebAuthn Relying Party. Assuming the authenticator uses a PIN for user verification, the authenticator itself is something you have while the PIN is something you know.

To initiate the WebAuthn authentication flow, the WebAuthn Relying Party indicates its intentions to the WebAuthn Client (i.e., the browser) via JavaScript. The WebAuthn Client communicates with the authenticator using a JavaScript API implemented in the browser. A roaming authenticator conforms to the FIDO Client to Authenticator Protocol.

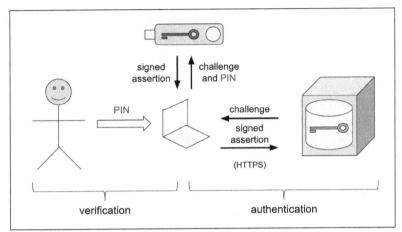

A typical Web Authentication (WebAuthn) flow.

WebAuthn does not strictly require a roaming hardware authenticator. Alternatively, a software authenticator (implemented on a smartphone, e.g.) or a platform authenticator (i.e., an authenticator implemented directly on the WebAuthn Client Device) may be used. Relevant examples of platform authenticators include Windows Hello and the Android operating system.

The illustrated flow relies on PIN-based user verification, which, in terms of usability, is only a modest improvement over ordinary password authentication. In practice, the use of biometrics for user verification can improve the usability of WebAuthn. The logistics behind biometrics are still poorly understood, however. There is a lingering misunderstanding among users that biometric data is transmitted over the network in the same manner as passwords, which is not the case.

Registration

When the WebAuthn Relying Party receives the signed authentication assertion from the browser, the digital signature on the assertion is verified using a trusted public key for the user. How does the WebAuthn Relying Party obtain that trusted public key in the first place?

To obtain a public key for the user, the WebAuthn Relying Party initiates a WebAuthn registration flow that is very similar to the authentication flow illustrated above. The primary difference is that the authenticator now signs an attestation statement with its attestation private key. The signed attestation statement contains a copy of the public key that the WebAuthn Relying Party ultimately uses to verify a signed authentication assertion. The attestation statement also contains metadata describing the authenticator itself.

The digital signature on the attestation statement is verified with the trusted attestation public key for that particular model of authenticator. How the WebAuthn Relying Party obtains its store of trusted attestation public keys is unspecified. One option is to use the FIDO metadata service.

The attestation type specified in the JavaScript determines the trust model. For instance, an attestation type called self-attestation may be desired, for which the trust model is essentially trust on first use.

Support

The WebAuthn Level 1 standard was published as a W3C Recommendation by the Web Authentication Working Group on 4 March 2019. WebAuthn is supported by the following web browsers: Google Chrome, Mozilla Firefox, Microsoft Edge, Apple Safari and the Opera web browser.

The desktop version of Google Chrome has supported WebAuthn since version 67. Firefox, which had not fully supported the previous FIDO U2F standard, included and enabled WebAuthn in Firefox version 60, released on May 9, 2018. An early Windows Insider release of Microsoft Edge implemented a version of WebAuthn that works with both Windows Hello as well as external security keys.

Existing FIDO U2F security keys are largely compatible with the WebAuthn standard, though WebAuthn added the ability to reference a unique per-account "user handle" identifier, which older authenticators are unable to store. One of the first FIDO2-compatible authenticators was the second-generation Security Key by Yubico, announced on April 10, 2018.

The first Security Level 2 certified FIDO2 key, called "Goldengate" was announced one year later by eWBM on April 8, 2019. and Dropbox announced support for WebAuthn logins (as a 2nd factor) on May 8, 2018.

API

WebAuthn implements an extension of the W3C's more general Credential Management API, which is an attempt to formalize the interaction between websites and web browsers when exchanging user credentials. The Web Authentication API extends the Credential Management `navigator. credentials.create()` and `navigator.credentials.get()` JavaScript methods so they accept a `publicKey` parameter. The `create()` method is used for registering public key authenticators as part of associating them with user accounts (possibly at initial account creation time but more likely when adding a new security device to an existing account) while the `get()` method is used for authenticating (such as when logging in).

To check if a browser supports WebAuthn, scripts should check if the `window.PublicKeyCredential` interface is defined. In addition to `PublicKeyCredential`, the standard also defines the `AuthenticatorResponse`, `AuthenticatorAttestationResponse`, and `AuthenticatorAssertionResponse` interfaces in addition to a variety of dictionaries and other datatypes.

The API does not allow direct access to or manipulation of private keys, beyond requesting their initial creation.

Criticism

In August 2018, Paragon Initiative Enterprises did a security audit of the upcoming WebAuthn standard. While they could not find any specific exploits, they revealed some serious weaknesses in the way the underlying cryptography is used and mandated by the standard.

The main points of criticism revolve around two potential issues that were problematic in other cryptographic systems in the past and therefore should be avoided in order to not fall victim to the same class of attacks:

- Through the mandated use of COSE (RFC 8152) WebAuthn also supports RSA with PKCS1v1.5 padding. This particular scheme of padding is known to be vulnerable to specific attacks for at least twenty years and it has been successfully attacked in other protocols and implementations of the RSA cryptosystem in the past. It is difficult to exploit under the given conditions in the context of WebAuthn, but given that there are more secure cryptographic primitives and padding schemes, this is still a bad choice and is not considered to be best practice among cryptographers any more.

- The FIDO alliance standardized on an asymmetric cryptographic scheme called ECDAA. This is a version of direct anonymous attestation based on elliptic curves and in the case of WebAuthn is meant to be used to verify the integrity of authenticators, while also preserving the privacy of users, as it does not allow for global correlation of handles. However, ECDAA does not incorporate some of the lessons that were learned in the last decades of research in the area of elliptic curve cryptography, as the chosen curve has some security deficits inherent to this type of curve, which reduces the security guarantees quite substantially. Furthermore, the ECDAA standard involves random, non-deterministic, signatures, which already has been a problem in the past.

Paragon Initiative Enterprises also criticized the way in which the standard was initially developed, as the proposal was not made public in advance and experienced cryptographers were not asked for suggestions and feedback. Hence the standard was not subject to broad cryptographic research from the academic world.

Despite these shortcomings Paragon Initiative Enterprises still encourage users to continue to use WebAuthn but have come up with some recommendations for potential implementors and developers of the standard that they hope can be implemented before the standard is finalized. Avoiding such mistakes as early as possible would prevent the industry from any challenges that are introduced by broken standards and the need for backwards compatibility.

ECDAA is only used in combination with device attestation. This particular feature of WebAuthn is not necessarily required for authentication to work. Current implementations allow the user to decide whether an attestation statement is sent during the registration ceremony. Independently, relying parties can choose to require attestation or not.

WEB API SECURITY

Web API security entails authenticating programs or users who are invoking a web API.

With ease of API integrations comes the difficult part of ensuring proper authentication (AUTHN) and authorization (AUTHZ). In a multitenant environment, proper security controls need to be put in place to only allow access on "need to have access basis" based on proper AUTHN and AUTHZ. Appropriate AUTHN schemes enable producers (API's or services) to properly identify consumers (clients or calling programs) and to evaluate their access level (authz). In other words, can a consumer invoke a particular method (business logic) based on credentials presented?

"Interface design flaws are widespread, from the world of crypto processors through sundry embedded systems right through to antivirus software and the operating system itself.

Method of Authentication and Authorization

Most common methods for authentication and authorization include:

- Static strings: These are like passwords that are provided by API's to consumers.

- Dynamic tokens: These are time based tokens obtained by caller from an authentication service.

- User-delegated tokens: These are tokens such as OAuth which are granted based on user authentication.

- Policy & attribute-based access control: Policies use attributes to define how APIs can be invoked using standards such as ALFA or XACML.

The above methods provide different level of security and ease of integration. Oftentimes, the easiest method of integration also offers weakest security model.

Static Strings

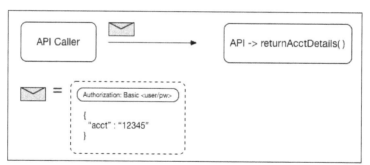

Basic Authentication Block Diagram.

In static strings method, the API caller or client embeds a string as a token in the request. This method is often referred as basic authentication. "From a security point of view, basic authentication is not very satisfactory. It means sending the user's password over the network in clear text for every single page accessed (unless a secure lower-level protocol, like SSL, is used to encrypt all transactions). Thus the user is very vulnerable to any packet sniffers on the net."

Dynamic Tokens

When an API is protected by a dynamic token, there is a time-based nonce inserted into the token. The token has a time to live (TTL) after which the client must acquire a new token. The API method has a time check algorithm, and if the token is expired, the request is forbidden. "An example of such token is JSON Web Token. The "exp" (expiration time) claim identifies the expiration time on or after which the JWT MUST NOT be accepted for processing."

User-delegated Token

This type of token is used in three-legged systems where an application needs to access an API on behalf of a user. Instead of revealing user id and password to the application, a user grants a token which encapsulates users permission for the application to invoke the API.

The OAuth 2.0 authorization framework enables a third-party application to obtain limited access to an HTTP service, either on behalf of a resource owner by orchestrating an approval interaction between the resource owner and the HTTP service, or by allowing the third-party application to obtain access on its own behalf.

Fine-Grained Authorization for APIs

Attribute-based Access Control

In this approach, there is a Policy Enforcement Point either within the API itself, in the API framework (as an interceptor or message handler), or as an API gateway (e.g. Kong) that intercepts the call to the API and / or the response back from the API. It converts it into an authorization request (typically in XACML) which it sends to a Policy Decision Point (PDP) e.g. AuthZForce or Axiomatics. The Policy Decision Point is configured with policies that implement dynamic access control that can use any number of user, resource, action, and context attributes to define which access is allowed or denied. Policies can be about:

- The resource (e.g. a bank account).

- The user (e.g. a customer).

- The context (e.g. time of day).

- A relationship (e.g. the customer to whom the account belongs).

Policies are expressed in ALFA or XACML.

WEBRTC

WebRTC (Web Real-Time Communication) is a technology which enables Web applications and sites to capture and optionally stream audio and/or video media, as well as to exchange arbitrary data between browsers without requiring an intermediary. The set of standards that comprise WebRTC makes it possible to share data and perform teleconferencing peer-to-peer, without requiring that the user installs plug-ins or any other third-party software.

WebRTC consists of several interrelated APIs and protocols which work together to achieve this.

WebRTC Concepts and Usage

WebRTC serves multiple purposes; together with the Media Capture and Streams API, they provide powerful multimedia capabilities to the Web, including support for audio and video conferencing, file exchange, screen sharing, identity management, and interfacing with legacy telephone systems including support for sending DTMF (touch-tone dialing) signals. Connections between peers can be made without requiring any special drivers or plug-ins, and can often be made without any intermediary servers.

Connections between two peers are represented by the RTCPeerConnection interface. Once a connection has been established and opened using RTCPeerConnection, media streams (MediaStreams) and/or data channels (RTCDataChannels) can be added to the connection.

Media streams can consist of any number of tracks of media information; tracks, which are represented by objects based on the MediaStreamTrack interface, may contain one of a number of types of media data, including audio, video, and text (such as subtitles or even chapter names). Most streams consist of at least one audio track and likely also a video track, and can be used to send and receive both live media or stored media information (such as a streamed movie).

You can also use the connection between two peers to exchange arbitrary binary data using the RTCDataChannel interface. This can be used for back-channel information, metadata exchange, game status packets, file transfers, or even as a primary channel for data transfer.

WebRTC Interfaces

Because WebRTC provides interfaces that work together to accomplish a variety of tasks, we have divided up the interfaces in the list below by category.

Connection Setup and Management

These interfaces are used to set up, open, and manage WebRTC connections. Included are interfaces representing peer media connections, data channels, and interfaces used when exchanging information on the capabilities of each peer in order to select the best possible configuration for a two-way media connection.

RTC Peer Connection

Represents a WebRTC connection between the local computer and a remote peer. It is used to handle efficient streaming of data between the two peers.

RTC Data Channel

Represents a bi-directional data channel between two peers of a connection.

RTC Data Channel Event

Represents events that occur while attaching a RTCDataChannel to a RTCPeerConnection. The only event sent with this interface is datachannel.

RTC Session Description

Represents the parameters of a session. Each RTCSessionDescription consists of a description type indicating which part of the offer/answer negotiation process it describes and of the SDP descriptor of the session.

RTC Session Description Callback

The RTC Session Description Callback is passed into the RTCPeerConnection object when requesting it to create offers or answers.

RTC Stats Report

Provides information detailing statistics for a connection or for an individual track on the connection; the report can be obtained by calling RTCPeerConnection.getStats(). Details about using WebRTC statistics can be found in WebRTC Statistics API.

RTC Ice Candidate

Represents a candidate Internet Connectivity Establishment (ICE) server for establishing an RTCPeerConnection.

RTC Ice Transport

Represents information about an ICE transport.

RTC Ice Server

Defines how to connect to a single ICE server (such as a STUN or TURN server).

RTC Peer Connection Ice Event

Represents events that occur in relation to ICE candidates with the target, usually an RTCPeerConnection. Only one event is of this type: icecandidate.

RTC Rtp Sender

Manages the encoding and transmission of data for a MediaS tream Track on an RTC Peer Connection.

RTC Rtp Receiver

Manages the reception and decoding of data for a MediaStreamTrack on an RTC Peer Connection.

RTC Rtp Contributing Source

Contains information about a given contributing source (CSRC) including the most recent time a packet that the source contributed was played out.

RTC Track Event

The interface used to represent a track event, which indicates that an RTCRtpReceiver object was added to the RTCPeerConnection object, indicating that a new incoming MediaStreamTrack was created and added to the RTCPeerConnection.

RTC Configuration

Used to provide configuration options for an RTCPeerConnection.

RTC Sctp Transport

Provides information which describes a Stream Control Transmission Protocol (SCTP) transport and also provides a way to access the underlying Datagram Transport Layer Security (DTLS) transport over which SCTP packets for all of an RTCPeerConnection's data channels are sent and received.

RTC Sctp Transport State

Indicates the state of an RTCSctpTransport instance.

Identity and Security

The WebRTC API includes a number of interfaces which are used to manage security and identity.

RTC Identity Provider

Enables a user agent is able to request that an identity assertion be generated or validated.

RTC Identity Assertion

Represents the identity of the remote peer of the current connection. If no peer has yet been set and verified this interface returns null. Once set it can't be changed.

RTC Identity Provider Registrar

Registers an identity provider (idP).

RTC Identity Event

Represents an identity assertion generated by an identity provider (idP). This is usually for an RTCPeerConnection. The only event sent with this type is identityresult.

RTC Identity Error Event

Represents an error associated with the identity provider (idP). This is usually for an RTCPeerConnection. Two events are sent with this type: idpassertionerror and idpvalidationerror.

RTC Certificate

Represents a certificate that an RTCPeerConnection uses to authenticate.

Telephony

These interfaces are related to interactivity with Public-Switched Telephone Networks (PTSNs).

RTCDTMF Sender

Manages the encoding and transmission of Dual-Tone Multi-Frequency (DTMF) signaling for an RTCPeerConnection.

RTCDTMF Tone Change Event

Used by the tonechange event to indicate that a DTMF tone has either begun or ended. This event does not bubble (except where otherwise stated) and is not cancelable (except where otherwise stated).

References

- Scott Gilbertson (2011-09-19). "Chrome 14 Adds Better Audio, 'Native Client' Support". Webmonkey. Wired. Retrieved 2012-07-04

- Flanagan, David (2006). JavaScript: The Definitive Guide. O'Reilly & Associates. pp. 312–313. ISBN 0-596-10199-6

- working-with-indexeddb, pwa, ilt, web: developers.google.com, Retrieved 28 March, 2019

- Strickland, Jonathan (18 March 2019). "What is WebAuthn". TechStuff. iHeartMedia. 20:35 minutes in. Retrieved 20 March 2019

Website Maintenance and Management

Website maintenance and management is referred as the act of checking website for issues and continuously keeping it updated and seamless. Various sub-fields included are web audits, website governance, website monitoring, website tracking, web content lifecycle, etc. The following chapter elucidates the varied aspects associated with website maintenance and management.

As search engine optimization became more well known and part of every business marketing strategy, website maintenance became key to the process. Frequently updating web page content and keyword information was crucial to encourage search engines to return to a site and look favorably on the optimization work.

As the economy started to change, keeping a fresh website became crucial to staying in business. Website visitors were often checking websites looking for reassurance that businesses were still operational. The problem was finding website content that hadn't been updated since the 2008 economic downturn and wondering if this was the last update from a defunct business.

In the past couple of years, Content Management Systems (CMS) have come into popularity. Websites are now being built with tools that allow a non-web developer to make updates to web pages. Could this mark the end of website maintenance? Actually, it has been our experience that maintenance requirements increase with the addition of a content management system. Many business owners don't want to take the time to learn the tools or the changes that are required cannot be performed within the CMS. We have noticed that we spend more time on sites equipped with CMS tools then the traditional coded sites.

Importance of Website Maintenance

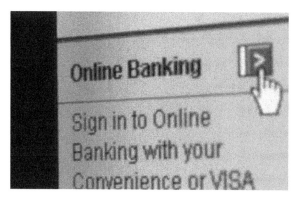

Website maintenance is important to any business, regardless of size. a website is a worldwide window into a business and it can have a big impact on how the value of a product or service is perceived. A well-maintained website is critical for real-time service industries. All businesses need regular website maintenance to attract and retain customers, maintain search engine rankings and present new information, products and services to the public. Website maintenance is also required to maintain the value of the website over time.

Customer Interest

A well-maintained website attracts new customers and maintains the interest levels of existing customers. a website should be customer centered and kept relevant by routinely refreshing the content and ensuring that customer contact points are in good working order. Routinely check that contact forms work, address and phone number listings are updated and products, services and price lists are current and correct.

Search Engines

Website maintenance is critical to search-engine rankings. Websites with old content rank lower in search engine listings. Some search engines, including Google, check a page's "if-modified-since" HTTP header to determine whether it is worth crawling. Failing to make frequent modifications could cause you to be pushed below active competitors in the listings and cost you business over time.

WEB AUDITS

Website audit is a full analysis of all the factors that affect website's visibility in search engines. This standard method gives a complete insight into any website, overall traffic and individual pages. Website audit is completed solely for marketing purposes. The goal is to detect weak points in campaigns that affect web performance.

The website audit starts from a general analysis of a website aimed at revealing the actions needed to improve search engine optimization (SEO). Many tools offer recommendations on how to raise the website rankings in search that can include on page and off page SEO audit such as broken links, duplicate meta descriptions and titles, HTML validation, website statistics, error pages, indexed pages and site speed. Site audit is applicable for all online businesses and improves different aspects of the websites.

Purpose

There are many reasons to do a website audit, but in most cases SEO and content marketing are the main ones. Website audit made for SEO purposes discovers weak spots of a website's SEO score and helps understand the state of SEO. Content audit is used to analyze the engagement and what changes have to be made to the content strategy to enhance the site's performance.

Types

There are multiple types of site audits, but the most well-known types of SEO audits are the following:

- Website health audits - Analyzing overall health of the website while revealing all issues that require immediate attention.

- Security audits - Accessing a site for potential vulnerability issues such as high value sites and high-risk verticals.

- Competitive site audits - The ability to monitor all gaps and opportunities for website promotion, and detect the benefits and drawbacks of competitors.

- Red flag and recovery audits - Analyzing a website for impending penalties and site metrics when there is an oncoming peril of algorithmic penalties.

- Conversion optimization audits - Accessing a site for possible technical and onsite conversion problems.

- Technical SEO audits - This often involves crawling the entire site, beginning with a review of site content, structure, and adherence to best practices such as web accessibility.

All of these audits can form a part of the same audit. Each one is made to make sure that you have powerful and reliable system in place. It shows the unidentified dangers that can bring you down, tells what needs to change and what's working well and what's not good, and gives practical recommendations and insights into what need to prioritize more. All website audits start with site health audits.

WEBSITE GOVERNANCE

Website governance is an organization's structure of staff and the technical systems, policies and procedures to maintain and manage a website. Website governance applies to both Internet and Intranet sites.

Areas of Responsibility

Governance of a website may include a wide variety of responsibilities, including online strategy, budgeting, systems and software administration, hosting, online marketing and communications, e-commerce, customer service, business development, online community and social media, web content development and workflows, content strategy, translation, website graphic design, user experience (analysis/design), information/data architecture, website analytics, security, archiving, outsourcing, accessibility, legal issues (for example, copyright, DRM, trademark, and privacy), information ethics, and training, among others. These areas may be the responsibility of several or single staff within an organization, depending on available resources and infrastructure, organizational needs and objectives, website size, and how content is managed and delivered. McGovern argues that there is a limit to the number of web pages that can be professionally managed by one person, although he does not set the outer limit, either in number of pages (in a centralized model of website governance) or in number of publishers (in a decentralized model of website governance).

Website Management Team

A website management team (WMT) can be defined as an authorizing body of a website responsible for setting and achieving high-level goals for a site. This body includes content owner stakeholders and site production staff. In some organizations, a chief web officer leads the WMT.

Website Governance Roles Organized as a Tactical Steering Team

Strategic site sponsor(s)

Tactical team leader

Content	Legal	Project Direction	Marketing and Editorial	User Experience	Creative	Production	Technical - software	Security	Quality Assurance
Content owner	Compliance content owner	Customer liaison	Marketing coordinator	Information architect	Art director	Technical/ Production director	Software architect	Security network engineer	Link, code and browser tester
Content author	Compliance author	Project manager	Web promotion marketer	Human Factors engineer	Web designer	CMS programmer	Lead Programmer	Encryption key manager	System acceptance tester
		Program manager/ Scrum master	Web editor	Interaction designer	Sound and motion designer	Client-side script programmer	Programmer	Security compliance analyst	Requirements tester
		Analyst	Copywriter		Illustrator	CSS presentation programmer	**Technical - hardware**		
						HTML programmer	Systems architect		
						Production administrator	System engineer		
						Content entry	Network engineer		
							Server administrator		
							Database administrator		
							Configuration manager		

Content owner roles | Site delivery tactical and operational roles

☐ = Core tactical team leads

Website management team: An example of a tactical steering team organized primarily by production roles.

Responsibilities and authorities of website staff may be grouped by strategic, tactical and operational roles, and may be organized as a cross-functional web team. A strategic site sponsor articulates the high-level vision of the site, and determines if the vision is adequately fulfilled; a tactical-level staff translates the vision into detail by prioritizing projects, specifying site design and negotiating placement of content. The tactical staff may be a group serving on a website governance board or steering team representing the main constituencies as defined by the organization's overall business plan.

Governance Models

Several models of website governance exist. Authors have focused on the content lifecycle; primary components, such as people, process, and standards; attributes, such as accountability, accessibility, participation across business areas, and standards; and type of governance structure (centralized, decentralized, or federated).

Through the Federal Web Managers Council, Federal agencies in the U.S. government collaborate to share common challenges, ideas, and best practices and improve the online delivery of U.S. government information and services. Harrison, the first co-chair of the Federal Web Managers Council, has proposed the 5 "R's" of web governance: Roles, Responsibilities, Relationships, Rules, and Review.

In a 2008 report, the United Nations Joint Inspection Unit reviewed the management of websites in United Nations system organizations and made eight recommendations to improve a website presence. These included website governance, strategy, and policies and guidelines; content management systems; and staffing, training, and funding.

In 2011 Jacoby introduced the Website Governance Functional Model. Based on a business reference model within Davenport's information ecology, the Website Governance Functional Model included at least 16 functional areas within an organization, along with the principles of project, information, and knowledge management.

In 2012 Jacoby introduced the Website Governance Modeling Tool, "designed to help Web managers and their stakeholders conceptualize and assess their organization's website governance.

WEBSITE MONITORING

Website monitoring is the process of testing and verifying that end-users can interact with a website or web application as expected. Website monitoring is often used by businesses to ensure website uptime, performance, and functionality is as expected.

Website monitoring companies provide organizations the ability to consistently monitor a website, or server function, and observe how it responds. The monitoring is often conducted from several locations around the world to a specific website, or server, in order to detect issues related to general Internet latency, network hop issues, and to prevent false positives caused by local or inter-connect problems. Monitoring companies generally report on these tests in a variety of reports, charts and graphs. When an error is detected monitoring services send out alerts via email, SMS, phone, SNMP trap, pager that may include diagnostic information, such as a network trace route, code capture of a web page's HTML file, a screen shot of a webpage, and even a video of a website failing. These diagnostics allow network administrators and webmasters to correct issues faster.

Monitoring gathers extensive data on website performance, such as load times, server response times, page element performance that is often analyzed and used to further optimize website performance.

Purpose

Monitoring is essential to ensure that a website is available to users, downtime is minimized, and performance can be optimized. Users that rely on a website, or an application, for work or pleasure will get frustrated or even stop using the application if it is not reliably available. Monitoring can cover many things that an application needs to function, like network connectivity, Domain Name System records, database connectivity, bandwidth, and computer resources like free RAM, CPU load, disk space, events, etc. Commonly measured metrics are response time and availability (or uptime), but consistency and reliability metrics are gaining popularity. Measuring a website's availability and reliability under various amounts of traffic is often referred to as load testing.

Website monitoring also helps benchmark the website against the performance of a competitors to help determine how well a site is performing. Website speed is also used as a metric for search engine rankings.

Website monitoring can be used to hold web hosting providers accountable to their service-level agreement. Most web hosts offer 99.9% uptime guarantee and, when uptime is less than that, individuals can be refunded for the excessive downtime. Note that not all hosts will refund individuals for excessive downtime so one must become familiar with the terms of service of their host.

Most paid website monitoring services will also offer security features such as virus and malware scanning which is of growing importance as websites become more complicated and integral to business.

Internal vs. External

Website monitoring can be done from both inside and outside of a corporate firewall. Traditional network management solutions focus on inside the firewall monitoring, whereas external performance monitoring will test and monitor performance issues across the Internet backbone and in some cases all the way to the end-user. Third-party website performance monitoring solutions can monitor internal (behind the firewall), external (customer-facing), or cloud-based Web applications.

Inside firewall monitoring is done by special hardware appliances which can help you determine if your internal applications' sluggish performance is caused by: design of applications, internal infrastructure, internal applications or connections to any public Internet.

External performance monitoring is also known as end-user monitoring or end-to-end performance monitoring.

Real user monitoring measures the performance and availability experienced by actual users, diagnoses individual incidents, and tracks the impact of a change.

Types of Protocol

A website monitoring service can check other internet protocols besides HTTP pages and HTTPS such as FTP, SMTP, POP3, ActiveSync, IMAP, DNS, SSH, Telnet, SSL, TCP, PING, UDP, SOAP, Domain Name Expiry, SSL Certificate Expiry and a range of ports. Monitoring frequency occurs at intervals of once every 4-hours to every 15-seconds. Typically, most website monitoring services test a server, or application, between once-per hour to once-per-minute.

Advanced monitoring services capture browser interactions with websites using macro recorders, or browser add-ons such as Selenium or iMacros. These services test a website by running a web browser through a typical website transaction (such as a shopping cart) or a custom scenario, in order to check for user experience issues, performance problems, and availability errors. Browser-driven monitoring services detect not only network and server issues, but also webpage object issues (such as slow loading Javascript, or third-party hosted page elements).

An implementation of time performance monitoring for the Apache HTTP Server is the mod_arm4 module.

Types of Monitoring

Users of website monitoring (typically network administrators, web masters, web operations personnel) may monitor a single page of a website, but can also monitor a complete business process (often referred to as multi-step transactions).

Servers Monitoring from Around the Globe

Website monitoring services usually have a number of servers around the globe – South America, Africa, North America, Europe, Africa, Asia, Australia and other locations. By having multiple servers in different geographic locations, monitoring service can determine if a web server is available across continents over the Internet. Some vendors claim that the more locations the better picture on your website availability while others say that three globally distributed stations are sufficient and more stations do not give more information.

Types

There are two main types of website monitoring:

- Synthetic monitoring also known as active monitoring, and

- Passive monitoring also known as real monitoring.

Notification Options: Alerts

As the information brought by website monitoring services is in most cases urgent and may be of crucial importance, various notification methods, often known as "alerts" are used: e-mail, IM, regular and cell phones, SMS, fax, pagers, Skype, RSS Feed, SNMP trap, URL notifications, etc.

There exists companies such as Monitor The Internet that provide website monitoring on a very granular level. You can monitor anything your VPS server can output. As long as MTI accepts it and includes it in their new release.

Website Monitoring Services

Website monitoring market is very competitive. There are 150+ active service providers and more than 100 documented to have gone out of business. Most of the providers offer a free plan with low-frequency monitoring.

WEBSITE TRACKING

Website tracking refers to the act of archiving existing websites and tracking changes to the website over time. Many applications exist for website tracking which can be applied to many different purposes.

Website Monitoring

Website monitoring allows interested parties to track the health of a website or web application. A software program can periodically check to see if a website is down, if broken links exist or if errors have occurred on specific pages. For example, a web developer who hosts and maintains a website for a customer may want to be notified instantly if the site goes down or if a web applications returns an error.

Monitoring the web is a critical component for marketing, sales and product support strategies. Over the past decade transactions on the web have significantly multiplied the use of dynamic web page, secure web sites and integrated search capabilities which requires tracking of user behavior on web sites.

Website Change Detection

Website change detection allows interested parties to be alerted when a website has changed. A web crawler can periodically scan a website to see if any changes have occurred since its last visit. Reasons to track website changes include:

- Enhanced automations:
  - Triggering in Event-driven programming.
  - Updating dependent automations (such as screen scraping programs).
  - Link rot mitigation.
  - Change trend monitoring.
- Triggering human actions:
  - Analyst classifications.
  - Updating documentation.
  - Competitive monitoring.
  - Compliance monitoring.
  - Enforcement monitoring.
  - Investigation monitoring.

Web Press Clippings

This is a parallel application to the offline business of press clippings. For web press clippings, a crawler needs to scour the Internet to find terms that match keywords the clipping service is looking for. So for instance, the Vice President of the United States may have staff looking at web press clippings to see what is being said about the Vice President on any given day. To do this, a web press clipping service (aka Media monitoring service) needs to monitor mainstream websites as well as blogs.

- Ereleases.com provides a list of web press clipping services.
- Google Alerts and OnWebChange.com provide notifications when keywords are found in newly indexed web content.
- RSS feeds can often be used in this case since these are the areas in which relevant content will be found.

Website Archiving

This type of service archives a website so that changes to the website over time can be seen. Unless archived, older versions of a website cannot be viewed and may be lost permanently. Fortunately there is at least one web service that tracks changes to most websites for free. Past information about a company can therefore be gleaned from this type of service, which can be very useful in some circumstances.

WEB CONTENT LIFECYCLE

The web content lifecycle is the multi-disciplinary and often complex process that web content undergoes as it is managed through various publishing stages.

Authors describe multiple "stages" (or "phases") in the web content lifecycle, along with a set of capabilities such as records management, digital asset management, collaboration, and version controlóthat may be supported by various technologies and processes. One recognized technology for managing the web content lifecycle is a web content management system.

Concepts often considered in the web content lifecycle include project management, information management, information architecture, and, more recently, content strategy, website governance, and semantic publishing.

Stages

Various authors have proposed different "stages" or "phases" in the content lifecycle. Broadly speaking, the stages include content creation/development, revision, distribution, and archiving. The lifecycle processes, actions, content status, and content management roles may differ from model to model based on organizational strategies, needs, requirements, and capabilities.

Two Stages

In 2003, McKeever described "two iterative phases": "the collection of content, and the delivery or publishing of that content on the Web." She also explains a Web Content Management (WCM) "four layer hierarchy"ócontent, activity, outlet, and audienceóintended to illustrate the breadth of WCM.

Three Stages

Bob Boiko's Content Management Bible emphasizes three major parts: collect (creation and editing is much more than simply collecting), manage (workflows, approvals, versioning, repository, etc.), and publish. These concepts are graphically displayed in a Content Management Possibilities poster developed by Boiko. The poster details such content management concepts as metadata, syndication, workflows, repositories, and databases.

Gerry McGovern also sees three "processes," designating them creation, editing, and publishing.

Four stages

JoAnn Hackos' Content Management for Dynamic Web Delivery argues for four "components": authoring, repository, assembly/linking, and publishing.

In Managing Enterprise Content, Ann Rockley argues for the planning of content reuse through four stages: create, review, manage, deliver. A stage can have sub-stages; for example, the "create" stage has three sub-stages: planning, design, and authoring and revision. She notes that content is often created by individuals working in isolation inside an enterprise (the coined term is the Content Silo Trap). To counter this content silo effect, she recommends using a "unified content strategy," "a repeatable method of identifying all content requirements up front, creating consistently structured content for reuse, managing that content in a definitive source, and assembling content on demand to meet your customersí needs."

Five Stages

Nakano described five "collaboration operations": Submit, Compare, Update, Merge, and Publish.

The State government of Victoria (Australia) produced a flowchart with a diagrammatic view of the web content lifecycle with five stages: Develop, Quality Approval, Publish, Unpublish, and Archive. Some of the stages include sub-stages (for example, Archive consists of Storage, Archived, and Disposed) intended to further delineate content status. In addition, this model depicts three aspectsó Status, Process, and Rolesóas part of the flow for web content. The four roles in this model are content author, content quality manager, business quality manager, and records manager.

The AIIM speaks of managing content to achieve business goals. AIIM ECM 101 Poster from 2003, and the AIIM Solving the ECM Puzzle Poster from 2005, present the same five stages: Capture, Manage, Store, Deliver, Preserve.

Six Stages

The Content Management Lifecycle Poster devised by CM Pros suggests six "steps":

- Plan,
- Develop,
- Manage,
- Deploy,
- Preserve,
- Evaluate.

Each step contains sub-steps. For example, step 1, Plan, consists of Align, Analyze, Model, and Design; and step 2, Develop, consists of Create, Capture, Collect, Categorize, and Edit.

There is also another six stage model based on the concept of product lifecycle:

- Goal setting,
- Creation,
- Publishing,
- Promoting,
- Maintaining,
- Retirement.

Seven Stages

Bob Doyle suggests seven stages of the Web content lifecycle:

- Organization,
- Creation,
- Storage,
- Workflow,
- Versioning,
- Publishing,
- Archives.

Doyle argues for seven stages based on the psychologist George A. Miller's famed magical number "seven plus or minus two" limit on human information processing. He notes this is merely a suggestion and that one should "add or subtract a couple of your own favorites."

Governance Rather than Workflow

In a 2005 article, Woods addressed governance of the content lifecycle. In his model, there are categories of issues to address, rather than a simple, cradle-to-grave pathway. He writes that most content governance questions fall into one of the following categories:

- Legacy Content Migration.
- Template Considerations.
- New Content Creation.
- Content Modification and Reuse.
- Version Control and Site Rollback.
- Content Rotation and the End of the Road.
- Monitoring Progress, Managing for Success.

More recently, Kristina Halvorson has humorously suggested 15 discrete steps in the web content lifecycle: Audit, Analyze, Strategize, Categorize, Structure, Create, Revise, Revise, Revise, Approve, Tag, Format, Publish, Update, Archive.

Role of Technologies

Enterprise content management as a business strategy might incorporate web content management:

When integrated with an ECM system, WCM enables organizations to automate the complete Web content lifecycle. As soon as new content is developed, the system ensures that it goes live the moment it is intended to not a minute earlier. By specifying timed releases and expiration dates, content is published to and removed from the Web according to recommendations, requirements and even regulations.

A web content management system can support and enhance certain processes because of automation, including document management, templates, and workflow management. However, the absence of well defined roles and process governance will greatly dilute the effectiveness of any technology intended to augment/enhance the publishing process overall.

Role of Information Management

Information management describes the "organization of and control over the structure, processing, and delivery of information." The goal of information lifecycle management is to use policies, operations, and infrastructure to manage information throughout its useful life. However, businesses struggle to manage their data and information.

The missing stage in all the major sources is the organization of information, structuring it where possible, for example using XML or RDF, which allows arbitrary metadata to be added to all information elements. This is the secret that the knowledge managers describe as turning mere data or information into knowledge. It allows information to be retrieved in a number of ways and reused or repurposed in many more.

Using semantic markup in the publishing process is part of semantic publishing. Tim-Berners Lee's original vision for the Semantic Web has yet to be realized, but many projects in various research areas are underway.

WEB CONTENT MANAGEMENT SYSTEM

A web content management system (WCM or WCMS) is a software content management system (CMS) specifically for web content. It provides website authoring, collaboration, and administration tools that help users with little knowledge of web programming languages or markup languages create and manage website content. A WCMS provides the foundation for collaboration, providing users the ability to manage documents and output for multiple author editing and participation. Most systems use a content repository or a database to store page content, metadata, and other information assets the system needs.

A presentation layer (template engine) displays the content to website visitors based on a set of templates, which are sometimes XSLT files.

Most systems use server side caching to improve performance. This works best when the WCMS is not changed often but visits happen regularly. Administration is also typically done through browser-based interfaces, but some systems require the use of a fat client.

Capabilities

A web content management system controls a dynamic collection of web material, including HTML documents, images, and other forms of media. A WCMS facilitates document control, auditing, editing, and timeline management. A WCMS typically has the following features:

- Automated templates:

    Create standard templates (usually HTML and XML) that users can apply to new and existing content, changing the appearance of all content from one central place.

- Access control:

    Some WCMS systems support user groups, which control how registered users interact with the site. A page on the site can be restricted to one or more groups. This means an anonymous user (someone not logged on), or a logged on user who is not a member of the group a page is restricted to, is denied access.

- Scalable expansion:

    Available in most modern WCMSs is the ability to expand a single implementation (one installation on one server) across multiple domains, depending on the server's settings. WCMS sites may be able to create microsites/web portals within a main site as well.

- Easily editable content:

    Once content is separated from the visual presentation of a site, it usually becomes much easier and quicker to edit and manipulate. Most WCMS software includes WYSIWYG editing tools allowing non-technical users to create and edit content.

- Scalable feature sets:

    Most WCMS software includes plug-ins or modules that can be easily installed to extend an existing site's functionality.

- Web standards upgrades:

    Active WCMS software usually receives regular updates that include new feature sets and keep the system up to current web standards.

- Workflow management:

    workflow is the process of creating cycles of sequential and parallel tasks that must be accomplished in the WCMS. For example, one or many content creators can submit a story, but it is not published until the copy editor cleans it up and the editor-in-chief approves it.

- Collaboration:

    WCMS software may act as a collaboration platform where many users retrieve and work on content. Changes can be tracked and authorized for publication or ignored reverting to old versions. Other advanced forms of collaboration allow multiple users to modify (or comment) a page at the same time in a collaboration session.

- Delegation:

    Some WCMS software allows for various user groups to have limited privileges over specific content on the website, spreading out the responsibility of content management.

- Document management:

    WCMS software may provide a means of collaboratively managing the life cycle of a document from initial creation time, through revisions, publication, archive, and document destruction.

- Content virtualization:

    WCMS software may provide a means of allowing each user to work within a virtual copy of the entire web site, document set, and/or code base. This enables viewing changes to multiple interdependent resources in context prior to submission.

- Content syndication:

    WCMS software often helps distribute content by generating RSS and Atom data feeds to other systems. They may also e-mail users when updates become available.

- Multilingual:

    Many WCMSs can display content in multiple languages.

- Versioning:

    Like document management systems, WCMS software may implement version control, by which users check pages in and out of the WCMS. Authorized editors can retrieve previous versions and work from a selected point. Versioning is useful for content that changes and requires updating, but it may be necessary to start from or reference a previous version.

Types

A WCMS can use one of three approaches: offline processing, online processing, and hybrid processing. These terms describe the deployment pattern for the WCMS in terms of when it applies presentation templates to render web pages from structured content.

Offline Processing

These systems, sometimes referred to as "static site generators", pre-process all content, applying templates before publication to generate web pages. Since pre-processing systems do not require a server to apply the templates at request time, they may also exist purely as design-time tools.

Online Processing

These systems apply templates on-demand. They may generate HTML when a user visits the page, or the user might receive pre-generated HTML from a web cache. Most open source WCMSs support add-ons that extended the system's capabilities. These include features like forums, blogs, wikis, web stores, photo galleries, and contact management. These are variously called modules, nodes, widgets, add-ons, or extensions.

Hybrid Processing

Some systems combine the offline and online approaches. Some systems write out executable code (e.g., JSP, ASP, PHP, ColdFusion, or Perl pages) rather than just static HTML. That way, personnel don't have to deploy the WCMS itself on every web server. Other hybrids operate in either an online or offline mode.

Advantages

- Low cost:

  Some content management systems are free, such as Drupal, eZ Publish, TYPO3, Joomla, Zesty.io, and WordPress. Others may be affordable based on size subscriptions. Although subscriptions can be expensive, overall the cost of not having to hire full-time developers can lower the total costs. Plus software can be bought based on need for many WCMSs.

- Easy customization:

  A universal layout is created, making pages have a similar theme and design without much code. Many WCMS tools use a drag and drop AJAX system for their design modes. It makes it easy for beginner users to create custom front-ends.

- Easy to use:

  WCMSs accommodate non-technical people. Simplicity in design of the admin UI lets website content managers and other users update content without much training in coding or system maintenance.

- Workflow management:

  WCMSs provide the facility to control how content is published, when it is published, and who publishes it. Some WCMSs allow administrators to set up rules for workflow management, guiding content managers through a series of steps required for each of their tasks.

- Good For SEO:

  WCMS websites also accommodate search engine optimization (SEO). Content freshness helps, as some search engines prefer websites with newer content. Social media plugins help build a community around content. RSS feeds automatically generated by blogs, or WCMS websites can increase the number of subscribers and readers to a site. URL rewriting can be implemented easily—clean URLs without parameters further help in SEO. Some plugins specifically help with website SEO.

Disadvantages

- Cost of implementations:

  Larger scale implementations may require training, planning, and certifications. Certain WCMSs may require hardware installation. Commitment to the software is required on bigger investments. Commitment to training, developing, and upkeep are costs incurred in any enterprise system.

- Cost of maintenance:

  Maintaining WCMSs may require license updates, upgrades, and hardware maintenance.

- Latency issues:

  Larger WCMSs can experience latency if hardware infrastructure is not up to date, databases are used incorrectly, or web cache files that reload every time data updates grow too large. Load balancing issues may also impair caching files.

- Tool mixing:

  Because the URLs of many WCMSs are dynamically generated with internal parameters and reference information, they are often not stable enough for static pages and other web tools, particularly search engines, to rely on them.

- Security:

  WCMS's are often forgotten about when hardware, software, and operating systems are patched for security threats. Due to lack of patching by the user, a hacker can use unpatched WCMS software to exploit vulnerabilities to enter an otherwise secure environment. WCMS's should be part of an overall, holistic security patch management program to maintain the highest possible security standards.

Advantages and Disadvantages of Content Management System

While all CMS software have their own particular advantages and disadvantages, some of the pros and cons are common for each.

Advantages of using a CMS

- Quick development and deployment time: Using a CMS can drastically speed up the process of developing a site.
- Open source CMSs are free to download and install.
- Advanced site functionality: Most systems allow the implementation of functionalities (forms, polls, quizzes, event calendars, etc.) that would otherwise be extremely hard to achieve.
- User-friendly: Gives people with little or no technical skills the ability to create, update or modify content.
- Reduces costs: Implementing an out-of-the-box CMS is definitely less costly than a custom one. Also, after users have learned some of the ins and outs of the CMS, they will be able to handle the basic functions on their own, and this reduces the costs of outside technical assistance as well.
- Easy maintenance and updates: Most CMSs are developed to be easy to maintain and update.
- Huge development communities for open source CMSs.

Disadvantages of using a CMS

- Hidden implementation costs for perfecting the system for users' needs.

- Server resources: Some CMSs (e.g. Joomla) can put a load on your server resources.

- Some technical skillset requirements: If users have an aversion to learning the basics of using a CMS, the usage of a CMS will not be as efficient. This means that hiring experienced staff or contracting technical help might be necessary.

- Maintenance: In the wrong hands, an unmaintained and outdated CMS can do a lot of harm to a website and lead to serious security vulnerabilities.

- Direct support: For community-based CMS systems, direct support may not be easy to find, and you have to rely on user forums and existing documentation.

References

- Robert Jacoby (October 26, 2011). "6 Concepts for the Future of Website Governance, Including a New Functional Model". Cmswire. Retrieved 2011-11-10

- What-is-website-maintenance: cybervise.com, Retrieved 29 April, 2019

- Rockley, Ann (2002). Managing Enterprise Content: A Unified Content Strategy. Reading, Mass: New Riders Press. P. 592. ISBN 0-7357-1306-5

- Website-maintenance-important-48199: smallbusiness.chron.com, Retrieved 30 May, 2019

- Costill, Albert. "SEO 101: How Important is Site Speed in 2014?". Search Engine Journal. Retrieved 25 October 2014

- Berners-Lee, T.; Hendler, J. (2001). "Publishing on the semantic web". Nature. 410 (6832): 1023ñ1024. Doi:10.1038/35074206. PMID 11323639

- Rockley, Ann (2002). Managing Enterprise Content: A Unified Content Strategy. Reading, Mass: New Riders Press. P. 592. ISBN 0-7357-1306-5

- Bob Doyle (September 2005). "Seven Stages of the CM Lifecycle". Econtentmag.com. Retrieved 20 July 2010

INDEX

CPSIA information can be obtained
at www.ICGtesting.com
Printed in the USA
LVHW060725010222
709759LV00069B/275